John Stott (NT)
Derek Tidball (Bible Themes)

The Message of Worship

*Celebrating the glory of
God in the whole of life*

The Bible Speaks Today: Bible Themes series

The Message of the Living God
His glory, his people, his world
Peter Lewis

The Message of the Resurrection
Christ is risen!
Paul Beasley-Murray

The Message of the Cross
Wisdom unsearchable, love indestructible
Derek Tidball

The Message of Salvation
By God's grace, for God's glory
Philip Graham Ryken

The Message of Creation
Encountering the Lord of the universe
David Wilkinson

The Message of Heaven and Hell
Grace and destiny
Bruce Milne

The Message of Mission
The glory of Christ in all time and space
Howard Peskett and Vinoth Ramachandra

The Message of Prayer
Approaching the throne of grace
Tim Chester

The Message of the Trinity
Life in God
Brian Edgar

The Message of Evil and Suffering
Light into darkness
Peter Hicks

The Message of the Holy Spirit
The Spirit of encounter
Keith Warrington

The Message of Holiness
Restoring God's masterpiece
Derek Tidball

The Message of Sonship
At home in God's household
Trevor Burke

The Message of the Word of God
The glory of God made known
Tim Meadowcroft

The Message of Women
Creation, grace and gender
Derek and Dianne Tidball

The Message of the Church
Assemble the people before me
Chris Green

The Message of the Person of Christ
The Word made flesh
Robert Letham

The Message of Worship
Celebrating the glory of God in the whole of life
John Risbridger

The Message of Worship

Celebrating the glory of God in the whole of life

John Risbridger

Minister and Team Leader at Above Bar Church, Southampton and Chair of Keswick Ministries

Inter-Varsity Press

InterVarsity Press
P.O. Box 1400
Downers Grove, IL 60515-1426
ivpress.com
email@ivpress.com

InterVarsity Press® is the book-publishing division of InterVarsity Christian Fellowship/USA®, a movement of students and faculty active on campus at hundreds of universities, colleges and schools of nursing in the United States of America, and a member movement of the International Fellowship of Evangelical Students. For information about local and regional activities, visit intervarsity.org.

ISBN 978-0-8308-2417-5 (print)
ISBN 978-0-8308-9916-6 (digital)

Printed in the United States of America ∞

As a member of the Green Press Initiative, InterVarsity Press is committed to protecting the environment and to the responsible use of natural resources. To learn more, visit greenpressinitiative.org.

Library of Congress Cataloging-in-Publication Data

Risbridger, John.
  The message of worship : celebrating the glory of god in the whole of life / John Risbridger, Minister and Team Leader at Above Bar Church, Southampton and Chair of Keswick Ministries.
    pages cm.—(The Bible speaks today series)
  Includes bibliographical references and index.
  ISBN 978-0-8308-2417-5 (pbk. : alk. paper)
  1. Worship in the Bible. 2. Worship--Biblical teaching. I. Title.
  BS680.W78R57 2015
  248.3—dc23

                                                              2015027490

| **P** | 17 | 16 | 15 | 14 | 13 | 12 | 11 | 10 | 9 | 8 | 7 | 6 | 5 | 4 | 3 | 2 | 1 |
| **Y** | 29 | 28 | 27 | 26 | 25 | 24 | 23 | 22 | 21 | 20 | 19 | 18 | 17 | 16 | 15 |

Contents

BST The Bible Speaks Today

GENERAL PREFACE

THE BIBLE SPEAKS TODAY describes three series of expositions, based on the books of the Old and New Testaments, and on Bible themes that run through the whole of Scripture. Each series is characterized by a threefold ideal:

- to expound the biblical text with accuracy
- to relate it to contemporary life, and
- to be readable.

These books are, therefore, not 'commentaries', for the commentary seeks rather to elucidate the text than to apply it, and tends to be a work rather of reference than of literature. Nor, on the other hand, do they contain the kinds of 'sermons' that attempt to be contemporary and readable without taking Scripture seriously enough. The contributors to *The Bible Speaks Today* series are all united in their convictions that God still speaks through what he has spoken, and that nothing is more necessary for the life, health and growth of Christians than that they should hear what the Spirit is saying to them through his ancient – yet ever modern – Word.

ALEC MOTYER
JOHN STOTT
DEREK TIDBALL
Series editors

Author's preface

I am neither a professional theologian nor a professional musician. Nonetheless, a deep hunger for biblical truth and a deep love of many types of music have both been woven into the fabric of my life from childhood until the present day. The home in which I grew up was a loving and godly one, in which the reading of Scripture was built into the rhythm of family life; it was also a musical home, in which a day would rarely pass without the sound of musical instruments and singing being heard. It was natural enough, then, that I became involved in music groups in churches and Christian Unions (I love to play the piano and I sing, though only at an amateur level in both cases) and that my Christian faith was always a singing faith. At the same time my sense of calling to Bible teaching and pastoral ministry was quite strong by my mid teenage years, and developed rapidly as I began to work in student ministry in my mid-twenties. However, it was only when Geoff Baker (who subsequently became a friend) invited me to become involved in 'leading worship' in larger Christian festivals[1] that the two threads became more tightly woven together and I began to search for a deeper biblical understanding of 'worship' and its relationship to congregational praise. This book is, in many ways, the fruit of that search.

Against that background, it is perhaps not surprising that I find it difficult to resonate with the tension between preacher/theologians on the one hand and musicians on the other that rarely seems far below the surface of many debates on the theme of worship. As a *pastor-teacher* I rejoice to receive Holy Scripture as God's word written, his glorious gift of self-revelation for our salvation, bearing infallible witness to the Living Word – his Son, our Saviour, Jesus Christ. As a *musician* I rejoice to welcome music as a wonderful gift of God in creation, possessing both the power to move the human

---

[1] Initially Word Alive (which was then a partnership between Spring Harvest, UCCF and the Proclamation Trust) and latterly in the Keswick Convention, in which I have remained involved ever since.

heart profoundly and the variety to engage every human culture and civilization. Scripture itself bears testimony to the pervasive presence and power of music in human experience, with its many songs and its many references to making music. For me then, one of the many joys of engaging in Christian worship is the opportunity it gives to bring together two of things I most love. For in congregational worship at its best, the power of music is employed both to address biblical truth to the human heart and to carry the response to that truth that the Holy Spirit brings forth.

This is not to limit our view of worship only to singing, for biblical worship is (as we shall quickly see) a response to God's revelation of himself, empowered by the Holy Spirit, which finds expression in every aspect of human life and experience. Nonetheless, there is a great deal of music in the Bible – its longest book is, after all, a book of songs – and I see no reason to be negative or suspicious of music and every reason to embrace its riches and harness its power responsibly for the glory of God and the blessing of his people.

Of course the reality is that churches have been divided and Christian unity has all too often been breached over competing ideas of the theology and practice of worship. Many things contribute to these difficulties: different of views of the gifts of the Holy Spirit and of communion; the respective value given to liturgical and extemporary prayer; the priorities attached to the missional, pastoral and instructional functions of the church; the weight given to congregational worship and whole-life worship in our thinking; and varying opinions on the place and style of music. Inevitably this book will touch on many of these areas, but my intention is not to court controversy, but simply to do my best to allow Scripture to speak, in the hope that the question 'What kind of worship do we like?' is gradually replaced by the better question: 'What kind of worship is it that God seeks?' My prayer is that this book may make some small contribution to reducing the heat and increasing the light in our well-worn debates, so that what A. W. Tozer once called 'the jewel of worship'[2] might gleam more brightly in our churches, as something associated less with painful division and more with joyful celebration and whole-life consecration.

The invitation to worship God is the highest privilege of human beings, a privilege squandered by human rebellion but gloriously restored to us through the death, resurrection and ascension of Christ. First and foremost, therefore, this book is a testimony to my own experience of the abundant grace of God in Jesus Christ. It

[2] A. W. Tozer, *Worship: The Missing Jewel of the Evangelical Church* (Harrisburg: Christian Publications, n. d.), p. 12, quoted in V. Roberts, *True Worship* (Carlisle: Authentic Media, 2002), p. 15.

follows a loosely trinitarian structure, with the main sections exploring the connection between worship and the purpose of the Father, the supremacy of the Son and the life of the Holy Spirit. Each section concludes with two chapters from the Psalms in which we hear a variety of worship 'voices', and learn to join in their distinctive songs.

Biblical worship is primarily a journey we are called to make in community with the people of God. For me the major parts of that journey have been made as part of Bethel Baptist Church Farnham, Cornerstone Evangelical Church Nottingham and Above Bar Church Southampton, and I am profoundly grateful for the formative influence that each has had on me. I particularly wish to record my warm thanks to my fellow elders, trustees and colleagues at Above Bar for granting me a period of sabbatical leave over the summer of 2014, during which the writing of most of this book took place. I also wish to express my deep gratitude to Derek Tidball, Philip Duce, Chris Jack, Richard Blake and my own father for their wise input, patient interest and unflinching support during the process of writing. The final and most heartfelt tribute must of course be to my immediate family for their patience and encouragement, and particularly to my dear wife, Alison, whose unfailing love, faithful support and vibrant faith both in joy and in sorrow have been the most precious human gifts of my life. It is to her that I wish this book to be dedicated.

JOHN RISBRIDGER
Above Bar Church, Southampton
February 2015

Abbreviations

BDAG	Bauer-Danker Lexicon, *A Greek-English Lexicon of the New Testament and Other Early Christian Literature* (3rd ed., Chicago: Chicago University Press, 2000)
BST	Bible Speaks Today
ESV	English Standard Version, Anglicized Version, 2002
ICC	International Critical Commentary
IVPNTC	IVP New Testament Commentary
JSOTSup	*Journal for the Study of the Old Testament Supplement*
KJV	King James Version
LXX	Septuagint
NAC	New American Commentary
NASB	New American Standard Bible
NBC	*New Bible Commentary* (3rd ed., Leicester: Inter-Varsity Press, 1994)
NBD	*New Bible Dictionary* (Leicester: Inter-Varsity Press, 1996)
NICNT	New International Commentary on the New Testament
NICOT	New International Commentary on the Old Testament
NIDNTT	*New International Dictionary of New Testament Theology*, ed. Colin Brown, 4 vols. (Grand Rapids: Zondervan, 1976 and Carlisle: Paternoster, 1986)
NIDOTTE	*New International Dictionary of Old Testament Theology and Exegesis*, ed. W. A. VanGemeren, 5 vols. (Grand Rapids: Zondervan, 1996 and Carlisle: Paternoster, 1997)
NIGTC	New International Greek Testament Commentary
NIV	New International Version
NIVAC	NIV Application Commentary

NLT	New Living Translation
NRSV	New Revised Standard Version, 1989–95
PNTC	Pillar New Testament Commentary
TNTC	Tyndale New Testament Commentary
TOTC	Tyndale Old Testament Commentary
WBC	Word Biblical Commentary

Select bibliography

Anderson, B. W. with S. Bishop, *Out of the Depths: the Psalms Speak for Us Today* (rev. ed., Louisville: Westminster John Knox Press, 2000).

Balchin, J. F., 'Colossians 1:15–20: An Early Christian Hymn? The Arguments from Style', *Vox Evangelica* 15 (1985), pp. 65–94.

Barnett, P., *The Second Epistle to the Corinthians*, NICNT (Grand Rapids: Eerdmans, 1997).

Barrett, C. K., *The Second Epistle to the Corinthians* (London: A & C Black, 1973).

Beale, G. K., *The Book of Revelation*, NIGTC (Grand Rapids: Eerdmans, 1999).

———, *The Temple and the Church's Mission* (Leicester: Apollos, 2004).

Beasley-Murray, G. R., *John*, WBC 26 (Waco: Word Books, 1987).

Begbie, J., *Resounding Truth: Christian Wisdom in the World of Music* (Grand Rapids: Baker Academic, 2007).

Belville, L. L., *2 Corinthians*, IVPNTC (Leicester: Inter-Varsity Press, 1996).

Best, H., *Music Through the Eyes of Faith* (San Francisco: HarperCollins, 1993).

Block, D. I., *For the Glory of God: Recovering a Biblical Theology of Worship* (Grand Rapids: Baker Academic, 2014).

Blomberg, C. L., *Jesus and the Gospels* (Leicester: Apollos, 1997).

Bugbee, B. and D. Cousins, *The Network Course Participant's Guide* (Grand Rapids: Zondervan, 2005).

Calvin, J., *Institutes of the Christian Religion*, trans. L. Battles (Louisville: The Westminster Press, 1960).

———, *Commentary on the Psalms*, vol. 1, <http://www.ccel.org/ccel/calvin/calcom08.i.html>.

Carson, D. A., *Showing the Spirit: A Theological Exposition of 1 Corinthians 12–14* (Grand Rapids: Baker Book House Company, 1987).

————, *The Gospel According to John* (Leicester: Inter-Varsity Press, 1991).

————, *The Cross in Christian Ministry* (Grand Rapids: Baker Books, 1993).

————, *Matthew*, Expositor's Bible Commentary, vol. 8 (Grand Rapids: Zondervan, 1995).

Carson, D. A. (ed.), *Worship: Adoration and Action* (Eugene: Wipf & Stock Publishers, 2002).

Chester, T., *Good News to the Poor* (Nottingham: Inter-Varsity Press, 2004).

Cockerill, G. L., *The Epistle to the Hebrews*, NICNT (Grand Rapids: Eerdmans, 2011).

Cole, A., *Exodus*, TOTC (Leicester: Inter-Varsity Press, 1973).

Craig, C. T., *The First Epistle to the Corinthians*, Interpreter's Bible, vol. 10 (New York: Doubleday, 1953).

Craigie, P. C. with M. E. Tate, *Psalms 1–50*, WBC 19 (rev. ed., Nashville: Thomas Nelson Inc., 2004).

Cranfield, C. E. B., *A Critical and Exegetical Commentary on the Epistle to the Romans*, ICC, vol. II (Edinburgh: T&T Clark, 1957).

Edwards, J., 'The Miscellanies', in *The Works of Jonathan Edwards*, vol. 13., ed. T. Schafer (New Haven: Yale University Press, 1994).

Enns, P., *Exodus*, NIVAC (Michigan: Zondervan, 2000).

Fee, G. D., *The First Epistle to the Corinthians*, NICNT (Grand Rapids: Eerdmans, 1987).

————, *God's Empowering Presence* (Peabody: Hendrickson Publishers, Inc., 1994).

————, *Philippians*, IVPNTC (Leicester: Inter-Varsity Press, 1999).

Fee, G. D. and D. Stuart, *How to Read the Bible for All Its Worth* (Grand Rapids: Zondervan, 1982).

France, R. T., *Matthew: Evangelist and Teacher* (Eugene: Wipf & Stock Publishers, 2004).

————, *Matthew*, NICNT (Grand Rapids: Eerdmans, 2007).

Garland, D. E., *2 Corinthians*, NAC 29 (Nashville: B&H Publishing, 1999).

Goldingay, J., *Songs from a Strange Land: Psalms 42–51* (Leicester: Inter-Varsity Press, 1978).

————, *Psalms: Psalms 42–89* (Michigan: Baker Academic, 2007).

Goulder, M. D., *The Psalms of the Sons of Korah*, JSOTSup 20 (Sheffield: Sheffield Academic Press, 1982).

Grudem, W. A., *The Gift of Prophecy in 1 Corinthians* (Washington DC: University Press of America, 1982).

————, *Systematic Theology* (Leicester: Inter-Varsity Press, 1994).

Gunkel, H., *The Psalms: A Form-Critical Introduction*, trans. T. M. Horner (Philadelphia: Fortress, 1967).

Hardyman, J., *Idols: God's Battle for Our Hearts* (Nottingham: Inter-Varsity Press, 2010).

Haugen, G. A., *Good News about Injustice* (Leicester: Inter-Varsity Press, 1999).

Hawthorne, G. F., R. P. Martin and D. G. Reid (eds.), *Dictionary of Paul and His Letters* (Leicester: Inter-Varsity Press, 1993).

Hoehner, H. W., *Ephesians: An Exegetical Commentary* (Grand Rapids: Baker Academic, 2003).

Hudson, N., *Imagine Church* (Nottingham: Inter-Varsity Press, 2012).

Jack, C., 'The Proskuneo Myth: When a Kiss Is Not a Kiss', in D. J. Cohen and M. Parsons (eds.), *In Praise of Worship: An Exploration of Text and Practice* (Eugene: Pickwick Publications, 2010).

Johnson, A. F., *1 Corinthians*, IVPNTC (Leicester: Inter-Varsity Press, 2004).

Keener, C. S., *Matthew*, IVPNTC (Leicester: Inter-Varsity Press, 1997).

Keller, T., *Counterfeit Gods* (London: Hodder & Stoughton, 2009).

———, *Center Church* (Grand Rapids: Zondervan, 2012).

Kidd, R. M., *With One Voice: Discovering Christ's Song in our Worship* (Grand Rapids: Baker Books, 2005).

Kidner, D., *Psalms 1–72*, TOTC (Leicester: Inter-Varsity Press, 1973).

———, *Psalms 73–150*, TOTC (Leicester: Inter-Varsity Press, 1975).

Lane, W. L., *Hebrews 9–13*, WBC 47b (Waco: Word Books, 1991).

Lewis, C. S., *Mere Christianity* (London: Fontana Books, 1952).

———, *Reflections on the Psalms* (London: Geoffrey Bles, 1958).

———, *Letters to Malcolm* (London: Geoffrey Bles, 1963/4).

———, 'The Weight of Glory', in *C. S. Lewis Essay Collection and other Short Pieces*, ed. L. Walmsley (London: Harper Collins Publishers, 2000).

Lewis, P. H., *The Glory of Christ* (London: Hodder & Stoughton, 1992).

Lincoln, A. T., *Ephesians*, WBC 42 (Waco: Word Books, 1990).

Longman, T. III and D. E. Garland, *The Psalms*, Expositor's Bible Commentary, vol. 5 (rev. ed., Grand Rapids: Zondervan, 2008).

Martin, R. P., *2 Corinthians*, WBC 40 (Waco: Word Books, 1991).

Moo, D. J., *The Epistle to the Romans*, NICNT (Grand Rapids: Eerdmans, 1996).

———, *The Letters to the Colossians and to Philemon*, PNTC (Nottingham: Apollos, 2008).

Morris, L., *1 Corinthians*, TNTC (Leicester: Inter-Varsity Press, 1985).

Nolland, J., *Luke 18:35–24:53*, WBC 35c (Waco: Word Books, 1993).

O'Brien, P. T., *Colossians, Philemon*, WBC 44 (Waco: Word Books, 1982).

——, *The Letter to the Hebrews*, PNTC (Nottingham: Apollos, 2010).

Ortland, R. C. Jr, *Revival Sent from God: What the Bible Teaches for the Church Today* (Leicester: Inter-Varsity Press, 2000).

Peckham, C. and M., *Sounds from Heaven: The Revival on the Isle of Lewis, 1949-1952* (Fearn, Ross-shire: Christian Focus Publications, 2009).

Perigo, J., 'Getting Past the Western vs. Indigenous Hymnody Debate: Viewing Turkish Hymnody through a Pneumatological Framework', presented at the 43rd Annual Meeting of the Society for Pentecostal Studies, 2014.

Peterson, D., *Engaging with God* (Leicester: Apollos, 1992).

——, *Encountering God Together* (Nottingham: Inter-Varsity Press, 2013).

Piper, J., *Desiring God: Meditations of a Christian Hedonist* (Leicester: Inter-Varsity Press, 1986).

——, *The Purifying Power of Living by Faith in Future Grace* (Colorado: Multnomah Books, 1995).

——, *The Dangerous Duty of Delight* (Colorado: Multnomah Books, 2001).

——, *Let the Nations Be Glad* (Leicester: Inter-Varsity Press, 2003).

Roberts, V., *True Worship* (Carlisle: Authentic Media, 2002).

Ross, A. P., *Recalling the Hope of Glory: Biblical Worship from the Garden to the New Creation* (Grand Rapids: Kregel Publications, 2006).

Schaeffer, F. A., *The Mark of the Christian* (Downers Grove: InterVarsity Press, 1970).

Schaeffer, F. A. and U. Middelmann, *Pollution and the Death of Man* (Leicester: Crossway, 1992).

Stott, J. R.W., *The Cross of Christ* (Leicester: Inter-Varsity Press, 1986).

——, *The Message of Romans*, BST (Leicester: Inter-Varsity Press, 1994).

Tate, M. E., *Psalms 51–100*, WBC 20 (Nashville: Thomas Nelson Inc., 2000).

Thiselton, A. C., *The First Epistle to the Corinthians*, NIGTC (Grand Rapids: Eerdmans, 2000).

Tidball, D., *The Message of the Cross*, BST (Leicester: Inter-Varsity Press, 2001).

——, *The Message of Leviticus*, BST (Leicester: Inter-Varsity Press, 2005).

Torrance, J. B., *Worship, Community and the Triune God of Grace*, expanded version of 1994 Didsbury lecture (Downers Grove: InterVarsity Press, 1997).

Wenham, G. J., *Genesis 1–15*, WBC 1 (Waco: Word Books, 1987).

Wilcock, M., *The Message of Psalms 1–72*, BST (Leicester: Inter-Varsity Press, 2001).

———, *The Message of Psalms 73–150*, BST (Leicester: Inter-Varsity Press, 2001).

Wright, C. J. H., *The Mission of God: Unlocking the Bible's Grand Narrative* (Downers Grove: InterVarsity Press and Nottingham: Inter-Varsity Press, 2006).

———, *The Mission of God's People* (Grand Rapids: Zondervan, 2010).

Wright, N. T., *The Climax of the Covenant* (Minneapolis: Fortress, 1992).

Part 1
Worship and the glory of God

Psalm 8; Hebrews 2:5–18
1. Worship and the music of creation

What if human beings are made for more than the pursuit of comfort and success? What if there is something more important than amassing personal wealth, maximizing shareholder value, increasing the number of our 'friends' on social media? What if human beings are not just '. . . machines built by DNA whose purpose is to make more copies of the same DNA'?[1] What if there is an ultimate meaning and purpose for our existence? What if we are made for ultimate joy? What if we are made to reflect and enjoy the glory of our Creator? What if we are made for worship?

The questions are so far-reaching in their implications that we are often inclined to avoid facing them. To recall Jostein Gaarder's memorable image,[2] we are like a family of parasites living on a long-haired rabbit, who prefer to remain close to the rabbit's skin, deep in the familiar warmth of the fur, rather than venturing to the surface to see a bigger picture of fields, hills, trees and sunshine. We prefer to keep our heads down and get on with the things we assume to be of greatest importance in life, rather than wrestling with the bigger questions, our responses to which determine our view of human identity, significance and purpose.

However, those questions do not go away. As Melvyn Bragg once put it,

> I think there's a feeling that this deep, instinctual, recurrent, dogged and majestic wonderful idea about the meaning of life

[1] R. Dawkins, Royal Institution Christmas Lecture, 'The Ultraviolet Garden', No. 4, 1991. Quoted in V. Ramachandra, *Subverting Global Myths: Theology and the Public Issues Shaping Our World* (London: SPCK Publishing, 2008), p. 187. Dawkins adds, '. . . It is every living object's sole reason for living.'

[2] J. Gaarder, *Sophie's World* (London: Phoenix House, Orien Books, 1995), p. 13.

simply cannot be denied. Back it comes – and not because people are young, naive and stupid or because they are burnt out and old, but it comes through thinking, through experience and it also comes of itself. It simply bubbles up and there it is – we have to address it.[3]

Failure to do so would be both tragic and unforgivable, like a high-prestige Lamborghini locked up forever in a garage showroom, that never discovered it was made for the open road. In the words of the great columnist Bernard Levin, 'To put it bluntly, have I time to discover why I was born before I die? . . . I am unable to believe it was an accident; and if it wasn't one, it must have a meaning.'[4] The witness of Scripture is that the meaning we long to find will elude us until we begin to search for it on the high ground of worship. We do not exist for ourselves; we exist for the glory of Another. As Augustine of Hippo put it long ago, 'Thou hast formed us for thyself and our hearts are restless till they find their rest in thee.'[5] We were made for worship.

This is a book about worship; but if worship truly provides the context of meaning for our whole human existence, this must be a book about much more than church music or even church services. A book about worship must ultimately be a book that helps us discover what it is to be human – and that takes us to the heart of Psalm 8.

1. Creation's majestic music (Ps. 8:1, 9)

> LORD, our Lord,
>   how majestic is your name in all the earth! (1, 9)

These are both the opening and closing words of the psalm, leaving us in no doubt as to the central theme that it celebrates. The creation is 'charged with the grandeur of God'.[6] It is the great theatre of his handiwork in which his magnificence and glory are displayed for all to see. 'The heavens declare the glory of God; the skies proclaim the work of his hands.'[7]

The vastness of the galaxies, the bewildering complexity of the human genome; the restless movement of the sea, the calm stillness

---

[3] Melvyn Bragg, interviewed in *Third Way*, January 1996.

[4] Quoted in N. Gumbel, *Questions of Life* (Eastbourne: Kingsway, 1993), p. 13.

[5] St Augustine, *The Confessions*, Bk 1, Ch. 1; < http://www.ccel.org/a/augustine/confessions/>.

[6] Gerard Manley Hopkins, 'God's Grandeur' (1877).

[7] Ps. 19:1.

of a misty lake at dawn; the majestic glory of the mountains, the intricate beauty of a single flower; the richness of human art and culture, the extravagant colours of a thousand sunsets painting the skies every evening: the whole creation is drawn together into one glorious anthem of worship, pulsating to the rhythm of joyful praise! This is precisely the vision of Psalm 148:

> Praise the LORD.
> Praise the LORD from the heavens;
>   praise him in the heights above.
> Praise him, all his angels;
>   praise him, all his heavenly hosts.
> Praise him, sun and moon;
>   praise him, all you shining stars.
> Praise him, you highest heavens
>   and you waters above the skies.
> Let them praise the name of the LORD,
>   for at his command they were created,
> and he established them for ever and ever –
>   he issued a decree that will never pass away.
> Praise the Lord from the earth,
>   you great sea creatures and all ocean depths,
> lightning and hail, snow and clouds,
>   stormy winds that do his bidding,
> you mountains and all hills,
>   fruit trees and all cedars,
> wild animals and all cattle,
>   small creatures and flying birds,
> kings of the earth and all nations,
>   you princes and all rulers on earth,
> young men and women,
>   old men and children.
> Let them praise the name of the LORD,
>   for his name alone is exalted;
>   his splendour is above the earth and the heavens.
> And he has raised up for his people a horn,
>   the praise of all his faithful servants,
>   of Israel, the people close to his heart.
> Praise the LORD.

It was with good reason that C. S. Lewis imagined Narnia brought into being by the majestic *song* of Aslan!

We find the same theme in the New Testament also. The apostle Paul argues in Romans 1 that the revelation of God's glory in creation

23

is so clear that every human being is without excuse for our failure to 'glorify him as God'. 'Since the creation of the world God's invisible qualities – his eternal power and divine nature – have been clearly seen, being understood from what has been made, so that people are without excuse.'[8] In Romans 11 he concludes his doxology with the same conviction: 'For from him and through him and for him [lit. 'to him'] are all things. To him be the glory for ever! Amen.'[9] Jonathan Edwards was surely right to insist that 'The end of the creation is that the creation might glorify [God]'.[10]

Like so many of the psalms, Psalm 8 is written from the particular perspective of Israel's faith (addressing God by his covenant name 'Yahweh'[11]), but with a global vision for the world – *how majestic is your name* [i.e. reputation and renown] *in all the earth* (1). The God of Israel was never merely a local, tribal deity; he was the Creator of the whole world. It followed that, while he had uniquely established his reign among his people in Jerusalem, his glory was seen not only in the life of Israel but in the vast richness and diversity of the whole of creation. The music of creation, therefore, is not just a single note, nor even a single melody, but a great symphony in which many voices are united in rich harmony, even as God is himself a union of Father, Son and Holy Spirit; one eternal community of unfailing love and perfect harmony. Gregory of Nyssa spoke of the 'diverse and variegated musical harmony' of creation, explaining that,

> . . . just as when the plectrum skilfully plucks the strings and produces a melody in the variety of the notes, since indeed there would be no melody at all if there were only one note in all the strings, so too the composition of the universe in the diversity of the things which are to be observed individually in the cosmos plucks itself by means of some structured and unchanging rhythm, producing the harmony of the parts in relation to the whole, and sings this polyphonic tune in everything.[12]

The creation exists for worship and its music is rich, beautiful and glorious, for it bears witness to a God who is rich, beautiful and glorious.

---

[8] Rom. 1:20–21.

[9] Rom. 11:36.

[10] J. Edwards, 'Miscellanies' No. 3, in *The Works of Jonathan Edwards*, vol. 13, ed. T. Schafer (New Haven: Yale University, 1994), p. 200.

[11] In most English translations the name Yahweh is indicated by writing 'Lord' in small capitals.

[12] Gregory of Nyssa, *Inscr* 31: 1–11, quoted by Hans Boersma, *Embodiment and Virtue in Gregory of Nyssa: An Anagogical Approach* (Oxford: Oxford University Press, 2013), pp. 75–76.

However, if creation is the great theatre of God's handiwork to display his magnificence and glory, then who makes up the audience to enjoy the show? The answer, according to Psalm 8, is that this is *our* role as human beings. Jonathan Edwards again: 'God is glorified not only by His glory's being seen, but by its being rejoiced in.'[13] We are created, in the famous words of the Westminster Shorter Catechism of 1647, to 'Glorify God *and enjoy him forever*' (emphasis added), which is why Psalm 8 turns in (what is at first sight) an unexpected direction.

2. Creation's lowly singers (Ps. 8:2–4)

You have set your glory
  in the heavens.
Through the praise [lit. the mouths] *of children and infants*
  you have established a stronghold against your enemies,
  *to silence the foe and the avenge*r (1b–2).

The contrast is almost more than we can bear. That the God whose majestic name echoes in all the earth and who has set his glory in the heavens, should give a role to *children and infants* to form a stronghold against his enemies, seems implausible; surely he should entrust that responsibility to mighty angels! That this God should form a stronghold against his enemies using the babbling noises that come from the mouths of these *children* seems impossible; surely they must be armed with more than mere words! Yet this is precisely what he has done, for while the psalms are frank in their analysis of human failure they are nonetheless strong in their assertion of human dignity. The first psalm, for example, begins with a portrait of the ideal human, living in the blessing of God and walking in the ways of God (Ps. 1:1–3). Psalms 2 to 7 explore the dark side of human existence from many angles. Psalm 8, however, is a reminder that, in the heart and will of God, the ideal is not altogether lost[14] (though it will remain thoroughly obscured until Christ appears, as we shall see). Within that ideal, human beings – though frail and finite (as the imagery of children and infants doubtless recognizes[15]) – are given a place of astonishing dignity and a role of great responsibility. We

[13] Edwards, 'The Miscellanies', No. 448, p. 495.
[14] T. Longman III and D. E. Garland, *The Psalms*, Expositor's Bible Commentary, vol. 5 (rev. ed., Grand Rapids: Zondervan, 2008), p. 137.
[15] When Jesus quotes Ps. 8 in Matt. 21 he is referring, in the first place, to literal children and infants. However, within Matthew's Gospel children frequently function as examples of the 'little ones' who are welcomed into the kingdom of God and who (in the final analysis) are all the 'poor in spirit' who know their need of God.

are created and called to be the 'lead-worshippers' within creation, celebrating the majesty of God in our praise!

The *enemies* (2) of God are those (whether fallen humans or fallen angels) who are unwilling to recognize the majestic glory of God revealed in creation. In their view, creation exists for their own autonomous glory and pleasure, not for the glory and pleasure of God. Theirs is a destructive voice of hostility, cynicism and reductionism. How is that voice to be overcome? Not with the wisdom of the wise, nor with strength of the powerful, but with the words of the weak; the words of *children and infants* (2), who notwithstanding their weakness, celebrate the glory and goodness of God, whose name is majestic in all the earth! The hostile voice of cynicism is silenced by the life-affirming, life-enriching, God-honouring voice of *praise*.[16]

This was exactly the way in which Jesus himself understood these words. We meet him in Matthew 21, where he has entered the Jerusalem temple, overturned the tables of its money changers and denounced the self-serving corruption of its life. The 'blind and the lame' are flocking to him (Matt. 21:14) and the children are praising him as the 'Son of David', the Messiah and King of his people (21:15); but the powerful religious establishment is becoming ever more blatant in its hostility.

'Do you hear what these children are saying?' they asked him.
'Yes,' replied Jesus, 'Have you never read,
   "From the lips of children and infants
     you, Lord, have called forth your praise"?'[17]

The Word had been made flesh and made his dwelling among them. They had seen his glory, the glory of the One and only who had come from the Father, 'full of grace and truth', but his own had not received him (John 1:14, 11). Yet, while the powerful became

---

[16] There is an apparent tension between the Hebrew of the Masoretic Text, which makes no direct reference to 'praise' (reflected in the ESV, 'Out of the mouth of babies and infants, you have established strength') and the Greek of the LXX which does (reflected in NIV 1984, 'From the lips of children and infants you have ordained praise'). It is clear that Jesus used the LXX when quoting Ps. 8 in Matt. 21:16, but less clear that this should be reflected in the translation of the psalm. See also Michael Wilcock, *The Message of Psalms 1-72*, BST (Leicester: Inter-Varsity Press, 2001), p. 38, who suggests that the LXX represents a somewhat free, but nonetheless faithful, translation of the original (given Dominical support in Matt. 21). The point is that, if the 'enemies' are understood to be those who refuse to recognize the majestic name of the Lord in all the earth, then the voice which will silence them is precisely the voice that *does* recognize that name, and that voice is (by definition) the voice of praise. The NIV 2011 seems to square the circle rather admirably with its dynamic rendering, 'Through the praise of children and infants you have established a stronghold . . .'

[17] Matt. 21:16.

ever more entrenched in their hostility, their voice was silenced by the worship of the weak and the praise of the children.

It is worth pausing to see the implications of these verses for a truly biblical view of creation, for while God's enemies refuse to recognize his glory within the creation, the *children* (2) (representing faithful humankind, albeit in our weakness and finitude) gladly confess his glory revealed *in all the earth* (1). So, far from encouraging a negative view of the material world, biblical faith sees the majesty of God revealed in creation and responds to that revelation with joyful praise! Christian faith has its feet firmly on the ground; it does not seek to escape from the material world to a higher 'spiritual' realm, but rather recognizes, embraces and enjoys the glory and goodness of God revealed within the physical creation. Christians, of all people, should be those who know how to enjoy the goodness of creation, sharing the delight of God in all he has made (cf. Gen. 1:31).

So, just as the creation in general exists to worship its Creator, so we human beings in particular are created for worship. However, while the worship to which we are called begins with words of praise and adoration, it does not finish there. Worship moves from adoration to action,[18] which is precisely the movement of Psalm 8 also.

3. Creation's glorious rulers (Ps. 8:5–8)

In my student days I spent a week one summer walking the Pembrokeshire Coastal Path with my fiancée, Alison (who is now my wife). We stayed several nights in the remote youth hostel on St David's Head and in the middle of one night someone set off the fire alarm. We all had to go outside and gather under the clear night sky. I had never experienced being outside in the middle of the night in such a remote setting, which was virtually free of light pollution. I still remember the almost overwhelming sense of awe and of smallness I felt, as I looked deeper into the night sky than I had ever looked before. Many people have had such experiences and for the writer of this psalm they were probably quite commonplace, living long before the development of most of the artificial forms of light with which we are familiar today.

> *When I consider your heavens,*
> *the work of your fingers,*

---

[18] See D. A. Carson (ed.), *Worship: Adoration and Action* (Eugene: Wipf & Stock Publishers, 2002).

> *the moon and the stars,*
> *which you have set in place,*
> *what is mankind that you are mindful of them,*
> *human beings that you care for them?* (3–4)

Verses 1 and 2 of the psalm have already prepared us for this, moving from God's glory, set *in the heavens* (1b), to the lips of *children and infants* (2) on earth. However, the contrast is now drawn out and painted in even sharper relief. The vast heavens (i.e. the cosmos) belong to God (*your heavens*) and are *the work of his fingers* (3). The shining moon and countless stars were set in place by him. How then could we possibly imagine that such a God would pay the slightest attention to us – *what is mankind that you are mindful of them?* (4a).

We can easily read verse 4 as if it is posing a merely rhetorical question, the purpose of which is to denigrate humankind and dismiss us as wholly unworthy of divine interest or concern. That is, however, to misread the psalm, for we have already established in verse 2 that God *is* mindful of us. He has given us a place of great dignity within creation; we clearly matter to him! The question of verse 4 is therefore a real question, not a rhetorical one: *What is mankind that you are mindful of them?* The purpose of the question is not to denigrate humanity but to force us to reflect on our inherent value and significance: given that God is so very great and yet still is mindful of us, what is the nature of the great dignity we possess? The answer is given in verse 5:

> *You have made them a little lower than the angels*[19]
> *and crowned them with glory and honour.*

Human beings are of the earth (Gen. 2:7); in that sense we are made lower than the angels. However, God has crowned us with glory and honour! The glory of God, which he has *set . . . in the heavens* (1) rests on the head of humankind, created (both male and female) in his image. The picture of a crown denotes authority to rule and the rule envisaged is an extension of the rule of God himself! ' "Glory and honour" are attributes of God's kingship extended to humanity's royal status'[20] and the scope of this rule is then spelt out in the remaining verses of the section.

---

[19] The obvious reading of the Hebrew (*'ĕlōhîm*) here is that we were made a little lower than God or the gods (see NRSV). However, the semantic range of the word includes the broader sense of heavenly beings, as reflected in LXX.

[20] Longman and Garland, *The Psalms*, p. 141.

You made them rulers over the works of your hands;
  you put everything under their feet:
all flocks and herds,
  and the animals of the wild,
the birds in the sky,
  and the fish in the sea,
all that swim the paths of the seas (6–8).

In the Ancient Near East when a city was conquered, the conquering king would sometimes place a statue of himself in the city as a reminder of his authority there. In Syria one such statue has been found which is described as 'the image and likeness' of the ruler.[21] So what is the 'image and likeness' of himself which the Lord, whose name is majestic in all the earth, has placed within creation as an expression of his rule and authority? The Bible is adamant that the living God cannot be faithfully represented by a lifeless statue, but that he has created human beings – into whom he himself breathed the 'breath of life'[22] – in his own likeness, to be his image within creation, the representatives of his rule.

Then God said, 'Let us make mankind in our image, in our likeness, so that they may rule over the fish in the sea and the birds in the sky, over the livestock and all the wild animals, and over all the creatures that move along the ground.'[23]

For generations theologians have debated precisely what this divine image-bearing entails for human beings,[24] but the text of Genesis itself makes it clear that, whatever else the image of God may mean for us, it does not mean less than a responsibility to rule within creation on his behalf. This is precisely the flow of thought in Psalm 8 also: human beings, crowned by God with glory and honour, are commissioned to rule over the works of his hands. These texts provide no mandate to domineer over or exploit creation, for our role is to represent a God who 'is good to all; [and] has compassion on all he has made'.[25] However, they do call us to the awesome responsibility of stewardship over the world that God

---

[21] E. Lucas, *Can We Believe Genesis Today?* (Leicester: Inter-Varsity Press, 2001), p. 175.

[22] Gen. 2:7.

[23] Gen. 1:26.

[24] For a full discussion see G. J. Wenham, *Genesis 1–15*, WBC 1 (Waco: Word, 1987), pp. 29–32.

[25] Ps. 145:9.

has made, so that creation functions well for his pleasure and our good.[26]

Built into the very order of creation, therefore, is both a calling for human beings to be worshippers, and a vision for worship that embraces both the praise of our lips (2) and the obedience of our lives (3–8). This 'whole-person' and 'whole-life' view of worship opens for us the richest possible vision for what it means to be human. Too often Christians have portrayed far too negative a view of human beings, as if the *only* thing God had to say about us was that we are wicked, fallen and sinful. As a result many people feel that God is against them, endlessly critical of them and always ready to 'rub their noses' in their failure (perhaps even with a hint of pleasure). Without doubt, Scripture faces the reality of our fallenness head-on, yet the Bible begins not with human failure but with human dignity; it ends not with human shame but with human glory; and between those two 'bookends' it offers a message not of despair but of *hope* for human beings. As Thomas Howard and J. I. Packer suggested some years ago, we have been too quick to surrender the label 'humanist' to the secularists; it is those whose allegiance is to biblical faith who can claim to be the true humanists.[27]

We are truly extraordinary creatures! We have the capacity to perceive what is ultimate (the glory of God) and to savour and enjoy it; we have the responsibility to reflect what is ultimate, representing God in creation and ruling over it on his behalf with justice and compassion – we are created to be worshippers of Yahweh.

But tragically this is not the whole of the human story.

4. Creation's great Restorer (Heb. 2:5–18)

Psalm 8 presents an ideal vision of human beings in which everything in creation is *under their feet* (8:6); that is, it is in its proper place, stewarded with wisdom, nurtured with care, functioning for the pleasure and glory of God and the blessing and flourishing of humankind. But life as we experience it is not like that. At the time of writing 200 schoolgirls are held captive by terrorists in Northern Nigeria; Syria has been shattered by civil war; 748 million people have no access to safe water;[28] and today a relative of mine suffering

---

[26] For an excellent summary of what this responsibility entails see C. J. H. Wright, *The Mission of God's People* (Grand Rapids: Zondervan, 2010), ch. 3, 'People who care for creation'.

[27] T. Howard and J. I. Packer, *Christianity: The True Humanism* (Vancouver: Regent College Publishing, 1985).

[28] Figures taken from <www.wateraid.org>.

from terminal cancer has been admitted for end-of-life care in a hospice. The writer to the Hebrews faces this reality with great candour in his exposition of Psalm 8: *In putting everything under them, God left nothing that is not subject to them. Yet **at present we do not see everything subject to them*** (8).

I lived my student years in a grand old house named Lenton Hurst on the campus of Nottingham University. It was originally built for William Goodacre Player, the youngest son of John Player, the tobacco tycoon. On first impressions, its former glories remained visible, with attractive gardens, sweeping bay windows and an oak-panelled entrance hall, but it didn't take anyone long to realize it wasn't so grand anymore. Paint was peeling, graffiti covered the oak panelling, mould was growing on the milk in the kitchen and the smell of stale beer was never far away! The old glory was still visible, but the house was now thoroughly spoilt.

The biblical narrative tells us that a similar tragedy has befallen us as human beings. The dignity for which we were made is still evident in us – we *are* extraordinary creatures – but we are also thoroughly spoilt. We were made to display the very glory of God but we have fallen short of that glory (Rom. 3:23; cf. Gen. 3) and exchanged our honour for shame (Rom. 1:21–26). So it is that we don't see everything in order and subject to us, subdued and stewarded with wisdom, love and ingenuity; instead we see nations in turmoil, creation under threat and people in pain. Is there any hope then? Could we scan history and have any hope of finding a human being who breaks the trend, who fits the ideal of Psalm 8?

. . . *at present we do not see everything subject to them. But we do see Jesus . . .* (8b–9). The first is a vision of *failed* humanity, the second a vision of *ultimate* humanity, for Jesus *fulfils* the ideal for humanity that Psalm 8 set out. He was the eternal Word of the Father (Heb. 1:1–2; cf. John 1:1), yet he was *made a little lower than the angels* – he became what he had not been, taking a true and full human nature to himself. He became like us, and yet *unlike us*, he is the true, unflawed image of God, radiating the Father's majesty: he is *crowned . . . with glory and honour* (9).

Yet, mysteriously, it is *because he suffered death* (9) that he is seen to be crowned in this way. How can this be? Only because he tasted *death for everyone* (9). Death is the final enemy of humanity, the punishment for our sin and the seal of our alienation from God; but Jesus has tasted it for us all, so that we can be freed from its power and reconciled to him. All, this, the writer insists, is the outworking of the gracious plan of God. In the beginning Adam stood in a garden and faced a choice between obedience and disobedience; he chose disobedience and dragged the human race into rebellion, guilt and death. Centuries later, Jesus – a new Adam – stood in another garden facing the same choice. Would he resist the Father's will or fulfil his plan of grace, walking the road to the cross in perfect obedience so as to free the human race from the grip of sin? Where Adam chose rebellion, Jesus chose obedience, revealing the true perfection of his humanity so that through his suffering and death he is indeed *crowned with glory and honour*!

The obedience of Jesus, the perfect human being, is therefore the basis for humanity's hope of restoration. In Genesis 3 the serpent promised Eve that the embracing of sin would make her 'like God'. The converse was true, however: together with Adam, she had *already* been created in the likeness of God, to be *crowned with glory and honour* (7) and the effect of their sin was to deprive them of that glory as they fell short of what they were made for. It was an act of *de-creation*.[29] Yet, through his death Jesus is *bringing many sons and daughters to glory* (10). The suffering of the cross is an act of *re-creation* through which our humanity is restored and we begin the journey of becoming the worshippers we were created to be. That journey of restoration will continue until its completion in the *new creation* when Christ returns to make 'everything new'[30] and 'the creation itself will be liberated from its bondage to decay and brought into *the freedom and glory of the children of God*'[31] – the children he first created (Ps. 8) to praise his majestic name and rule creation on his behalf.

5. Conclusion: Created for worship

One of my all-time favourite Christmas presents was a camera I received in my teenage years. It wasn't my first camera, but the others had all been cheap, schoolboy cameras that produced fuzzy images which were often poorly exposed. This, however, was a *proper* camera, with a big lens and sophisticated exposure control, and the only way I could get it was to forgo all the usual presents and ask my relatives to contribute to the camera instead. When I finally bought it everything about it oozed quality: the sound of the shutter; the crispness of the focus, the precision of the exposure control. I never picked up my old cameras again. As I held the *new* one in my hands I knew that, at last, I had the real thing! In the same way, when we

---

[29] I am indebted to Steve Timmis for this language which he uses in his summary of the biblical narrative: Creation; de-creation (fall); re-creation (salvation); new creation (consummation).

[30] Rev. 21:5.

[31] Rom. 8:21, emphasis added.

grasp a clear vision of the glory of God[32] we realize that we have found the 'real thing', the thing of supreme worth and ultimate significance. The glory of humanity is that we were created to recognize, reflect and rejoice in the glory of God – that is, we were created to be worshippers.

Some might think it strange that God should create us to worship him, as if he needed a race of sentient beings to buttress a fragile ego for all eternity. However, it is not divine insecurity but divine love that stands behind the creation. If the glory of God is indeed of supreme worth and ultimate significance, it must follow that God's first delight and joy is in his own glory[33] as Father, Son and Holy Spirit perceive that glory in each other and respond in ceaseless love and mutual delight. Yet in his generous love, God the Holy Trinity has chosen freely to share this infinite joy, by creating us in his image to be worshippers who delight in what he delights in and reflect his glory in creation.

To miss this calling to infinite joy and to squander our lives in the pursuit of lesser joys is the greatest tragedy of all. In the words of C. S. Lewis, 'We are half-hearted creatures, fooling about with drink and sex and ambition when infinite joy is offered us, like an ignorant child who wants to go on making mud pies in a slum because he cannot imagine what is meant by the offer of a holiday at the sea. We are far too easily pleased.'[34]

---

[32] The Hebrew word for glory (*kābôd*) is about weight, substance, worth. God's glory is his inherent majesty, his unveiled magnificence, his overwhelming and absolute significance, his inner perfection and beauty. It may be helpful to distinguish between his *essential* glory (what he is in himself), his *expressed* glory (his revelation of his glory in creation, in Scripture and supremely in Christ) and his *reputational* glory (the esteem in which he is held by those whom he has created).

[33] 'God's glory is uppermost in his own affections. In everything he does, his purpose is to preserve and display that glory ... he delights in his glory above all things' (J. Piper, *Desiring God: Meditations of a Christian Hedonist* [Leicester: Inter-Varsity Press, 1986], p. 31).

[34] C. S. Lewis, 'The Weight of Glory', in *Essay Collection and Other Short Pieces*, ed. L. Walmsley (London: HarperCollins Publishers, 2000), p. 96.

Exodus 3 – 4
2. Worship and the story of salvation

The desire to be free is an almost universal human aspiration and a key motivating factor behind many of the iconic political struggles of the last century. Nelson Mandela's autobiography, recounting the story of his own people's struggle against the oppressive rule of apartheid in South Africa was entitled *Long Walk to* **Freedom**.[1] As I write, it is twenty-five years to the day since the tanks of the Chinese government rolled onto Tiananmen Square to crush the pro-democracy movement which had been demonstrating there to advance their vision of political *freedom*. Almost forty-five years earlier, on 6 June 1944, 170,000 Allied troops landed on the beaches of Normandy on D-Day, to strike the decisive blow against the occupying Nazi forces which began the restoration of *freedom* to continental Europe. Further back in history, the first amendment of the Constitution[2] of the United States famously set out to protect *freedom* of religion, *freedom* of speech and *freedom* of the press.

We desire freedom and, at times, have been willing to pay a heavy price to secure it, but the notion of freedom is not as straightforward as it may at first seem. None of us is truly free to 'do whatever we want to do' – genetics, socialization, gravity and limited resources make certain of that! In any case, the dream of unrestrained freedom all too easily becomes the nightmare of bondage and compulsion. The 'freedom' to misuse drugs or alcohol, look at pornography or feed sexual addictions frequently leaves people gripped by new oppressive forces which are very hard to break. Furthermore, personal freedom cannot exist in a vacuum; the exercise of my freedom may impose constraints on the freedom of others. What if

[1] N. Mandela, *Long Walk to Freedom* (London: Abacus, 1995).
[2] The first article of the Bill of Rights.

my 'freedom' to purchase low-cost food and clothing means that those who produce these goods are held in conditions of grinding poverty from which they cannot escape? What if my 'freedom' to listen to loud music outside my home deprives my neighbour of the freedom to live in peace? What if I want to use my 'freedom' to engage in corrupt practices which undermine the economy to the detriment of the whole society? May I not have to accept certain limitations on my freedom so as to protect the freedom of others? Nelson Mandela expressed it well, 'to be free is not merely to cast off one's chains, but to live in a way that respects and enhances the freedom of others'.[3]

No book in the Bible speaks into the quest for freedom more powerfully than the book of Exodus. The fledgling nation of Israel had moved to Egypt in order to survive the famine in Canaan (see Gen. 41 – 50). However, as they grew and prospered, the Israelites were increasingly viewed as a threat to the people of Egypt. So it was that they became a slave people, languishing under cruel oppression. God, nonetheless, had not forgotten them or the promises he had made to their forefathers. He had a plan to rescue them from slavery. The book of Exodus tells how that plan was fulfilled. It is no wonder that this text has had such resonance for so many oppressed peoples across the world – and rightly so, for it is a dramatic demonstration in history of God's heart to 'work righteousness and justice for *all* the oppressed'.[4]

However, we misread the book of Exodus if we see it *only* as a dramatic narrative of rescue and emancipation; it is also a definitive manifesto of freedom. Its vision of freedom is not only that of casting off oppression, still less that of the autonomous human being possessing the liberty to do whatever they may desire. No, Exodus casts a vision of freedom that is altogether more compelling. The freedom into which Israel is redeemed is (potentially, at least) a *freedom to be who they were created to be*: it is freedom to know God; freedom to nourish their souls with his glory and order their lives by his holiness; it is freedom to *worship*. On no fewer than seven occasions[5] in the first ten chapters we hear God's call, 'Let my people go, *so that they may worship me.*' In the great story of salvation it is God's purpose to call to himself a *worshipping community* that drives the narrative along.

God had a plan to rescue Israel, but he also had a person through whom that plan would be put into action: Moses, the reluctant

[3] Mandela, *Long Walk*, p. 751.
[4] Ps. 103:6.
[5] See Exod. 4:23; 7:16; 8:1, 20; 9:1, 13; 10:3. There are also several references where the Pharaoh says something very similar.

35

servant of the Lord. In many senses Moses' own story mirrored the story of his people. Like the rest of them, he was born in Egypt and was immediately subject to the murderous intent of Pharaoh who had ordered the killing of all the Israelite boys that were born. Yet, just as Moses would one day lead the nation out of the waters of the Red Sea to safety, so God arranged for the daughter of Pharaoh to draw the infant Moses[6] out of the waters of the river Nile to safety and adopt him as her son. So began Moses' privileged upbringing in Pharaoh's household – until he put his life in peril by killing an Egyptian who was beating one of the Israelite slaves (Exod. 2:11–15). As a result, Moses ended up 'a foreigner in a foreign land',[7] even as his people were foreigners in Egypt. Moses fled to Midian where he stayed with a priest named Reuel (Jethro) who became his father-in-law (Exod. 3:1). He stayed in Midian for many long years, tending Jethro's flocks as a shepherd, while his people's suffering in Egypt continued. Then, shortly before he was eighty (cf. Exod. 7:7), Moses had an encounter with God that would change his life forever and transform the destiny of his people.

1. Worship: the sign of salvation (3:1–12)

So now, go. I am sending **you** *to Pharaoh to bring my people the Israelites out of Egypt* (10).

Those were the words that shattered the peace of Moses' life as a shepherd in Midian and summoned him out of rural obscurity onto the world stage. God had seen the misery of his people and decided to *come down to rescue them*, bringing *them up* out of Egypt and into the Promised Land (8). The bombshell for Moses, however, was that God would accomplish this rescue *through him*! We can feel him reeling from shock as he responds, '*Who am I that I should go to Pharaoh and bring the Israelites out of Egypt?*' (11). Who was he indeed? An obscure shepherd in Midian; a man wanted for murder in Egypt; an Israelite who was always an outsider among his people, having grown up in Egypt's royal household. God's response is deeply significant: *I will be with you. And this will be the sign to you that it is I who have sent you: when you have brought the people out of Egypt, you* [plural – i.e., you, the nation of Israel] *will worship God on this mountain* (12).

Moses' reaction may be understandable, but his question is misdirected: the thing that matters is not who Moses is but who will go with him. What is less clear, though, is how the sign that God offers

---

[6] The name Moses sounds like the Hebrew for *draw out*. See NIV fn. for Exod. 2:10.
[7] Exod. 2:22.

is meant to reassure the reluctant Moses, for he will only see the sign after he has brought the people out of Egypt. Some commentators attempt to resolve this by suggesting that the sign is really the burning bush which first drew Moses into this encounter (2–3), but that does not appear to be the natural reading of the text. Perhaps we need to approach this sign slightly differently.

Imagine for a moment that you are going to visit a friend for the first time. They give you instructions for finding their home (or, more likely, a postcode for your satnav!) and then add, 'You'll know you've found the right house when you see the bright yellow door.' The yellow door is a 'sign', but the purpose of the sign is not to persuade you to begin the journey, but to reassure you that you have found the right house when you arrive. Perhaps Moses' sign here is similar.

a. Moses worships on Mount Horeb (Sinai)

We begin by reflecting on what the phrase *you* [i.e. the nation] *will worship God on this mountain* (12) meant to Moses when he first heard it. The mountain was Mount *Horeb, the mountain of God* (1), known also as Mount Sinai. Moses had been tending his father-in-law's flocks when he arrived at the mountain. He was drawn to the sight of a bush that was burning with fire. At the edge of the desert this was not perhaps so unusual, but this bush was not consumed by the fire. Moses goes to investigate, but as he approaches the bush, God calls to him by name and warns him not to come any closer, *'Take off yours sandals,*[8] *for the place where you are standing is holy ground'* (5). Fire in Scripture is often a sign of God's presence and, in particular, of his holiness.[9] Clearly that is the case here: the ground is holy because the God of holiness is present, revealing himself to Moses.

It may well be that in the long years of his exile in Midian Moses had been distant from the God of his fathers. Nonetheless, the God who speaks from the burning bush is not a new God to him, but rather *the God of* [his] *father, the God of Abraham, the God of Isaac and the God of Jacob* (6). Moses responds to this encounter with God's holiness in reverent worship and holy fear, hiding *his face, because he was afraid to look at God.* However, the burning bush is a revelation not only of God's holiness but also of his grace: the bush

[8] Note the comment of Peter Enns: 'This is a sign of reverence common in the Ancient Near East, a practice that continues to this day' (*Exodus*, NIVAC [Michigan: Zondervan, 2000], p. 98). Cf. Josh. 5:15.

[9] See, for example, Gen. 3:24; Exod. 19:18; 13:21; 32:10, as highlighted in A. Cole, *Exodus* TOTC (Leicester: Inter-Varsity Press, 1973), p. 64.

burns with holy fire *but the bush is not consumed.* In the same way God is not showing himself to Moses to destroy him but to reveal grace to him. He has seen the suffering of his people and plans to rescue them (7–9). To this word of grace Moses was called to respond in faith, obediently stepping forward to fulfil his strategic role within God's plan of salvation (10). It is clear then that Moses himself had *worshipped God on this mountain* (12): he had encountered God's holy presence and responded with homage and holy fear; he had heard God's saving word and was preparing to take the first steps of obedient faith.

b. Israel will worship on Mount Horeb (Sinai)

So when God speaks of the whole, redeemed nation of Israel gathering to worship on the same mountain, he is saying that, once again, Moses' experience will prefigure the experience of his people. They will encounter God's holiness as he has encountered it; they will hear his saving word as he has heard it; they will worship as he has worshipped. This will be the authenticating sign to Moses that God had sent *him* to rescue his people and claim them as his own. The worship of God's people will be the sign of his work of salvation. So the promised sign is given not to impart faith to the reluctant Moses[10] but to confirm and authenticate his faith following his obedience.[11]

Exodus 19 – 24 records the fulfilment of this promise to Moses. The people he had led out of slavery in Egypt now gather at Mount Sinai. First they encounter God's holy presence as he reveals himself in holy fire and the people tremble in reverent fear:

> On the morning of the third day there was thunder and lightning, with a thick cloud over the mountain, and a very loud trumpet blast. Everyone in the camp trembled. Then Moses led the people out of the camp to meet with God, and they stood at the foot of the mountain. Mount Sinai was covered with smoke, because the LORD descended on it in fire. The smoke billowed up from it like smoke from a furnace, and the whole mountain trembled violently.[12]

[10] Other than in the sense that he knew of the authenticity of his own experience on Mount Horeb and could therefore be confident in the reality of what was promised.

[11] Rather as in Luke 2:12, where the shepherds see the sign of the infant Jesus wrapped in strips of cloth lying in a manger only after they have obeyed the angelic call and gone to search for him.

[12] Exod. 19:16–18.

Next they hear the gracious word of God's covenant, which confirms their salvation and teaches them to shape their lives by his holiness:

And God spoke all these words:
'I am the LORD your God, who brought you out of Egypt, out of the land of slavery.
You shall have no other gods before me.'[13]

Finally the people respond with worship (Exod. 24:1), pledging their obedience and loyalty: 'When Moses went and told the people all the LORD's words and laws, they responded with one voice, "Everything the LORD has said we will do."'[14]

So it was that Moses worshipped on *the mountain of God*, together with his people and in that moment he knew that God had indeed sent him to save them. In the New Testament too, it was when Peter heard Cornelius and his household 'speaking in tongues and *praising God*'[15] that they knew that they had received the Holy Spirit and were sealed as God's own. Authentic worship was (and is) a key sign of salvation.

2. Worship: the goal of salvation (3:13 – 4:26)

It is easy to be rather harsh on Moses as we explore his dialogue with God that followed the shattering realization that God intended to rescue his people *through him*. There is little evidence that God responded to Moses' many questions with anything other than understanding and patience, until his final attempt to sidestep God's call altogether. Indeed, given the significance of God's responses to those questions, we should perhaps conclude that Moses was displaying a teachable and humble spirit that was actually quite appropriate. The dialogue focuses on two key challenges facing Moses:

a. How would Moses persuade his fellow Israelites to believe him?

Moses wonders how he should reply if the Israelites ask him for the *name* of the God who has sent him (3:13). God responds by using his covenant name, Yahweh (3:14–15).[16] It is often assumed that this

---

[13] Exod. 20:1–3.
[14] Exod. 24:3.
[15] Acts 10:46, emphasis added.
[16] Reflected in most English translations by using small capitals for 'the LORD'. It is not entirely clear whether the name God gives is 'I AM' or the (related) 'Yahweh'. Enns (*Exodus*, p. 106) suggests a more encompassing response: 'I am YHWH, the 'I AM', the God of the patriarchs.'

is the first time that the name Yahweh is revealed to Israel, and that the revelation of this new name to Moses will confirm to them that he is called to speak on God's behalf.[17] It could equally be that the name was already known both to Israel[18] and to Moses, but that his long sojourn in Midian had left him uncertain whether this was the appropriate name to use in the circumstances. Either way, the giving of the covenant name provides the basis for a further exposition of God's plan to rescue Israel and bring them into the land.

Moses is not yet sufficiently reassured. *'What if they do not believe me or listen to me and say, "The LORD did not appear to you"?'* (4:1). With great patience, the Lord responds by giving Moses a series of miraculous signs to perform in the presence of the Israelites – his staff becoming *a snake*; his hand made *leprous* and then healed; the water of the Nile turned to blood (4:2–9). In all this, Moses' primary concern seems to be the reaction of his own people, but the signs were not given only (or even primarily) to persuade them.

b. How would Moses persuade Pharaoh to let the Israelites go?

The Lord has to keep bringing Moses back to this challenge. His instructions are clear. Moses is to go to Pharaoh and tell him to let the people go on *a three-day journey* into the desert to make sacrifices to their God (3:18).[19] Of course it seemed impossible that Pharaoh would accept such a request unless forced to do so, so God promises, *'I will stretch out my hand and strike the Egyptians with all the wonders that I will perform among them. After that, he will let you go'* (3:20).

Moses' questions are all dealt with, but still he is not persuaded. He finally steps over the mark as he complains of his lack of eloquence and begs God to send someone else. The Lord reminds him that the ability to speak is God-given, but agrees to send Moses' brother, Aaron, to be his mouthpiece (4:10–17). As Moses sets out to Egypt at last, the Lord spells out the task that lies ahead of him, and explains how the conflict will come to a head such that Pharaoh is finally persuaded.

The LORD said to Moses, 'When you return to Egypt, see that you perform before Pharaoh all the wonders I have given you the

---

[17] See Cole, *Exodus*, p. 69.

[18] Enns argues that the statement in v. 15, 'This is my name *forever*' indicates past, present and future, i.e. 'this has always been and will always be my name' (Enns, *Exodus*, p. 106).

[19] The reference to a three-day journey need not be read as deceptive. It could simply indicate the length of the journey to Sinai rather than implying that they will return.

power to do. But I will harden his heart so that he will not let the people go. Then say to Pharaoh, 'This is what the LORD says: Israel is my firstborn son, and I told you, "Let my son go, so that he may worship me." But you refused to let him go; so I will kill your firstborn son.' (4:21–23)

In some mysterious sense the hardening of Pharaoh's heart will not be only his business; God will also be at work, for he is sovereign in this great drama. Time after time, Moses will go to Pharaoh demanding the release of his people and time after time Pharaoh will refuse. After nine devastating plagues, Moses must deliver this dire message from the Lord. God had chosen Israel as his *firstborn son* but Pharaoh has refused to release God's firstborn son to him and so God will claim the firstborn sons of Egypt for himself. Pharaoh will finally be persuaded to let Israel go through this great act of judgment – a judgment from which Israel will be protected only through the blood of the Passover lamb.[20]

I have two daughters who have learned to play various musical instruments and participated in local orchestras and ensembles as they have grown up. Both of them have had to spend many hours practising their instruments at home and rehearsing with fellow musicians. At times the requirement for more and more rehearsing has seemed rather to take over their free time. It can be difficult in the busyness of life to remember that the purpose of learning the instruments is not really to participate in rehearsals but to make beautiful music for all of us to enjoy! However, when the concert comes and the first notes of the orchestra sound, all the rehearsing seems worthwhile. Sometimes, as we read the story of salvation we can get so consumed in the detail that we forget to ask what it is all for. That is the question to which the Lord now draws Moses' attention.

c. What is the reason for releasing Israel from Egypt?

The Lord insists that Pharaoh must let Israel go from Egypt *in order that they may worship him*. He does not merely save them *from* slavery but *for* worship. Worship is the goal of salvation, the calling of holy liberty and joy which defines what it means to be the *firstborn son* of God. This should not surprise us, of course. For if human beings were created for worship[21] and yet have fallen short of this God-given calling, we would expect that the goal of God's work in

---

[20] See Exod. 11 and 12; cf. 1 Cor. 5:7.
[21] As we understood from Ps. 8 in the first chapter of this book.

salvation would be to restore them to that calling again. That is precisely what the Exodus narrative affirms time after time.

It is worth noting that the Hebrew word here for 'worship' (*'bd*) has a wide range of meaning. For example, the same word is used to describe Israel's bond-service in Egypt,[22] which could hardly be said to be worship! Some translations[23] therefore opt for the language of service rather than that of worship in this passage. However, the parallel with Exodus 5:1 ('Let my people go so that they may hold a festival to me in the wilderness'[24]) strongly points towards the idea of worship[25] (or at least suggests that the 'service' envisaged is specifically religious service).[26]

As he makes his journey back to Egypt, Moses is given a final reminder of the holiness of the God he has been called to serve (4:24–26). The details are uncertain,[27] but the point seems to be that if Moses is to lead his people to become the worshippers God calls them to be, he must first make sure his own house and family are in order by obeying the covenant requirement to circumcise his own son.[28] This is surely a salutary reminder about the importance of personal integrity for would-be worship leaders in every generation. So, chastened after this close brush with God's holiness,[29] Moses (along with his brother, Aaron) goes to the leaders of his people to explain all that God has said to him.

3. Worship: the response to salvation (4:27–31)

Moses' fears about his reception among his people prove groundless. When they hear his message and see the signs he performs, we read, *they believed. And when they heard that the LORD was concerned*

---

[22] See Exod. 6:5.

[23] E.g. ESV: '*Let my son go that he may serve me*'. Also KJV.

[24] See also Exod. 3:18.

[25] So NIV, NRSV.

[26] 'The verb . . . is often used theologically with respect to the cult of Israel in its service and care for the tabernacle, temple, its appurtenances, and its personnel . . . Thus the verb refers to the performance of the cult in the sense of worship, honour, serve in a purely religious sense, in addition to caring (*'bd*) for its physical upkeep and maintenance. The goal of the Exodus was the worship (*'bd*) of the Lord at Sinai (Exod 3:12; cf 1 Chron 28:9; Mal 3:18), "To serve Yahweh" (*'bd yhwh*) is found 56x (e.g. Exod 4:23; Deut 6:13; 1 Sam. 7:3; Psa 100:2; Jer 2:20). All referring to worship, cultic service of faithfully keeping his covenant as his people' (*NIDOTTE*, vol. 3, pp. 305–306).

[27] See, for example, the fuller discussion in Enns, *Exodus*, pp. 132–134.

[28] In some respects this is an OT equivalent of the NT warning to teachers in the church that they will be 'judged more strictly' (Jas 3:1).

[29] I owe this phrase to my friend Julian Hardyman of Eden Baptist Church, Cambridge.

about them and had seen their misery, they bowed down and worshipped (4:31). The word used here for worship was linked with physical prostration[30] as an expression of homage and gratitude to God – what David Peterson describes as 'grateful submission'.[31] The people hear that God is concerned for them, that he has a plan to come to set them free from slavery and free to worship. They see the signs of his power which confirm the reliability of his word. They are therefore moved with awe and gratitude and bow their heads and (quite possibly, literally) prostrate themselves before this great, majestic God who is also the covenant God of unfailing love. A few chapters later, God's word is fulfilled and the people walk free from Egypt and see their enemies destroyed in the Red Sea. In response to the experience of salvation they sing 'the song of Moses'.[32] In the same way, in the New Testament book of Revelation, those who have 'washed their robes and made them white in the blood of the Lamb' are 'before the throne of God, and worship him day and night within his temple'.[33] Worship was (and still is) the response to salvation.

4. Conclusion: Worship and the ongoing story of salvation

a. Exodus opens a window onto the nature of biblical worship

Since God's purpose in saving Israel from Egypt was to make them into a worshipping community, it follows that the life into which he led them (unfolded in the remaining chapters of Exodus) will give us a key model for what God intends a worshipping community to be. Those chapters focus *first* on God's word to his people, the law (Exod. 20 – 24), through which he establishes his covenant with them; and *second* on God's presence among his people, the tabernacle (Exod. 25 – 40, see especially 25:8), through which they encounter his majestic glory for themselves (see Exod. 40:34–38).

The presence of God in the community of his people was both a joyful and a sobering reality in Scripture, because the God who made his dwelling among them was the holy God, whose righteous wrath is provoked by human sin.[34] 'Everything that is employed in offering

---

[30] The word is *ḥāwâ*: 'Worship, bow (down), make/do obeisance' (*NIDOTTE*, vol. 2, p. 42).

[31] D. Peterson, *Engaging with God* (Leicester: Apollos, 1992), p. 63.

[32] Exod. 15.

[33] Rev. 7:14–15, NRSV.

[34] The power of God's wrath to destroy in response to human sin is evident in a number of OT narratives. See for example Exod. 32:33–35; Lev. 10; Num. 16.

him worship – whether priests, sacrificial animals, altars or pots and pans – has to be set apart for his exclusive use and must partake of his holy character. His holiness must never be breached, compromised or trivialized.'[35] How then could this perfect God of holiness live among a flawed and sinful people without destroying them in judgment? The answer lay in the elaborate system of animal sacrifice which stood at the heart of Israel's tabernacle worship.[36] The book of Leviticus sets out the detail and we shall return to it in chapter 9 of this book, but at its heart was the following principle: 'For the life of a creature is in the blood, and I have given it to you to make atonement for yourselves on the altar; it is the blood that makes atonement for one's life.'[37] In other words, through the shedding of sacrificial blood, the life of the animal victim was being forfeited in place of the life of the sinful human worshipper. Only in this way was it possible for fallen and flawed human beings to live with the presence of God among them. In Scripture there was no true worship without atonement and no true atonement without the shedding of sacrificial blood.

From this analysis two foundational principles emerge to shape a biblical understanding of worship:

1. A worshipping community is centred on the saving word of God and responds with faith and obedience.
2. A worshipping community encounters the living presence of God through the atoning grace of God, and responds with awe, gratitude and praise.

This pattern was prefigured (as we saw) in Moses' own experience of worship on Mount Horeb (3:1–12). In fact we can go back still further to Eden itself where God spoke his word to Adam (Gen. 2:16), setting out before him the God-centred life that would bring him satisfaction and joy, and where God shared his presence with Adam, walking with him in the cool of the day (Gen. 3:8). The New Testament scholar G. K. Beale (drawing on strong evidence in Jewish tradition) has identified numerous indications in the Old Testament that the Garden of Eden was seen as the first and archetypal temple, upon which the subsequent temples were based.[38] Adam was created to worship, just as Israel was saved to worship.

[35] D. Tidball, *The Message of Leviticus*, BST (Leicester: Inter-Varsity Press, 2005), p. 32.
[36] See the connection in Exod. 29:42–46.
[37] Lev. 17:11.
[38] G. K. Beale, *The Temple and the Church's Mission* (Leicester: Apollos, 2004), pp. 66–80.

It follows that the worship the Father seeks[39] is deeply shaped by Scripture and its message of salvation, which is read, expounded, explored, applied, treasured and received with grateful and obedient faith. It also follows that the worship the Father seeks is deeply experiential as God's people encounter his living, transforming presence among them and find themselves moved to respond in awe, wonder, thankfulness and trembling joy. It follows lastly that true worshippers are those who respond to the initiative God himself has taken. Scripture could hardly be clearer in its rejection of human attempts to construct gods conjured up by our own imagination (Isa. 44:9–18), which seek to second-guess his word (Isa. 40:13–14) and manipulate his powerful presence (Acts 8:18–24). From start to finish, the Bible's story is a story of *grace*; a story of God's initiative to do for us what we cannot do for ourselves by offering us unmerited mercy and undeserved love. Worship in the Bible is never a bridge that we build out to him but simply a responsive journey we make to cross the bridge he has built out to us. He speaks his word and gives his presence; we his worshipping people simply respond to what he has done.

b. Exodus establishes the pattern for worship which the coming of Jesus fulfils

This pattern of worship runs right through into the New Testament, for Jesus comes as the true Word of God (John 1:1, 14) and the true temple of God (John 2:20–22), anointed with his living presence by the Holy Spirit (John 1:32). His coming therefore brings to fulfilment all that the book of Exodus has begun to establish. In him a new covenant 'people of God' come to Christ to receive the word he gives (the gospel) and drink the Spirit he pours out generously on all who believe (John 7:37–39; cf. John 1:32–33). So, with the coming of Christ, 'a time has come' when a new community of worshippers 'worship the Father in the *Spirit* [God's presence] and in truth [God's word]'. These are precisely the 'true' worshippers for 'they are the kind of worshippers the Father seeks'.[40] As God acted through Moses to rescue Israel from Egypt to make them into a worshipping community, so God has acted in Christ through the sacrifice of the cross and the victory of the resurrection, to rescue a global people from the darkness of sin in order to make them the kind of worshippers he seeks. The continuing story of salvation still moves to the music of worship.

[39] See John 4:23.
[40] John 4:23.

c. Worship therefore remains the sign and goal of salvation and the proper response to it

Having seen the trajectory thrown by these passages right into the world of the New Testament, we can confidently apply their insights to ourselves. As a serving pastor and member of a leadership team within a busy and growing church there are many calls on my time. Sermons must be written, funds raised, members of the congregation visited, vision statements agreed, partnerships established and leaders trained. In such a world the easy option is simply to hand the worship life of the church over to our team of highly talented musicians (of whom many are deeply spiritual people) as if it were simply a specialized ministry for musical people. Certainly the gifts of such people must be honoured and their spiritual leadership given space to flourish,[41] but if worship is the sign and goal of salvation and the proper response to it, then I must see that the nurturing of a worshipping community lies at the heart of my responsibilities.

At one level this is obvious since, if the word of God is central to the nature of worship, then my work of preaching and teaching that word is a crucial investment in the worship of our church community. However, I need to go further than that, for it is all too possible for churches to be rich in their sermons but poor in their congregational worship. A worshipping community is a community of word and Spirit, a community hungry to grow in understanding of God and transforming experience of his presence. A worshipping community therefore does not simply hear God's word preached; it comes to that word expecting to encounter the living presence of God among his people by his Holy Spirit; it receives that word with a joyful heart and a teachable spirit and it responds to it with repentance, faith, celebration and obedience.

My task as a pastor, then, is to seek to build such a worshipping community of expectant, responsive disciples of Christ, not to create a platform for 'my ministry'. That means (among other things) that I will always seek to preach as a 'lead-worshipper', allowing the congregation to see something of how the word is leading me to respond in praise, wonder, faith and obedience. It also means leaving space within services to nurture the congregation's response to God, working closely with others whose gifts can help us express that response meaningfully and appropriately. It means that I will be concerned for new believers to grow as worshippers, learning to praise God with grateful hearts and live obedient lives for his glory.

---

[41] Practice will vary, of course, but ideally services will be put together in a way which allows the preacher, the service leaders and the lead musician to bring their contribution both to its preparation and its leadership.

Since they were created and saved for worship, learning to worship will be a key authenticating sign of their salvation. It will also be for them a discovery of the true freedom in which they will thrive as Christians and as human beings.

Exodus 32 – 34; Isaiah 1
3. Worship catastrophe

It is a fairly large church and the time is 10:25 on Sunday morning. The service will soon begin, but the 'band' is still trying to rehearse. To be more exact, one lone guitarist is playing a few chords – the other musicians are all ill with a virus and unable to come. A fuse has blown on the mixing desk so the sound system is down. The projector bulb has failed so there are no song words on the big screen. The service leader has a heavy cold and very little voice. The visiting preacher's car has broken down and they are at least an hour away from the church building. The welcome team have lost their warm smiles because the coffee has run out. Longstanding members of the church are reminiscing about the good old days of the minister, the piano and the hymnbook when nothing could go wrong! The service leader attempts to offer a welcome, which no one can hear. The guitarist steps forward and, with no sound system to help her, tries to start the first song . . .

It's a worship catastrophe isn't it? Everything has gone wrong! Well, perhaps it is less of a catastrophe than we think. Perhaps it would do us all good sometimes to have a 'stripped down' service in which many of the normal props were taken away. Indeed, the real catastrophe may well be that the criteria we use to evaluate 'good worship' are so far removed from what matters most to God. Of course it is a good thing to seek to do things well: good music, good sound systems and visuals, welcome teams who reflect the welcoming God, and well-prepared, faithful sermons all play an important part in our church gatherings. However, it would be a much greater 'worship catastrophe' if we had all the things we believe make up a 'good' service, but the congregation sang loudly while their hearts were set on money, wealth and power and were closed to the needs of the poor and oppressed. It would be a much greater worship catastrophe if the preacher delivered a fine sermon but was fiddling

their annual tax return or the lead musician gave a stunning performance while holding bitterness in their heart against someone in the
church with a different musical taste. It would be a much greater
worship catastrophe if our worship experience was *perfect for us* but
we didn't even notice that God had been displaced from the centre,
the Bible neglected and the Holy Spirit grieved.

After seeing God's mighty hand save them powerfully from their
slavery in Egypt, experiencing God's majestic presence at Sinai and
hearing his word in the law, the young nation of Israel seemed to be
set up for generations of faithful worship. However, the story of
Israel echoed all too tragically the story of the human race as a whole.
The people chosen to be the community of Yahweh's worshippers
failed to live up that calling. Instead their history was marred by
one worship catastrophe after another. We will focus on two particular chapters, but the fault lines they expose run through the whole
story.

1. Idolatry: when worship is misdirected (Exod. 32 – 34)

Calvin's idea of the human heart as an 'idol factory'[1] has been
helpfully explored by a number of authors recently,[2] moving the
discussion beyond the familiar associations of gods of wood and
stone that are too easily dismissed as primitive by contemporary
people. An idol can be anything – including a great many good things
– which takes the place of God as the object of our worship. We can
idolize our relationship with another human being, when their
approval becomes too important to us. We can idolize our Christian
service, when we need to be 'doing ministry' of some kind in order
to feel secure about ourselves. We can idolize body-image, wealth,
reputation, influence over others or even our favourite Christian
leaders.[3] Some idols are relatively obvious, lying on the 'surface' of
our lives, while others are subtle and 'deep', connecting with our
basic human desires for a sense of security, identity, significance and
self-worth.[4]

Central to our problem with idolatry is the fickleness of our hearts.
Our experience of God may be powerful and recent but we can still

---

[1] 'Man's nature is a perpetual factory of idols' (J. Calvin, *Institutes of the Christian Religion*, trans. L. Battles [Louisville: The Westminster Press, 1960], I: 11.8).
[2] See J. Hardyman, *Idols: God's Battle for Our Hearts* (Nottingham: Inter-Varsity Press, 2010) and T. Keller, *Counterfeit Gods* (London: Hodder & Stoughton, 2009).
[3] Julian Hardyman quotes Luther's definition in his Larger Catechism: 'A god is that to which we look for all good and in which we find refuge in every time of need . . . That to which your heart clings and entrusts itself is really your God' (*Idols*, p. 21).
[4] Keller's discussion of this distinction is very insightful: *Counterfeit Gods*, pp. 64ff.

be tempted to trust someone or something else in his place. That was Israel's experience, so soon after God had set them free from Egypt to be his worshippers.

a. The catastrophe (Exod. 32:1–8)

When the people saw that Moses was so long in coming down from the mountain, they gathered round Aaron and said, 'Come, make us gods who will go before us. As for this fellow Moses who brought us up out of Egypt, we don't know what has happened to him.' (1)

Israel's fall into idolatry begins with a sense of disconnection from God and disillusionment with the mediator he had given. Moses was on Mount Sinai for forty days (Exod. 24:18) receiving the law from God, inscribed on tablets of stone. God had already displayed something of his glory to the people (Exod. 19) but the tabernacle was not yet set up; their only access to God was through the direct mediation of Moses who was nowhere to be seen! So how would they remain in touch with the God who had brought them out of Egypt? Had he rescued them from slavery only to abandon them in the desert?

Ironically Moses was at that very moment on the mountain receiving God's instructions for building the tabernacle, through which his presence among his people would be maintained for generations. The people, though, had run out of patience and took matters (quite literally) into their own hands. If Moses was not delivering on their expectations, they would make their own meeting place between heaven and earth; they would establish their own way to God and his blessings. So they challenged Aaron, *make us gods*[5] *who will go before us* and Aaron caved in to their pressure, making the calf-idol from the people's gold.

Scholars tell us that ancient people saw their idols not as gods but as visible representations of their gods. 'Specifically it was thought that calves or bulls functioned as pedestals for the gods seated or standing over them.'[6] It is likely, then, that what the Israelites thought they were doing was not replacing Yahweh, but creating their own

---

[5] Here (and in v. 4) either the singular (a god) or the plural (gods) are possible translations as is indicated by the NIV footnote, because the Hebrew *'ĕlōhîm* takes the same form in both cases. However, the plural forms of the verbs and pronouns in v. 4 indicate that the plural reading is probably correct. The point then is that, by constructing the calf, the Israelites have become polytheists whether they like it or not!

[6] P. Enns, *Exodus*, NIVAC (Michigan: Zondervan, 2000), p. 569.

means of access to him.[7] God's analysis, however, is very different: like all human attempts at constructing our own religion, the golden calf *does* in fact take his place and so deprives him of his glory. The text uses many devices to make this point: the gold that the people should be using to construct a dwelling place for Yahweh is used instead to make the idol (2–4a); the people explicitly link the calf statue to their deliverance from Egypt (4b); the festival to which Yahweh had called them in the desert (Exod. 5.1) now involves offerings being made on *an altar in front of the calf* (5–6); the eating and drinking of Israel's elders who saw Yahweh (Exod. 24:11) is now parodied by those who see the calf (6b); the people who 'bowed down and worshipped'[8] Yahweh when they first heard his message of salvation now *bow down* to the calf (8b); Moses' victory song (Exod. 15) is replaced by a new song *in the camp* (17–18). When he sees what has happened, Moses' grief-stricken cry to the Lord leaves us in no doubt as to how we should view what Israel has done: *So Moses went back to the* LORD *and said, 'Oh, what a great sin these people have committed!* **They have made themselves gods of gold**' (31).

The same conclusion is drawn still more starkly in Psalm 106:

> At Horeb they made a calf
> and worshipped an idol cast from metal.
> *They exchanged their glorious God*
> *for an image of a bull*, which eats grass.
> *They forgot the God who saved them*,
> who had done great things in Egypt,
> miracles in the land of Ham
> and awesome deeds by the Red Sea.[9]

Impatient with God's timing and indifferent to God's mediator, Israel desired a god they could see, a god who would conform to their expectations and 'go on ahead of them'. So they 'exchanged the truth about God for a lie, and worshipped and served created things rather than the Creator'.[10] Doubtless this is why God had already warned the nation both against the worshipping of other gods and the making of images as objects of worship (see Exod. 20:1–4 and cf. Exod. 23:13, 20–33). The nation redeemed for worship had become

---

[7] This may well be the reason that Exodus places this episode inbetween the two extended accounts of the establishing of the tabernacle, for the golden calf represents the human attempt to do precisely what God had ordained that the tabernacle should do.

[8] Exod. 4:31.

[9] Ps. 106:19–22, emphasis added.

[10] Rom. 1:25.

a people mired in idolatry – just as the human race as a whole, whom God created to worship him in the beginning, had fallen from their high calling into disobedience.[11]

The story of the golden calf was a worship catastrophe that would set the tone for many other such catastrophes in Old Testament history.[12] However, it remains a powerful insight for people in every generation into the nature of idolatry. It reminds us, *first*, of the fickleness of our hearts that can receive God's blessings with joy one moment and dethrone him the next. *Second*, it highlights the danger of assuming that God's ways, his timing and his way of working will always fit with our expectations, because when they do not we will be tempted to trust something else in his place. Of course a God who always fitted our expectations would be a mere projection of our own values and preoccupations, so to worship him would be to worship ourselves. If we want to avoid worship catastrophe we need to be clear that God is not like us; we must expect that sometimes he will surprise us, confuse us and even perplex us. *Third*, it warns us against taking our religion into our own hands and seeking to construct our own spirituality at times when we may feel disconnected from God. This was probably what the Israelites *thought* they were doing in constructing the golden calf, when what they were *actually* doing was putting their faith in a self-made religion and so putting it in the place of the true God. *Fourth*, it warns us against the desire to make our own visible images of God. Of course the God who is there does have a visible representation on earth, but that is not anything we make, but something he has made. He has created *us*, human beings, in his image, and appointed us as his representatives on earth. Idolatry is a terrible reversal of that order in which we seek to re-make God in our image, seeking to construct 'the God we like to believe in'. *Finally*, it exposes how rarely we call idolatry by its name. Instead we hide behind elaborate rationalizations of our behaviour when the fact is that, for all our pretence, we have stopped looking to God for our flourishing and have allowed something (or someone) else to take his place.

b. The judgment (Exod. 32:9–29)

And God spoke all these words:
'I am the LORD your God, who brought you out of Egypt, out of the land of slavery.

[11] Gen. 3 and see ch. 1 of this book. Enns quotes Terence E. Fretheim, 'It is Genesis 3 all over again' (Enns, *Exodus*, p. 589).
[12] See, for example, the moving analysis of idolatry in the prophet Hosea, and Isaiah's cutting exposé in Isa. 44:9–20.

'You shall have no other gods before me.

'You shall not make for yourself an image in the form of anything in heaven above or on the earth beneath or in the waters below. You shall not bow down to them or worship them; for I, the LORD your God, am a jealous God . . .'[13]

These are opening words of the famous Ten Commandments which God had given to Israel and which the nation had promised to obey (see Exod. 24:3). It is immediately obvious that, in making the golden calf and bowing before it, they had flagrantly disregarded virtually every sentence within these verses. It is certain that the Lord will act in judgment. In his first response he ominously describes Israel to Moses as *your* people, *whom* **you** *brought out of Egypt* (32:7) and concludes tersely, '*I have seen these people . . . and they are a stiff-necked people. Now leave me alone so that my anger may burn against them and that I may destroy them. Then I will make you into a great nation*' (9–10).

As we shall see, God relents from this course in response to Moses' plea, but still he orders a great slaughter within the camp (27–29) and strikes the people with a plague (32:35). To our ears these judgments may seem harsh, but that is because we are looking from this side of the cross. Throughout Scripture, unless sin is dealt with, its penalty is death (Gen. 2:17; Rom. 6:23), and that is what is being reflected here, for at this point in the story there is no tabernacle, no sacrificial system and therefore no obvious means of atonement.

What was still more devastating was God's word to Moses that, though he and the people should go on up to the Promised Land, they will make the journey without his presence among them (3), just as Adam and Eve had been banished from Eden, the first temple of God's presence,[14] following their disobedience. Israel's idolatry has threatened their entire status as the people of God. Ironically, hope now rests only with the mediator God has given them (Moses), the rejection of whom had precipitated this crisis in the first place.

c. The mediator (Exod. 32:30 – 33:23)

The propensity to re-make God in the image of our expectations is not unique to this generation of Israelites; it is a temptation that faces theologians today. Convinced as we (rightly) are of God's unchanging nature, complete knowledge and full sovereignty, we can fail to take seriously passages in Scripture like these, where God is presented

---

[13] Exod. 20:1–5.
[14] See ch. 2 of this book.

as being persuaded by a human intervention and changing his mind accordingly. Is this all just a piece of choreographed theatre in which God behaves like the most cynical of public servants, going through the pretence of a consultation while doing what he intended to do all along? Or is it that God is fickle and is outmanoeuvred by Moses? Neither of these responses is very adequate!

At one level we are up against one of the deepest mysteries of the God of the Bible, who is revealed as being both completely sovereign over all of his creation and at the same time authentically personal, making real responses to people (as he is clearly doing to Moses in this passage). We assume such a vision of God every time we address him in the sublime opening words of the Lord's Prayer. He is 'Our Father' – the personal God who interacts with us his children; and he is 'in heaven' – the sovereign God in the ultimate seat of all authority. How exactly he is able to be both is beyond our capacity fully to comprehend.[15] However, since he is revealed as both, we embrace the mystery and humbly worship the God we do not (expect to) understand.

At another level one of the key purposes of this passage is to reveal to us our need for a mediator with God. The judgments God announces are not idle threats: death and separation from his presence are precisely what his justice demands in the face of human sin and rebellion. Yet the God who judges human sin, *himself provides the mediator* in order that the judgment may be averted. Both the announcement of judgment and the turning aside of judgment are the work of the one God of justice and love. Psalm 106 is our guide once again:

> [The LORD] said he would destroy them –
> had not Moses, *his chosen one*,
> stood in the breach before him
> to keep his wrath from destroying them.[16]

So, having received the announcement of God's judgment, Moses *sought the favour* of the covenant God (32:11). The people of Israel are *his* people, the people *he* has redeemed to display his glory in the world. Surely, then, God will not abandon them and so bring shame on his name (32:12–13). However, the highest point of Moses' ministry of mediation comes a little later after he has instructed the Levites to put to the sword three thousand of their fellow-Israelites.

[15] For a full discussion see D. A. Carson, *Divine Sovereignty and Human Responsibility: Biblical Perspectives in Tension* (London: HarperCollins, 1994).
[16] Ps. 106:23.

The next day Moses said to the people, 'You have committed a great sin. But now I will go up to the LORD; perhaps I can make atonement for your sin.'

So Moses went back to the LORD and said, 'Oh, what a great sin these people have committed! They have made themselves gods of gold. But now, please forgive their sin – but if not, then blot me out of the book you have written' (30–32).

Though he has received all the instructions for the sacrificial system, Moses understands that full atonement will require more than an animal sacrifice; it will require a human mediator who offers themselves up to death for the sin of the people. Such a ministry of reconciliation is beyond Moses of course, but generations later God will provide exactly the mediator that Moses envisaged here. On the cross God made his own Son Jesus, to 'become sin' for us, though he was without sin himself, in order that we should 'become the righteousness of God in him'.[17] Nonetheless, God accepted Moses' work as a mediator, and the people were restored (17).

d. The restoration (Exod. 34)

In October 2012 Mark Rothko's widely-acclaimed painting *Black on Maroon* was vandalized with graffiti ink while on display in London's Tate Modern gallery. Much of the painting's interest and subtlety arose from the multiple layers of different materials Rothko had used to build it up, but the graffiti ink penetrated several of these layers, in some places soaking right through to the back of the canvas. The restoration of the painting was a huge technical challenge requiring eighteen months of painstaking restoration by the Collection Care Team at Tate, but on 13 May 2014 the work was put back on public view, fully restored to its former condition.

Exodus 34 records the full restoration of Israel, following their worship catastrophe and the judgment that had followed it. Moses is called back onto Mount Sinai to have two new stone tablets engraved with the words of the Ten Commandments, since he had smashed the previous tablets to pieces when he saw the golden calf (32:19). God appears in glory to Moses and proclaims *his name, the LORD* to him, confirming that he remains the covenant God who forgives the sins of his people, while not leaving the guilty unpunished (6–8). Moses' final prayer of mediation repeats his request

[17] 2 Cor. 5:21.

for the Lord to go with his people and accept them as his own (8–9) and God renews his covenant with the nation (10–27). The catastrophe is over; the restoration is complete.

2. Hypocrisy: when worship is meaningless (Isa. 1)

She thought it a bit strange that he was so keen for her to be out with a friend for the afternoon, but made little of it until she returned and saw cars on their drive. It was just a few days since her fortieth birthday and when she walked through the front door she was greeted with champagne and a cheering crowd of friends. Her husband had arranged a surprise celebration and left a huge bouquet of flowers prominently displayed in the lounge with a touchingly romantic note written in his own hand. She tried hard, but it didn't take long for her friends to sense the tension in the room. After the meal he began to make a short speech – slightly too gushing perhaps, but full of charm. She listened for a few minutes but could finally bear it no longer.

'The party is over,' she cried, rising to her feet as the guests shuffled uneasily. 'This whole event means nothing. It is just a show designed to make *him* look good and to cover up the fact that he is a self-absorbed, controlling man and a nightmare to live with!' The guests made a swift, polite exit, leaving the not-so-happy couple alone to try and repair their relationship . . .

> Hear the word of the LORD,
>   you rulers of Sodom;
> listen to the instruction of our God,
>   you people of Gomorrah!
> 'The multitude of your sacrifices –
>   what are they to me?' says the LORD.
> 'I have more than enough of burnt offerings,
>   of rams and the fat of fattened animals;
> I have no pleasure
>   in the blood of bulls and lambs and goats.
> When you come to appear before me,
>   who has asked this of you,
>   this trampling of my courts?
> Stop bringing meaningless offerings!
>   Your incense is detestable to me.
> New Moons, Sabbaths and convocations –
>   I cannot bear your worthless assemblies.
> Your New Moon feasts and your appointed festivals
>   I hate with all my being.

They have become a burden to me;
I am weary of bearing them.
When you spread out your hands in prayer,
I hide my eyes from you;
even when you offer many prayers,
I am not listening.' (10–15)

These words are truly shocking. The cities of Sodom and Gomorrah were proverbial in the Old Testament for barefaced sin and over-whelming judgment, so what could have brought the people of God to a point where he would address them in this way? The sacrifices and offerings had all been prescribed by God, along with the various feasts and festivals, so why does he now describe them as worthless and wearying? What is it that can make worship meaningless?

The worship to which Israel was called was to respond to the presence of God with praise and wonder and to respond to the word of God with the obedience of faith.[18] So Israel's first worship catastrophe (idolatry) reflected their failure to fulfil the first half of this calling: they were seeking the presence and blessing of God from that which was not God (i.e. the golden calf). However, Israel's second worship catastrophe (hypocrisy) reflects their failure to fulfil the second half of their calling: they are rebelling against the word of God and failing to *listen to [his] instruction* (10), despite all the fine words they say to him.

According to the opening verse of the chapter, Isaiah exercised his prophetic ministry in the latter part of the eighth century BC and the beginning of the seventh. During that period King Uzziah's reign of relative stability gave way to years of international turbulence (with the rise of the Assyrian superpower) and of internal religious and social decline (with a growing tension between a rich, powerful elite and a needy people). Isaiah's message concerns the southern kingdom of Judah and, in particular, the city of Jerusalem (Isa. 1:1). For him Jerusalem encompasses both the earthly city (whose judgment he announces) and the heavenly city – God's new creation, which will be the fulfilment of all the earthly Jerusalem was called to be.

a. Diagnosis: Judah's worship is undermined by their disobedience (2–17)

The Lord begins to speaks (2–3) with the pain of a parent whose children had been brought up well but turned out badly. God loved the whole nation of Israel as *his* child. He had given them everything

[18] See ch. 2 of this book.

they possessed and taught them everything they knew but they turned their backs on him. Isaiah then takes up the theme, with a lament for his people (4–9). At the heart of their guilt is their rejection of Yahweh their God, for sin is not simply the breaking of rules; it is the rejecting of the God who revealed *himself* in the law he gave.

> *They have forsaken the LORD;*
>   *they have spurned the Holy One of Israel*
>   *and turned their backs on him* (4b).

The desperate consequences for Judah are movingly portrayed in the image of a victim who has been beaten and brutalized and is covered with *wounds and bruises* (5–6). An invading army (Assyria) will overrun the nation (7), place Jerusalem (Zion) *under siege* (8) and come close to destroying it completely (9).

What then is the remedy? We might imagine the answer would be a renewal of Judah's religious life. However, the shock of Isaiah's message is that their religious life is deeply tied up with their sin. Their many sacrifices mean nothing to God (11); their temple worship is an unwelcome act of trespass in his dwelling place (12); their offerings and festivals are worse than meaningless – God 'hates them with all his being' (13–14); their prayers fail to reach his throne, for heaven's door is closed to them (15a). This is roughly equivalent to God saying to our churches, 'Your services mean nothing to me; your endless songs are empty words and your sermons mere platitudes. Your communion celebrations are meaningless rituals and I cannot bear your Easter events and wicked carol services. Who asked you to come to church anyway?' If that shocks us, it is because it is meant to.

But why this rejection of Judah's religious life? What is the nature of their worship catastrophe? It is that the hands spread out in prayer (15a) *are full of blood* (15b). They have done evil in God's sight, failing to *do right* or *seek justice*, or to *defend the oppressed, take up the cause of the fatherless* or *plead the case of the widow* (16–17). Isaiah's contemporary, the prophet Amos, would make much the same charge against the northern kingdom of Israel (see esp. Amos 5:21–24). Both prophets agree that, though we may say fine words to God or carry out elaborate rituals, our worship is hypocritical, meaningless and offensive in his sight if we rebel against his word, closing our ears to the cry of the oppressed and the poor. Judah's problem was that they thought worship was an *alternative* to obedience. Isaiah's message is that it is precisely in such obedience that authentic worship finds its true expression.

Centuries later, the prophet Malachi spoke to the people of God in very similar terms, after their return from exile.[19] Not only were they guilty of the same sins of social injustice (Mal. 3:5), their worship had degenerated into a begrudging boredom,[20] in which they were holding back their tithes (Mal. 3:6–12) and bringing blemished animals for their offerings (Mal. 1:6–14). '"But you say, 'What a weariness this is', and you snort at it," says the LORD of hosts.'[21] Once the heart to honour God in the obedience of our lives is lost, it is only a matter of time before our worship deteriorates into a dull, mechanical routine, devoid of any true devotion or life.

Returning to Isaiah, it is true that his message is particularly addressed to Judah's leaders (10) and that they were called to lead the people of God *constituted as a nation*. Does it follow that his emphasis on public righteousness and social justice is not relevant to New Testament believers scattered through the nations? Should we instead place our focus exclusively on (narrowly-defined) evangelism as we call people to personal salvation? Without doubt, there are examples of Christians whose focus on seeking justice has become so strong that they have lost their focus on clear gospel proclamation.[22] Without doubt, Christians living as a minority in predominantly non-Christian societies cannot always expect the state to legislate in favour of specifically Christian values. However, we cannot distance ourselves from Isaiah's challenge.[23] Jesus, after all, echoed Isaiah's message strongly when he challenged the religious elite of his own time: 'Woe to you Pharisees, because you give God a tenth of your mint, rue and all other kinds of garden herbs, but you neglect justice

---

[19] Malachi is generally believed to have ministered in the Persian era.

[20] 'The priests find the temple services boring and the people, following their example, are stingy and deceitful' (J. T. H. Adamson, *NBC*, p. 807).

[21] Mal. 1:13, ESV.

[22] Don Carson's analysis of movements which have proclaimed the gospel in the first generation, assumed the gospel in the next and denied the gospel in the third needs to be taken seriously. (See D. A. Carson *The Cross in Christian Ministry* [Grand Rapids: Baker, 1993], p. 63). However, there are many counter examples; this process is by no means inevitable for Christians who actively seek social justice.

[23] Gary A. Haughen quotes Carl F. Henry, speaking about the evangelical movement of the eighteenth and nineteenth centuries: 'Their evangelical movement was spiritually and morally vital because it strove for justice and also invited humanity to regeneration, forgiveness and power for righteousness. If the church preaches only divine forgiveness and does not affirm justice, she implies that God treats immorality and sin lightly. If the church proclaims only justice, we shall all die in unforgiven sin and without the Spirit's empowerment for righteousness. We should be equally troubled that we lag in championing justice and in fulfilling our evangelistic mandate' (G. A. Haugen, *Good News About Injustice* [Leicester: Inter-Varsity Press, 1999], p. 64).

and the love of God. You should have practised the latter without leaving the former undone.'[24]

In his challenging book, *Good News to the Poor*, Tim Chester identifies three key reasons why Christians should continue to do right, seek justice, defend the oppressed and take up the cause of the fatherless and the widow.[25]

- *The character of God* – the call for God's people to do right and to seek justice rests on the character of God who 'loves righteousness and justice'[26] and his character does not change.
- *The reign of God* – which we were created to express and reflect in our just stewardship of creation and to which we call people to re-submit when we preach the gospel of repentance and faith.
- *The grace of God* – who, in Christ, has 'brought good news to the poor'[27] and calls us to welcome and embrace them (Luke 14:12–14).

As in Isaiah's time and context so also in our own, disobedient neglect of our responsibilities to those in need, empties our worship of its meaning in the sight of God.

b. Invitation: Judah can be forgiven if they turn from their sins (18–20)

> 'Come now, let us settle the matter,'
>   says the LORD.
> 'Though your sins are like scarlet,
>   they shall be as white as snow;
> though they are red as crimson,
>   they shall be like wool.' (18)

The answer to Judah's hypocrisy lies not with their religious life, but with their God and his gracious invitation to come to him to *settle the matter* (18). There is no attempt here to downplay the significance of their sin, which blushes scarlet with shame and blood-red crimson with guilt. Nonetheless, if they will face their sin and bring it to God they will find complete forgiveness in him, as they are washed *as white as snow* and pure as fresh *wool*.

How will the God who loves justice forgive the guilty? Surely there is no justice in pretending that they have not sinned or that

---

[24] Luke 11:42.
[25] T. Chester, *Good News to the Poor* (Nottingham: Inter-Varsity Press, 2004), p. 34.
[26] Ps. 33:5.
[27] Luke 4:18.

their sin is not worthy of punishment. It is not until chapter 53 that Isaiah answers that question. The Lord will send his true Servant, who will perfectly embody everything Israel was called to be, not faltering until 'he establishes justice on earth'.[28] This Servant will 'be pierced' for the transgressions of the people as the Lord lays 'on him the iniquity of us all'.[29] This is the source of true hope for the beaten and brutalized figure of Isaiah 1:5–6, who will find healing because God's Servant was wounded for him, and peace because the Servant bore the punishment in his place. The invitation of Isaiah 1 is therefore an invitation for us, because Jesus is the Servant whose suffering has made forgiveness possible. As Peter would write, centuries later,

> 'He himself bore our sins' in his body on the cross, so that we might die to sins and live for righteousness; 'by his wounds you have been healed'. For 'you were like sheep going astray', but now you have returned to the Shepherd and Overseer of your souls.[30]

c. Future: Jerusalem will be judged now but will ultimately be restored (21–31)

The tragedy of Isaiah's time is that the people largely resisted the gracious invitation of God and so the (once) holy city of Jerusalem continued to decline. Justice and righteousness gave way to murder and violence as corrupt rulers used their power to feather their own nests (21–23). The city would therefore come under God's judgment (24–25).

However, there is a surprising twist. Sin and judgment will not have the last word in Jerusalem. The hand God *turns against them* in judgment (25), will also be a hand of purging and restoration. From the burnt-out shell of the old city will arise a new, restored Jerusalem, to be known as *the City of Righteousness, the Faithful City* (26). Suddenly Isaiah's vision breaks beyond the confines of its immediate historical context in the eighth century BC, and opens out into a thrilling vista of God's cosmic plan. The new Jerusalem he describes has yet to be seen in the fullness of its purity and glory, but at the end of his prophecy Isaiah describes it again. This time it is set within the context of God's promise of a whole new creation in which he will rejoice forever.

---

[28] Isa. 42:1–4.
[29] Isa. 53:5–6 . N. T. Wright describes these verses in a blog post as 'the clearest and most uncompromising statement of penal substitution you could find'.
[30] 1 Pet. 2:24–25.

> See, I will create
>   new heavens and a new earth.
> The former things will not be remembered,
>   nor will they come to mind.
> But be glad and rejoice for ever
>   in what I will create,
> for I will create Jerusalem to be a delight
>   and its people a joy.
> I will rejoice over Jerusalem
>   and take delight in my people;
> the sound of weeping and of crying
>   will be heard in it no more.[31]

There is hope beyond the worship catastrophes this chapter has explored, for the God of justice and judgment is also the God of salvation and unfailing love. However, Isaiah leaves us pondering to which city we belong: the old Jerusalem, that is proud in its worship but disobedient in its life, idolatrous in its heart and under God's judgment; or the new Jerusalem, known for its justice, righteousness and faithfulness. The answer to that question ultimately turns not on our performance as worshippers but on our response to the gracious invitation of the Lord, to face our failure, bring it to his abundant grace and find full forgiveness in his unfailing, covenant love.

[31] Isa. 65:17–19.

Matthew 1 – 4
4. The perfect worshipper

There is so much to celebrate and so much from which we can learn in the worship of Israel. As we have seen, theirs is a story of the birth, rescue, building and testing of the people of God as a community of worship. At its heart, their worship was to be a response of obedient faith to his word and of joyful reverence to his holy presence.

Israel's worship was expressed not just in the tabernacle/temple but in the whole of life. They understood that the world was not to be carved up into sacred and secular spheres, but that all of life belonged to God, 'The earth is the LORD's, and everything in it'![1] Their law taught them what would please God in every aspect of their lives, their tradition of wisdom gave them resources to navigate life's complexities with faith, and their poetry gave them a rich spirituality to know and respond to God in every season of life.

Israel's worship bequeathed to the people of God for all time the riches of the Psalms, the exploration of which will make up a significant portion of this book. Suffused with a majestic vision of the glory of God, the Psalms are still deeply (sometimes shockingly) honest about the struggles of human frailty. Nonetheless, their poetry and music open our hearts to God for his healing and blessing and lift our hearts to God for his glory and praise. Though written in a very different time and culture to our own, their ability to speak to the human heart (and, just as significantly, to speak *for* the human heart) is undiminished. It is hardly surprising, then, that they remain to this day one of the most significant sources of inspiration for the worship of the people of God.

Israel's worship maintained a sense of the transcendence and holiness of God and of the severity of human failure and sin. The thick curtain separating the Most Holy Place in the tabernacle/temple

---

[1] Ps. 24:1.

from the people demonstrated that, while God lived among his people, his holiness was such that human beings could not ordinarily approach him (see Exod. 26:31–35; cf. Lev. 16:1–2). The extensive system of animal sacrifices enabled Israelites to express their thanks and gratitude to God[2] but it was also a powerful statement to them of the seriousness[3] with which he approached their sin. In particular it reminded them that atonement for sin could only be made through the offering of sacrificial blood – as the writer to the Hebrews concluded, 'without the shedding of blood there is no forgiveness'.[4] At the same time, the sacrifices were a powerful reminder that there were resources in God to bridge the great gap between fallen humanity and the God of transcendent holiness – resources which would become fully evident in the coming of Christ – so that he could extend grace towards the penitent.

Israel's worship, finally, fostered among the people of God a great tradition of *remembering* their story, the story of how God had acted for them. They had once been a slave people – powerless and oppressed; foreigners held captive in an alien land. Yet God had stepped into their history, set them free, claimed them as his own and taught them how to live for his glory. The great psalms of salvation-history kept the story alive at the heart of their worship (e.g. Pss 105, 107 and 136). The rhythms of Sabbath rest, Jubilee liberation[5] and annual festivals encouraged them to re-live the story and pass it on to a new generation (supremely the festival of Passover, which re-enacted the deliverance from Egypt).[6] Israel was to never to forget the desperation of their slavery in Egypt or the dignity of what God had made them in his grace.

However, for all the undoubted riches and the many high points of Israel's worship, the Old Testament leaves us with an inescapable sense that their calling to be the model worshipping community remained largely unfulfilled. We have already explored some of the 'worship catastrophes' that marred their story. We have also heard some of the voices of the prophets, warning them of judgment and calling them back to the Lord with increasing urgency – words that went largely unheeded. Eventually, having rebelled against the word of God and failed truly to acknowledge the holiness of his presence among them, the worshipping community experienced the unthinkable: they were sent away into exile and their temple – the dwelling place of their God – was burnt to the ground.

---

[2] For example the 'fellowship offering', see Lev. 7:11–18.
[3] See the 'sin offering' and the 'guilt offering' in Lev. 4 – 6.
[4] Heb. 9:22.
[5] See Lev. 25, esp. vv. 38, 42 and 55.
[6] See Exod. 12, note esp. vv. 26–27.

The LORD, the God of their ancestors, sent word to them through his messengers again and again, because he had pity on his people and on his dwelling-place. But they mocked God's messengers, despised his words and scoffed at his prophets until the wrath of the LORD was aroused against his people and there was no remedy. He brought up against them the king of the Babylonians, who killed their young men with the sword in the sanctuary, and did not spare young men or young women, the elderly or the infirm. God gave them all into the hands of Nebuchadnezzar. He carried to Babylon all the articles from the temple of God, both large and small, and the treasures of the LORD's temple and the treasures of the king and his officials. They set fire to God's temple and broke down the wall of Jerusalem; they burned all the palaces and destroyed everything of value there.[7]

We are left wondering whether there will ever be an Israelite who will fulfil all that it meant to be the 'firstborn son' of Yahweh, faithfully offering to him the worship that is due to his majestic name.

Stand on a bridge sometime and look down on a river flowing through a tight gorge after a period of heavy rain. All the swollen streams and tributaries from higher up the river are pushing huge volumes of water downstream until all of it converges in the narrow width of the gorge and thunders through. All the power of the river is concentrated into that one, deafening, white rush of water beneath your feet. The experience of reading the early chapters of Matthew's Gospel can be rather similar. Numerous 'streams' of promise and expectation have flowed across the centuries of the Old Testament story: the blessing of the nations through the offspring of Abraham (Gen. 12:1–3); the forgiveness of sins through the suffering of the Lord's Servant (Isa. 53); the establishing of an everlasting kingdom through the victory of the great Davidic king (2 Sam. 7:11–16); the coming of God himself to purify his people (Mal. 3:1–4), to name but a few. The people are waiting, but the promises remain unfulfilled until at last all the streams converge in a single place. As C. S. Lewis put it, 'The whole thing narrows and narrows, until it comes down to a little point, small as the point of a spear – a Jewish girl and her prayers.'[8] All the power of the ongoing story of salvation is now invested in one person: the son of that prayerful Jewish woman, introduced to us by Matthew's gospel as, *Jesus the Messiah, the Son of David, the Son of Abraham* (1:1).

[7] 2 Chr. 36:15–19.
[8] C. S. Lewis, *God in the Dock* (Grand Rapids: Eerdmans, 2014), p. 81.

1. Jesus: the true Israelite (Matt. 1 – 3)

Matthew's Gospel starts with a carefully constructed genealogy of Jesus, which gives us a brief overview of the story of Israel (1:1–17). Matthew concludes his genealogy with these words: *Thus there were fourteen generations in all from Abraham to David, fourteen from David to the exile to Babylon, and fourteen from the exile to the Messiah* (1:17).

Comparison with other biblical genealogies demonstrates that Matthew had to be quite selective[9] to encapsulate the story in these three blocks of fourteen generations, suggesting that the number is both significant and symbolic. Scholars have proposed a number of different explanations and no clear consensus has emerged.[10] What is clear though, is that Matthew saw *Abraham, David* and Jesus *the Messiah* as the three key figures which gave Israel's story its shape and significance (see vv. 1 and 17). It is also clear that, while Abraham and David shape the first and second block respectively by being the *first* in those blocks, Jesus gives shape to the third block (and so to the whole genealogy) by being the *last*: the conclusion and fulfilment

[9] For an extensive discussion of the detail see D. A. Carson, *Matthew*, Expositor's Bible Commentary, vol. 8 (Grand Rapids: Zondervan, 1995), pp. 60–70. This kind of selectivity is entirely within the conventions of how such genealogies were put together at the time, being crafted to make a particular point, rather than simply to give a 'list'. M. D. Johnson, quoted in R. T. France, *Matthew*, NICNT (Grand Rapids: Eerdmans, 2007), p. 33, fn. 23, confirms that in Hebrew thought, genealogies served 'apologetic purposes, both nationalistic and theological. As such, a kind of midrashic exegesis could be utilized to construct genealogies that communicated the convictions of the author.'

[10] So, for example, R. T. France suggests that, since the actual genealogies of the OT indicate fourteen generations from Abraham to David, and the central section on the period of the monarchy requires only modest adjustment to make fourteen, so Matthew has adjusted the third block to make a symmetrical structure which centred on the monarchic period, to set up his conclusion that Jesus, the Messiah, is the true, kingly Son of David (*Matthew*, pp. 31–32). D. A. Carson (*Matthew*, pp. 69–70) sees it as an example of *gematria*, recognizing that, if numerical values are assigned to the Hebrew consonants, the name of David has a numerical value of fourteen, again underlining the royal emphasis in the genealogy. I remain drawn to the proposal of Hendrickson and Goodspeed (discussed in Carson, *Matthew*, p. 69) who see the three blocks of fourteen as six lots of seven generations, recognizing the importance of the number seven in Scripture as symbolic of completion and fulfilment. The six sevens are therefore awaiting completion and fulfilment in the seventh seven, which is the age of the kingdom inaugurated by Jesus, the fulfilment of everything to which the story of Israel was pointing. The main objection to this proposal is that Matthew's scheme is not six blocks of seven but three blocks of fourteen. However, the story would not naturally fall into six blocks, so that option was scarcely open to him. But very little hangs on our decision, since the king was understood to be the representative of the nation, so to say that Jesus is the true king is ultimately to acknowledge him as the true Israelite.

of the story so far. He is the true Son/Seed of Abraham who will bring to fulfilment the promise of blessing to the nations; he is the true Son of David who will fulfil the promise of an everlasting kingdom; he is the conquering Messiah who will bring to ultimate fulfilment the promise of return from exile as he dies 'the righteous for the unrighteous, *to bring us to God*'.[11] R. T. France concludes that the aim of the genealogy is 'to locate Jesus within the story of God's people as its intended climax, and to do it with a special focus on the Davidic monarchy'.[12] In other words, Jesus is *the true Israelite*, fulfilling all that Israel was called to be.

The same emphasis runs all the way through the opening chapters of Matthew, which are punctuated with Old Testament quotations and allusions. In each case these references are said to be fulfilled in some way by Jesus.[13] So for example consider these scriptures.

- His birth to a virgin mother (1:22–23), fulfilling Isaiah's prophecy of a virgin with child (Isa. 7:14).
- His birth in Bethlehem (2:4–6), fulfilling Micah's prophecy of a shepherd-ruler born there (Mic. 5:2–4).
- His refuge in Egypt (2:13–15), fulfilling Hosea's prophecy, 'Out of Egypt I called my son' (Hos. 1:11).
- The slaughter of the innocents (2:16–18), fulfilling Jeremiah's vision of a grieving mother (Jer. 31:15).
- His childhood in Nazareth (2:23), fulfilling the expectation that the Messiah would arise from obscurity and be despised.[14]
- The declaration of his sonship at his baptism (3:13–17), fulfilling a series of Old Testament declarations about a son and a servant (see Psa. 2:7; Gen. 22:2; Isa. 42:1).
- His testing/tempting in the desert (4:1–11), fulfilling Israel's experience of testing in the wilderness.[15]

[11] 1 Pet. 3:18.

[12] *Matthew*, p. 33.

[13] R. T. France has argued that the motif of fulfilment is the key distinctive of Matthew's Gospel, see R. T. France, *Matthew: Evangelist and Teacher* (Eugene: Wipf & Stock Publishers, 2004), pp. 166–205. The 'fulfilment formula' introduces five OT allusions in chs. 1 and 2, but these are not the only such allusions. 'Narrative echoes of other biblical scenes and language are woven together into a complex web of scripture foreshadowing, which has all found its fulfilment in the coming of the Messiah' (France, *Matthew*, p. 40).

[14] Attempts to tie this to a specific OT verse have been largely unsuccessful. We know, however, that in the first century Nazareth had become proverbial for something being obscure and worthy only of rejection (see John 1:46 and Acts 24:5). Such a designation for the Messiah was foreseen in the OT (e.g. Ps. 22:6–8; Isa 53:2–3). See Carson, *Matthew*, pp. 96–97; France, *Matthew*, pp. 91–95.

[15] Matthew is often accused here of poor handling of the OT scriptures and, without doubt, there are many complexities, though they are not insurmountable. France, *Matthew*, pp. 10–14 and 40–45 provides a useful summary of the main issues.

Listing the events out like this enables us to experience the sense of déjà vu that Matthew has built into these chapters. He describes someone whose arrival in history is due to the particular intervention of God and is promised in advance, whose life is protected through a desperate journey to Egypt, whose time in Egypt is associated with the death of children, who is called out of Egypt by the initiative of God, who emerges from obscurity to be rejected by many, who is led through water and into the wilderness where he is tested. Clearly he is speaking of the early life of Jesus[16] but he sets out the events in such a way as to mirror closely the story of Israel. In a way that foreshadowed the life of Christ, Israel as a nation was called to be God's 'firstborn son',[17] was brought forth into the world by God's own intervention in fulfilment of his promise to Abraham, had survived in Egypt until God called them out and had come via the waters of the Red Sea into the wilderness where God had tested them. Matthew is underlining the point he made through the genealogy in a way which, while subtle, is very striking: the events of Jesus' early life demonstrate that his story grows out of Israel's story as its climax and fulfilment. Jesus is the true Israelite, God's true firstborn Son in whom is all his delight. Clearly Jesus' sonship is unique, moving far beyond the sonship to which God had called Israel. Nonetheless, that sonship is not less than the perfect fulfilment of all God had called Israel to be.

However, when God called Israel out of Egypt to be his 'firstborn son', his express purpose was that they should worship him (Exod. 4:23) and, as we have already seen, Israel never fully reflected in its life all that this calling entailed. Indeed their failure was at times catastrophic (not least as they journeyed through the wilderness having escaped from Egypt). What, then, will be the outcome when Jesus, the true firstborn Son of God, is similarly tested in the wilderness?

2. Jesus: the true worshipper (4:1–11)[18]

The *forty days and forty nights* (2) duration of Jesus' testing/tempting are almost certainly an echo of Israel's forty years of testing in the wilderness (Matt. 4:2; Luke 4:2; cf. Deut. 8:2). The fact that all the scriptures Jesus uses to counter the temptations are drawn from the chapters in Deuteronomy which recount those forty years establishes

[16] There is no reason to suppose that Matthew's account is less than historical here – see France, *Matthew*, p. 43, fn. 8 – but it is clearly more than just historical.
[17] Exod. 4:22.
[18] D. Peterson, *Engaging with God* (Leicester: Apollos, 1992), pp. 109–112 takes a similar approach to my argument in this section.

the connection beyond doubt. Most of what those forty days and nights entailed for Jesus is not recorded for us, but it seems that the period of testing concluded with the three temptations here. The first two appear to build towards the third, which is in some way the climax, as Jesus is led *up by the Spirit into the wilderness* (1, ESV), then up further onto the highest point of the temple (5) and finally to a *very high mountain* (8).[19]

There are many helpful ways in which these temptations have been expounded and applied, but the striking thing for our purposes is to note that the final, climactic temptation is about worship. *'All this I will give you,'* boasts the devil, speaking of *the kingdoms of the world, 'if you will bow down and worship me'* (9). We have already seen that God had called Israel to be his firstborn son and to leave Egypt in order to worship him, so it will hardly surprise us that the question of worship will crop up in this climactic temptation to God's true firstborn Son. What we will discover, however, is that throughout these verses the issue of worship is never far below the surface.

a. Doubting the sufficiency of the word of God: Turning stones to bread (2–4)

The temptation to use our power for ourselves is one which most of us experience and it is certainly practically helpful to reflect on how Jesus handles that temptation here. However, this passage is about Jesus before it is about us and so our priority must be to see what *he* believed its particular significance to be. The power of this temptation doubtless arises from his extreme hunger after such a long period of fasting and from the incongruity of a 'Son of God' going hungry in the desert. After all, God had provided manna and quail for Israel in the desert, so there seems to be no requirement for him to be hungry. Furthermore he had the power (as he would show in his ministry) to create food, so why not use that power for himself? Scripture does not generally regard bodily appetites as intrinsically sinful but Jesus was insistent that they must not take first place in our lives; there is something still more important.

> So do not worry, saying, 'What shall we eat?' or 'What shall we drink?' or 'What shall we wear?' For the pagans run after all these things and your heavenly Father knows that you need them. But

[19] Luke's account reverses the last two temptations. It is not certain which of the two accounts reflects the actual chronology, but the balance probably tips towards Matthew's account – not least because he seems to include more chronological markers in his account ('then' in vv. 5 and 11; again in v. 8).

seek first his kingdom and his righteousness, and all these things will be given to you as well.[20]

Jesus exemplified this attitude himself rather strikingly while in Samaria, when his disciples urged him to eat something. 'He said to them, "I have food to eat that you know nothing about." Then his disciples said to each other, "Could someone have brought him food?" "My food," said Jesus, "is to do the will of him who sent me and to finish his work." '[21]

For Jesus, ultimate satisfaction came not from eating bread, but from hearing and obeying the word of his Father. The primary significance of this temptation for Jesus, then, was that it threatened to place something other than the word of God at the centre of his life, as his true source of nourishment and satisfaction. This is precisely the focus of Jesus' resolute response as he quotes from Deuteronomy 8:3: *Jesus answered, 'It is written: "Man shall not live on bread alone, but on every word that comes from the mouth of God." '* (4). Jesus refuses to turn away from the central priority of receiving and fulfilling the word of God. Such a response to the *word* of God is, as we saw in Exodus, central to being a faithful worshipper of Yahweh.

b. Doubting the reality of the presence of God: Testing at the temple (5–7)

The second element which, according to the book of Exodus, stands at the heart of faithful worship, is a right response to the *presence* of God. It is surely significant, therefore that the second temptation concerns a vision of *the temple* (5),[22] the place of God's presence among his people. Jesus' response to the first temptation, *'It is written . . .'* is now thrown back at him by the devil. He challenges Jesus to throw himself from the temple's *highest point*, on the basis that *it is written* that God had promised to send his angels to protect him. The temptation threatens to turn Jesus' world view on its head, so that God is expected to serve him when in fact he had been sent to serve the Father and fulfil his purposes.[23]

---

[20] Matt. 6:31–33.
[21] John 4:32–34.
[22] France notes the comparison with Ezekiel's visionary experiences of the Jerusalem temple while he is an exile beside the Kebar river in Babylon. There is, of course, no mountain that literally provides a vision of all the kingdoms of the earth, so it is likely that, in both the final temptation and this one, some kind of visionary experience is being described (*Matthew*, p. 132).
[23] See C. S. Keener, *Matthew*, IVPNTC (Leicester: Inter-Varsity Press, 1997), p. 92.

This too is a familiar temptation: we are prone to act as if God exists for the satisfaction of our needs rather than accepting that we exist to participate in his mission. Still Jesus' response goes further again. He quotes from Deuteronomy 6:16 where Moses told the people, 'Do not put the LORD your God to the test'. It is a reference back to Israel's grumbling in Exodus 17 where they complained that Moses had brought them out of Egypt only to die in the desert. Their sin was not that they requested water, but that they did not trust that God was present to help and provide for them, though they had seen his wonders in Egypt. Their angry demand for water therefore became a test of the reality of his presence among them: 'They tested the LORD saying, "Is the LORD among us or not?"'[24] Jesus understands the temptation to throw himself from the temple in exactly the same way: it is a test of the reality of God's presence, represented by the very temple on which he stands. So will Jesus trust the reality of God's holy presence among his people or will he put it to the test as the devil is encouraging him to do? Again Jesus is resolute: he will honour God's presence and will not put it to the test.

Trusting the sufficiency of God's word and reality of God's presence: Jesus has shown himself to be the perfect worshipper, according to the model set out in Exodus. These priorities are seen throughout his ministry, culminating in the cleansing of the temple from its corruption and in the decision in Gethsemane to walk the path of obedience to the cross (Matt. 21:12–17; 26:36–46). It is no surprise, then, that the issue of worship comes out into the open in the final temptation.

c. Giving up the worship of God: Testing on the mountain (8–11)

Matthew's Gospel will end with Jesus on a mountain commissioning the Twelve to go and make disciples, having been given 'all authority in heaven and on earth'.[25] The path to that mountain has been the path of obedience, suffering and final vindication (supremely in his death and resurrection). Here at the start of the Gospel, the devil takes Jesus to another mountain and offers him *all the kingdoms of the world and their splendour* (8), not by following the path of obedience to his Father but by abandoning his Father and giving himself to the worship of Satan. It is a temptation to seek a shortcut to success, though we might note that the 'success' on offer is only the kingdoms of the earth, for Satan has no authority in heaven to give away. Again this is something many of us experience in different

[24] Exod. 17:7.
[25] Matt. 28:18.

ways: financial 'success' through corrupt transactions; career 'success' through riding roughshod over competitors; relational 'success' by sexual enticement; ministry 'success' through the careful cultivation of our reputation. However, Jesus again sees through the presenting temptation to the real issue that lies behind it: the issue of worship. Israel had repeatedly given in on this issue and succumbed to idolatry and disobedience. Jesus, by contrast, is resolute and quotes from Deuteronomy 6:13: *Jesus said to him, 'Away from me, Satan! For it is written: "Worship the Lord your God, and serve him only."'* (10). He is therefore the perfect worshipper; the true Israelite who fulfilled all that Israel was called to be. In the words of M. D. Goulder, 'Where Israel of old stumbled and fell, Christ the new Israel stood firm.'[26]

3. The perfect worship of Jesus

We are more used to thinking of Jesus as the object of our worship than as an example of perfect worship. The two are linked however, for according to this passage, it is in the perfection of Jesus' worship that he is revealed to be the true, beloved Son of the Father, who is worshipped with the Father and the Spirit. The perfect worship of Jesus is not merely of academic interest but is of direct interest to us in at least three ways.

a. His perfect worship qualifies him to bear our sins on the cross

The failure to worship lies at the heart of human sin, for which we are rightly subject to God's wrath and condemnation. However, precisely because he fulfilled all that Israel was called to be as the worshipper of Yahweh, Jesus was qualified to be their representative and so their substitute (and, by extension, ours too). He could therefore offer 'himself without blemish to God [so as to] purify our consciences from dead works to worship the living God'.[27] It is our failure to worship that necessitates the cross; it is Jesus' perfect worship that makes the cross possible – it is our restoration to be 'worshippers of the living God' that is the goal of the cross.

b. His perfect worship counts for us

Paul's favourite term to describe Christian identity is to say that we are 'in Christ'. To be a Christian, therefore, is to be incorporated into the one who is the perfect worshipper, who never fails in his

---

[26] M. D. Goulder, *Midrash and Lection in Matthew* (London: SPCK, 1974), p. 245, quoted in France, *Matthew*, p. 128.
[27] Heb. 9:14, NRSV.

obedience to God's word and never fails to honour the holiness of God's presence. 'It is because of him [i.e. God] that you are in Christ Jesus, who has become for us wisdom from God – that is, *our* righteousness, holiness and redemption. Therefore, as it is written: "Let the one who boasts boast in the Lord."'[28] To be righteous in the sight of God is to fulfil his purpose for our lives: that is, ultimately, to worship him. Our righteousness derives from being 'in Christ Jesus', for his perfect worship counts for us.

c. His perfect worship makes our (imperfect) worship acceptable

Even on my best days, my experience of worship falls short of what I desire it to be, let alone what it should be in the sight of God – both in terms of daily obedience to God's word and living experience of his presence. It is easy to become discouraged therefore. However, there is an alternative, for as Christian people 'in Christ' our worship – in all its imperfection – is offered to God *through Christ*, the perfect worshipper and so made acceptable in his sight. He is the perfectly obedient worshipper (Heb. 4:15), the perfect sacrifice (Heb. 9 – 10) and the final, great High Priest of the new covenant (Heb. 7 – 8). The inauguration of his unshakable kingdom therefore becomes the basis for a new covenant worship which is truly 'acceptable' in the sight of God (Heb. 12:28). This knowledge frees us from negative introspection (from which there is no escape) to focus our attention on the sufficiency and God-delighting perfection of Christ whose worship never falls short. '*Through Jesus, therefore*, let us continually offer to God a sacrifice of praise – the fruit of lips that confess his name.'[29]

In the words of James Torrance, 'Christ is presented to us as the Son living a life of union and communion with the Father in the Spirit, presenting Himself in our humanity through the eternal Spirit to the Father on behalf of humankind. By His Spirit he draws men and women to participate both in his life of worship and communion with the Father and in his mission from the Father to the world.'[30]

The perfect worship of Jesus is good news for us!

---

[28] 1 Cor. 1:30–31, emphasis added.
[29] Heb. 13:15, emphasis added.
[30] J. B. Torrance, *Worship, Community and the Triune God of Grace*, expanded version of 1994 Didsbury lecture (Downers Grove: InterVarsity Press, 1997). Many of these themes are developed further in ch. 9 of this book.

John 4:1–42
5. In Spirit and truth

It was Sunday morning and Gordon[1] was listening to his radio. He felt the pain of broken relationships and the sting of regret over decisions he had made in his past. He was not in any way a religious man; indeed he felt sure that God would have no interest in him (if he did exist after all). A song began to play on his radio and, as he listened to it, Gordon found himself thinking a strange thought: perhaps he should go to church. He tried to push the idea away, reasoning that no-one in a church would accept him if they knew what he was really like, but in the end he went along and was surprised at the welcome he received and how much he enjoyed the service. He signed up for an Alpha course and just a few months later, as he was baptized in our church, he shared his story of God's grace in his life. Gordon had encountered the living Christ and his life was being transformed.

The fourth chapter of John's Gospel describes one of the Bible's great life-transforming encounters with Jesus. In the previous chapter Jesus was in Jerusalem, engaging with Nicodemus, an eminent Jewish theologian of his day. Now he is on his way north to Galilee, passing through the less familiar surroundings of Samaria. In the eyes of Jewish people at the time, Samaria was a region of racial impurity and religious compromise.[2] In the middle of the day Jesus stops to rest beside Jacob's well while his disciples go to buy food, and there he meets a woman who has come to draw water.

---

[1] Not his real name.

[2] Samaria was originally the name of the capital of the northern kingdom of Israel, which was exiled to Assyria in 722 BC. After taking most of the population into exile, the Assyrians brought foreigners into Samaria (2 Kgs 17:24), who blended with the surviving Israelites, bringing practices from their own religions with them (2 Kgs 17:29–34). See D. A. Carson, *The Gospel According to John* (Leicester: Inter-Varsity Press, 1991), p. 216.

The contrast with Nicodemus could hardly be greater. He was male, Jewish, influential, a theological heavyweight and deeply respected; she is female, a Samaritan, a nobody, unschooled, and she has come to draw water in the middle of the day (a hint, at least, that she has no place among the 'respectable' who would come to the well in groups in the cool of the day). Jesus, however, is no more embarrassed by her status as something of a social outcast than he was intimidated by Nicodemus' standing as 'Israel's teacher'.[3] He speaks to her, asking her *for a drink*. She is taken aback that Jesus, a Jewish man, would speak to her, a Samaritan woman. For all her lack of social standing, the many compromises of her life and the mixed-up history of her people, the woman finds that Jesus is taking her seriously. In the conversation that ensues, he opens up to her what is arguably the most definitive teaching on worship in the New Testament, explaining the impact of his coming on the nature of true worship (23). He begins by turning the conversation in a direction that she would never have imagined.

1. Jesus gives the living water of the Spirit, because he is greater than Jacob (10–15)

A few years ago I had the privilege of speaking at the dedication service for a translation of the whole Bible into the language of the Chumburung people of central Ghana.[4] The service took place in the village of Kmundi, where I stayed for over a week. One of the many memories of the visit that stands out in my mind is just how much of life in the village revolved around water: the need for a reliable source; the time taken to carry it around; the problem of storage; the potentially catastrophic consequences of poorly maintained pumps failing. In the Western world, fresh drinking water is largely taken for granted; in Kmundi it was a scarce resource on which life itself clearly depended.

It would have been much the same in the dry and arid land of Samaria. The concept of *living water* (10) that Jesus introduces would therefore have made immediate sense (superficially, at least) and had an instant, powerful appeal. What could be more attractive in a hot dry land than a spring of fresh, running water that did not run dry? However, Jesus is saying as much about himself as he is about water. He tells the woman that if she knew what he could give and understood who he was, their roles would have been immediately reversed and she would have been asking him for water. The woman is

[3] John 3:10.
[4] Members of our church, Keir and Gillian Hansford, had given about four decades of their lives to coordinating the project, working alongside local translators.

understandably confused. Jesus has no way of reaching deep into the well, so how could he possibly provide her with water? Or could it be that the water about which he is talking was not from Jacob's well at all? *Are you greater than our father Jacob, who gave us the well and drank from it himself as did also his sons and his livestock?* (12). The woman was speaking better than she knew – as others frequently do in John's Gospel. Jesus is indeed greater than Jacob, the father of Israel's twelve tribes, and the kind of water he is offering is greater than anything that could be drawn from Jacob's well. *Jesus answered, 'Everyone who drinks this water will be thirsty again, but whoever drinks the water I give them will never thirst. Indeed, the water I give them will become in them a spring of water welling up to eternal life'* (13–14).

Doubtless we need to imagine fuses blowing in the woman's mind as she tries to process what Jesus is saying. Her response (15) certainly suggests that she has not truly understood. At the end of John 1, Jesus had spoken of his own ministry fulfilling Jacob's vision of a ladder from heaven with 'the angels of God ascending and descending *on the Son of Man*'.[5] The idea is that a newly-constituted people of God will look to Jesus in the way Israel had looked to Jacob as their founding father. Jacob had dug a well to provide water for his descendants,[6] but the water Jesus will supply to those who look to him will be of an altogether different kind. It will satisfy them so deeply that *they will never thirst* and it will *become in them a spring of water welling* ['gushing', NRSV] *up to eternal life* (14). Clearly then, Jesus is greater than Jacob. But what exactly is the water that he claims to give?

The imagery of water is pervasive within the Hebrew Scriptures. As their Shepherd, the Lord leads his people 'beside quiet waters' (Ps. 23); Jeremiah castigated the people for forsaking the Lord who is the 'spring of living water' (Jer. 2:13); Isaiah promised 'water on the thirsty land' (Isa. 44:3) and joyful drawing of 'water from the wells of salvation' (Isa. 12:3); Zechariah promised 'living water flowing from Jerusalem' (Zech. 14:8); and Ezekiel prophesied a river from the temple which would make everything live wherever it flowed (Ezek. 47:9). The image, then, speaks of the people of God experiencing for themselves his promised blessing, his glorious life, his boundless grace and his transforming power. In Isaiah it is explicitly through the out-poured Holy Spirit that they come into this experience. 'For I will pour water on the thirsty land, and streams

---

[5] John 1:51, emphasis added.
[6] See Carson, *John*, p. 217 for the location of the well, which, he says, has not run dry to this day.

on the dry ground; *I will pour out my Spirit* on your offspring, and my blessing on your descendants.'[7]

Jesus makes precisely the same link, just a few chapters later in John.

> On the last and greatest day of the festival, Jesus stood and said in a loud voice, 'Let anyone who is thirsty come to me and drink. Whoever believes in me, as Scripture has said, rivers of living water will flow from within them.' *By this he meant the Spirit*, whom those who believed in him were later to receive.[8]

John the Baptist had already witnessed that the Holy Spirit had 'come down from heaven like a dove' and remained on Jesus, and concluded that Jesus was 'the one who will baptise with the Holy Spirit'.[9] Jesus, who is anointed by the Holy Spirit, will give the same Spirit to his people, and the imagery of baptism suggests that this 'giving' will be one of overwhelming abundance. In exactly the same way, John concludes his third chapter speaking of God giving 'the Spirit without limit'[10] to his Son and then describes this encounter in Samaria in which he promises to give the living water of the Spirit. Again, this 'giving' will be so abundant that he will become in those who receive him, *a spring of water welling up to eternal life* (14). The Spirit Jesus gives is the eschatological Spirit, who brings the life of the future into the present. In the language of the synoptic Gospels, he brings into present experience the life and power of the coming kingdom of God. In the language of Paul he is the 'deposit' in our hearts, 'guaranteeing what is to come'.[11] In the language of John he is the beginning of eternal life, the living presence of the everlasting God in our hearts.

When Jesus was tempted in the wilderness, we saw how he honoured the presence of God among his people by refusing to put him to the test (Matt. 4:5–7).[12] Now in his encounter with the Samaritan woman we discover that he brings the same presence of God to his people, by the gift of the Holy Spirit. He is, after all, Immanuel, God with us (Matt. 1:22–23); the 'Word who became flesh and made his dwelling [lit. 'pitched his tabernacle'[13]] among us';[14] the one who promised to destroy the temple and 'raise it again

---

[7] Isa. 44:3, emphasis added.
[8] John 7:37–39, emphasis added.
[9] John 1:32–33.
[10] John 3:34.
[11] 2 Cor. 1:22.
[12] See the discussion in the previous chapter of this book.
[13] Carson, *John*, p. 219.
[14] John 1:14.

in three days' (John 2:19–21); the one who has opened the way into God's presence through his sacrifice on the cross. All that the tabernacle/temple had modelled and foreshadowed, Jesus fulfilled, through his death and resurrection and the gift of his Holy Spirit.[15] It follows that those who wish to be true worshippers, responding with joyful reverence to the presence of God, must now learn to worship at the feet of Christ.

2. Jesus speaks the truth from God because he is a prophet (15–19)

Most of us will have experienced being in a conversation with someone and gradually sensing that they know a lot more about us than we had expected. It can be rather unnerving! We may therefore feel a deal of sympathy for the Samaritan woman at this point in her encounter with Jesus (though it was through her being confronted with the truth that she ultimately gained her freedom).[16] Of course, Jesus' knowledge of her did not come from a piece of social espionage but from God-given, prophetic insight, as the woman herself understood (19).

Jesus, perceiving the moral complexities of her personal life, asks her to call her husband. She acknowledges that she has no husband and, while he gently commends her for speaking truthfully, Jesus reveals the whole truth of her situation. Whether as a result of bereavement, divorce or some combination of the two, the woman has had five husbands and now lives with a man to whom she is not married. Suddenly the reason for her shame-ridden, lonely visits to Jacob's well in the middle of the day becomes all too clear. Whatever the circumstances that had led to the ending of her previous marriages, Jewish tradition would have frowned on her for marrying more than three times[17] and thoroughly disapproved of her current living arrangements. Jesus has spoken truth from God directly into her life and, uncomfortable though it must have been for her, she acknowledges what has happened. *'Sir,' the woman said, 'I can see that you are a prophet'* (19).

At a pastoral level, Jesus' words have turned the key that opens up the woman's life. We know from her testimony to her friends that it

---

[15] For a fuller exposition of this theme see G. K. Beale, *The Temple and the Church's Mission* (Leicester: Apollos, 2004), pp. 169–200.

[16] See John 8:31–32.

[17] 'Technically it was not contrary to the Mosaic law for a woman to be married five times, but Jewish teachers forbade a woman to be married more than twice or at most (in the eyes of some) three times' (G. R. Beasley-Murray, *John*, WBC 26 [Waco: Word Books, 1987], p. 61).

was this experience which persuaded her that Jesus may indeed be *the Messiah* (29). Having brought her sins out into the open, Jesus has left her with nowhere to find refuge other than in the grace he is ready to extend to her. He is 'the Lamb of God, who takes away the sin of the world'[18] but that process can only begin in a person's life when they face the reality of their sin, as the woman is doing here.

At a theological level, Jesus has taken another step towards revealing who he really is. David Peterson explains that, 'The Samaritans expected a *Taheb* (lit. the one who returns), who would be a prophet like Moses (Deut. 18:15-18), rather than a Davidic Messiah'.[19] Jesus is more than a prophet but he is not less than a prophet, for he speaks truth from God to the people (as the woman has just experienced). We cannot be sure at this stage whether she believes him to be '*the* prophet' (i.e. the *Taheb*) or just another prophet, but by the end of the dialogue her thinking is certainly moving towards the former (25). Nonetheless, what has become clear is that Jesus not only honours the word of God (as he showed in his temptation in the wilderness), he is also the bringer of that word. This is exactly what John has led us to expect from the first verse of his Gospel, when he introduced Jesus to us as 'the Word' of God. As the Word of God, Jesus had spoken God's truth into the life of the startled Nathaniel (John 1:47–49). He is the 'one whom God has sent' who 'speaks the words of God'[20] and will later say of himself that he is 'the way, the truth and the life'.[21] The God who revealed himself through the law has now revealed himself climactically in Christ (Heb. 1:1–4), who is the fulfilment of all its many promises and 'types' (Col. 1:16–17). It follows that those who wish to be true worshippers, responding with faithful obedience to the word of God, must now come to sit at the feet of Christ to receive that word. When they do they will discover his word to be the fuel that makes the fire of worship burn.

3. Jesus inaugurates the era of true worship because he is the Messiah (20–42)

The service is over and there is a tangible sense of hushed reflection as the impact of a challenging sermon is felt. For at least one section of the church, however, the service had fallen short of their expectations: the enthusiasm of the church's new drummer had (in their view) simply got out of hand. 'You really couldn't hear a thing!' they

---

[18] John 1:29.
[19] D. Peterson, *Engaging with God* (Leicester: Apollos, 1992), pp. 97–98.
[20] John 3:34.
[21] John 14:6.

complained, as they joined the queue for coffee. Within just a few seconds the challenge of the sermon was entirely forgotten; drowned out by a few minutes of worship controversy!

The scenario is fictional but sadly takes all too little imagination to envisage. Few strategies are more effective for evading the uncomfortable challenge of the word of God than stirring up some controversy about worship. Many have suggested that this is the strategy of the Samaritan woman who, feeling the heat of Jesus' prophetic insight, sought refuge in a well-worn argument about worship that had raged for years between Jews and Samaritans. That may or may not be the case[22] but the change of subject is certainly abrupt. The really striking thing though is that Jesus makes no attempt to turn the conversation back to the woman's personal life. For him, talk about worship is not evading the real issue; it *is* the real issue.

The background is that the Samaritans recognized the authority only of the first five books of the Hebrew canon and therefore did not accept Jerusalem or its temple (which came much later in the Old Testament). Abraham's first altar had been built in Shechem (Gen. 12:6–7), just adjacent to Mount Gerizim in Samaria, and Mount Gerizim itself was the place from which God had instructed blessings to be shouted to his people. For these (and other) reasons, the Samaritans placed their temple on Mount Gerizim. Faithful Jews hated any temple to Yahweh other than the one in Jerusalem and John Hyrcanus, the Hasmonean ruler of Judea, destroyed the Samaritans' in *c.* 128 BC,[23] fuelling religious tensions between the two communities. So what about Jesus: where does he believe to be the right place for worship?

According to Jesus the debate the woman has raised is rapidly approaching its sell-by date. The whole discussion is all but obsolete, because a new era is about to dawn where true worship will no longer be concerned with place (21).[24] Indeed, the new era has already come in one sense, because Jesus has *come*.[25] In another sense the defining events of Jesus' death, resurrection, ascension and giving of the Holy Spirit, are all still future at this point so the new era is still *coming* (23). *Yet a time is coming and has now come when the true worshippers will worship the Father in the Spirit and in truth, for they are*

---

[22] Carson, *John*, p. 221, and Beasley-Murray, *John*, p. 61, both suggest on the contrary that she raises the issue simply because Jesus is a prophet and she is therefore curious about his insight into the controversy.

[23] *NBD*, p. 406.

[24] Although Jesus does make clear his allegiance to the whole Hebrew canon and therefore to the Jerusalem temple in v. 22.

[25] V. 21 is lit. 'the hour is coming' (see ESV). In John's Gospel such references to 'the hour' refer to the coming of Jesus and in particular his death, resurrection and glorification (e.g. John 12:23–25).

the kind of worshippers the Father seeks. God is spirit, and his worshippers must worship in the Spirit and in truth (23–24).

It is immediately clear that the whole conversation has been leading to this point, for Jesus has revealed himself to the woman precisely as the giver of the Spirit and the revealer of truth. In the new era, it will be these two transformational realities – the Spirit of God and the word of God – that will characterize true worship, not the tired controversies about temples that had long divided the Jewish people and the Samaritans. On reflection we may go further: the *entire history of salvation* has been leading to this point. For the same God who called Israel out of slavery in Egypt to worship him has now come in Christ to call a people from all the nations from slavery to sin to worship him. And, just as God enabled Israel to worship by giving them the truth of his law and the reality of his presence (in the tabernacle/temple),[26] so in Christ he has enabled a new kind of worship, by giving us the truth of the gospel and the reality of his presence by the Holy Spirit.

This new worship breaks new ground and reaches new heights. The truth of the gospel is given not just to one nation but to all nations; the presence of the Spirit is encountered not just in special religious buildings but in all the different spaces of life; and because the ultimate sacrifice for sin has been offered, worshippers are not kept at a distance but invited 'to enter the Most Holy Place by the blood of Jesus' and so to 'draw near to God'.[27] The history of the early church bears this out. In the power of the Holy Spirit, the truth of the gospel spread from Jerusalem through Judea, Samaria and to the ends of the earth (Acts 1:8), so that the worship of Yahweh became a movement of global celebration. Furthermore, the working of the Holy Spirit was not focused in special buildings;[28] his intimate and powerful presence was experienced in the homes of Christian families (e.g. 1 Cor. 16:19), the households of God-fearing Gentiles,[29] the public spaces of cities[30] and even in the prisons (Acts 16:23–25) of the Roman Empire. The worship of Yahweh had moved out of the temple and into streets, homes and communities.

[26] I argue in ch. 2 of this book that this is determinative for the structure of the whole book of Exodus.

[27] Heb. 10:19–22, see the fuller discussion in ch. 10 of this book.

[28] It is true, of course, that the early Christians met in the temple courts, but there is no evidence in the rest of Scripture that they built special buildings or invested particular places with a unique sense of the presence of God. Of course church buildings can be very useful, but it is the community of God's people and not the building that constitutes the true temple of the Holy Spirit.

[29] See the moving story of Cornelius in Acts 10.

[30] E.g. the lecture hall of Tyrannus in Ephesus (Acts 19:9) and the Areopagus in Athens (Acts 17:16–34).

Such worshippers are *the kind of worshippers the Father seeks* (23) because *God is spirit* (24). It is doubtful that Jesus is making an abstract metaphysical statement about the nature of God (i.e. that he is spiritual rather than physical). From the beginning of the Old Testament, the work of the Spirit revealed God to be life-giving, creative, powerful, holy, renewing, inscrutable, untameable and miraculous. The worship that is energized and inspired by the same Spirit (which we might expect to reflect some of his characteristics) is therefore 'fitting' to the God who *is spirit*.

The coming of Jesus, then, has established a new community of true worshippers for the Father's glory and pleasure. The truth of his gospel and the gift of his Spirit has introduced a new era which transforms the worship of the people of God.

The purpose of God in sending his son to die and rise and live and be at the right hand of God the Father was that he might restore to us the missing jewel, the jewel of worship; that we might come back and learn to do again that which we were created to do in the first place – to worship the Lord in the beauty of holiness, to spend our time in awesome wonder and adoration of God, feeling it and expressing it and letting it get into our labours and doing nothing except as an act of worship to Almighty God through his son Jesus Christ.[31]

If the calling and restoration of fallen people to become worshippers of Yahweh really was so central to Jesus' ministry (and I believe it was), perhaps it is not so surprising that he ran with the woman's question about worship rather than turning her back to the failures of her personal life which he had exposed. After all, if her heart were so changed that she began to respond to God's truth in obedient faith and to his holy presence with reverent joy (that is to say she became a true worshipper), then her personal life would soon be turned around. John does not provide all the details, but he leaves us in little doubt that the process of transformation had begun. In her initial response the woman is cautious but seems to be reaching for something as she speaks of the time when *the Messiah* will come (25). She may already be wondering if he is standing before her, but Jesus' response removes all ambiguity. '*I, the one speaking to you – I am he*' (26). Within a short time, the testimony of this transformed woman has led many Samaritans from her town to believe in him and to conclude that *this man really is the Saviour of the world* (42).

[31] A. W. Tozer, *Worship: The Missing Jewel of the Evangelical Church* (Harrisburg: Christian Publications, n. d.), p. 12, quoted in V. Roberts, *True Worship* (Carlisle: Authentic Media, 2002), p. 15.

4. Conclusion: Worship in Spirit and truth

David Peterson concludes his reflections on this passage by saying, 'New-covenant worship is essentially the engagement with God that he has made possible through the revelation of himself in Jesus Christ and the life he has made available through the Holy Spirit.'[32]

What then does it mean for this new-covenant, *in-Spirit-and-truth* worship to be nurtured in practice?[33] I offer three suggestions, which I will apply mainly to our congregational worship, but which are also relevant to the worship of our whole lives.

a. Centred on Christ

The new era of worship dawns because (and only because) Christ has come. It is in coming to him that we learn to be the true worshippers whom the Father is seeking. Coming to Christ is clearly central to how we become Christians, but it is also important for the ongoing worship of the church. We are not called to worship 'God-in-general' but specifically the God who is the Father of our Lord Jesus Christ and who has drawn us into fellowship with himself by the Holy Spirit. It is alarmingly easy to sing through a whole block of worship songs and hymns and find few if any explicit reference to Christ or to the central gospel events. Our corporate praying often fails to reflect adequately the trinitarian nature of our faith, as we retreat a little sloppily into generic conceptions of 'God'. At its best, well-used liturgy can be helpful in providing a helpful, Christocentric structure for our worship, leading us to appropriate celebration, confession and consecration. However, it is equally important for those of us in non-liturgical traditions (like my own) to keep a similar christocentricity in our worship. We should aim to ensure that every worship service is, at its heart, a renewed 'coming' to Christ. We do this by choosing songs which tell his story, declare his majesty and celebrate his grace; we do it by offering prayers that magnify his goodness, seek his forgiving grace and look for the advance of his kingdom; we do it by preaching sermons which help people understand his message, hear his call to discipleship and find their place in his mission. We are not just theists; we are Christians!

---

[32] Peterson, *Engaging with God*, p. 100.
[33] Peterson's later book *Encountering God Together* (Nottingham: Inter-Varsity Press, 2013) is in many ways his own, very helpful reflection on this question.

b. Grounded in truth

For me one of the great challenges of corporate worship is putting together services which cohere and make sense, rather than being a disjointed collection of the songs that are 'in' this month, with a few disconnected prayers and a semi-detached sermon. The worship that the Father seeks is neither a feel-good show, nor a mechanical tradition, nor a rehearsing of my personal hobby horses and preferences; it is specifically a response to the truth of Scripture, as it is fulfilled in Jesus. That truth, then, needs to set the agenda for our worship, with the words of Scripture itself shaping and motivating our praise. So I always want to be able to answer the question, 'What is this whole service about and how will each part contribute to that theme?' I then seek to plan the various elements together into a single 'flow' of worship that unpacks and develops that theme in different ways and enables the congregation to respond to it. The worship the Father is seeking is grounded in Christian truth.

c. Engaged with the Holy Spirit

D. A. Carson has pointed out that, in the original language, one preposition, 'in', governs both 'Spirit' and 'truth'. We are not, therefore, considering two different kinds of worship – one 'in Spirit' and the other 'in truth' – but a single reality of worship that is simultaneously 'in Spirit and truth'.[34] Throughout Scripture there is the closest possible relationship between the word and the Spirit, which work together like two scissor blades. However, that does not mean that the Spirit *is* the word, or that to be engaged with the Holy Spirit is simply the same thing as to listen to the word. It is not sufficient simply to carry on our Bible study and leave the Holy Spirit entirely in the background. On the contrary, the worship the Father seeks is specifically and intentionally engaged with the Holy Spirit. We are, after all, making an astonishing claim: God the Holy Spirit is among us! Are we really to imagine that such a majestic, holy presence is barely to be recognized, acknowledged or felt? Surely his presence is to be welcomed, revered and honoured among us, as we open our lives to respond to the direction of God's word. His work of enlightening our minds (1 Cor. 2:10–16), stirring our affections (Gal. 5:22–23), convicting our hearts (John 16:8–11), assuring us of our adoption (Rom. 8:15–16) and satisfying our souls (John 7:37–38) is to be expected, experienced and embraced. His many and varied gifts for the building up of the body are to be used with

---

[34] Carson, *John*, p. 225.

wisdom, gratitude and discipline. And if we truly believe that the Holy Spirit is present in our worship, should we not anticipate some surprises? For 'the wind blows wherever it pleases. You hear its sound, but you cannot tell where it comes from or where it is going.'[35]

[35] John 3:8.

Revelation 4 and 7
6. The ultimate worship

Immediately after I left university I joined the national graduate training scheme for managers in the British National Health Service. The explicit goal of the training was to nurture the top managers of the future for the nation's hospitals and community health care services. One of the most notable features of the scheme was the high level of access trainees were given to senior managers. In reality we were very junior and very green, yet we were personally coached by the chief executives of hospitals and District Health Authorities[1] and even had occasional access to regional and national directors. The rationale was very straightforward: our trainers wanted us to get a vision of what our future could be, so as to nurture our ambition and accelerate the development of our careers.

1. A pilgrim people (Rev. 4)

The perspective of the New Testament is very similar. The people of God are a pilgrim people; a people on a journey to the new creation; a people whose life in the present is to be shaped by their vision of the future. The writer to the Hebrews contrasts the fear of God's people under the old covenant with their joyful security under the new covenant (see Heb. 12:18–24). He insists that we have not come to Mount Sinai (the place where the old covenant was received) but 'to Mount Zion, to the city of the living God, the heavenly Jerusalem'[2] (the place where the new covenant is finally consummated). This heavenly city echoes with the worship both of myriad angels 'in joyful assembly' and of 'the church of the firstborn, whose names are written in heaven'.[3] It is the centre

---

[1] Which have, of course, long been reorganized out of existence!
[2] Heb. 12:22.
[3] Heb. 12:23.

of a glorious 'kingdom' which will not be 'shaken' by the final judgment but will endure, and this confidence of our future participation in the ultimate worship of heaven becomes the basis for our thankful praise and reverent worship in the present (Heb. 12:28–29).

There is no better place to catch a vision of this ultimate worship than the early chapters of the book of Revelation. Allen Ross points out that in the fourth and fifth chapters there are five hymns sung by heavenly choirs[4] built in to the vision of God's throne and his plan of salvation. If, as Greg Beale suggests, the twenty-four elders in the heavenly entourage are heavenly representatives of the whole people of God and the four living creatures of the animate creation,[5] then this heavenly worship provides a powerful model to inspire and shape our worship on earth.

The language is significant here. Throughout Scripture the idea of 'worship' is clearly much broader than singing God's praise; worship is about living the whole of life for the glory of God. Does this therefore mean that we should be cautious about using the language of worship to describe Christians praising God together? I think not, because the writer of the book of Revelation uses the language of worship to describe these heavenly exclamations of praise. In the fourth chapter, they praise God for his sovereign rule over creation:

> *Whenever the living creatures give glory, honour and thanks to him who sits on the throne and who lives for ever and ever, the twenty-four elders **fall down before him who sits on the throne and worship him** who lives for ever and ever. They lay their crowns before the throne and say:*
> > *'You are worthy, our Lord and God,*
> > *to receive glory and honour and power,*
> > *for you created all things,*
> > *and by your will they were created*
> > *and have their being.' (9–11)*

In the fifth chapter, they praise God for his great plan of salvation, centred on Christ, 'the lamb . . . at the centre of the throne'[6] and the

---

[4] A. Ross, *Recalling the Hope of Glory* (Grand Rapids: Kregel Publications, 2006), pp. 481–488.

[5] G. K. Beale, *The Book of Revelation*, NIGTC (Grand Rapids: Eerdmans, 1999), pp. 322, 332. Their designation as *living* creatures suggests this and they are portrayed as constantly doing what the creation itself does: namely to bear ceaseless witness to the majestic glory of God.

[6] Rev. 5:6.

final verse of the chapter concludes, 'The four living creatures said, "Amen", and the *elders fell down and worshipped*'.[7]

So, while it is important to teach people a broad vision of worship, we must not lose the language of worship to describe what we do when, together as God's people, we stand in awe of God's holiness and praise him with thanksgiving.

The model of worship we find in Revelation 4 is particularly helpful. The heavenly worship is (as true worship always is) a response to revelation. In this case, it is a response to a revelation of the holiness and authority of God's throne. A number of features of their worship stand out.

a. They celebrate God's holiness and eternal sovereignty (8)

The *four living creatures* represent the creation. Their ceaseless praise celebrates God's sovereignty over creation, acknowledging that his rule is good since it is governed by his holiness, and that it will last forever since he is eternal. Their words draw on those of the seraphim in Isaiah's vision (Isa. 6:1–3), affirming that God is *holy, holy, holy*. In other words, God is not merely 'holy', nor even very holy ('holy, holy'); he is unimaginably holy ('holy, holy holy'), white-hot holy through and through without the slightest hint of corruption or impurity.[8] His goodness, faithfulness, beauty, wisdom and love are perfect and complete. He is therefore worthy of all our praise, love, trust and joy. This is the God who lives among his people by the Holy Spirit and we respond to him in worship, standing in awe of his holiness and loving him for it.

b. They humble themselves before him (9–10)

Next the focus shifts to *the twenty-four elders*, representing the people of God through all time. In response to the worship of the living creatures they *fall down before* the Lord (10a), as John had done when he saw a vision of the exalted Christ in the first chapter (Rev. 1:17). They also *lay their crowns* before his *throne* (10b), for all glory belongs to him and nothing must compete with it. The word used here for worship (*proskyneō*) has sometimes been said to imply a sense of intimacy with God, because it is linked to the idea of kissing. However, while the origins of the word may be 'the custom

---

[7] Rev. 5:14, emphasis added.

[8] 'Holiness is supremely the truth about God, and his holiness is in itself so far beyond human thought that a "super-superlative" has to be invented to express it' (A. Motyer, *The Prophecy of Isaiah* [Leicester: Inter-Varsity Press, 1993], pp. 76–77).

of prostrating oneself before persons and kissing their feet or their garment, the ground etc',[9] Chris Jack has demonstrated clearly that, in biblical usage, 'not only has the physical gesture of kissing disappeared, but so has any inference of the concept'.[10] In Scripture it is strongly associated with the idea of 'falling down' before the Lord, as it is here in Revelation. Prostration is the fundamental posture of worship, whether the literal prostration of the body or the inner prostration of the heart. It recognizes that God is God and we are not; it acknowledges that he is the Creator and we are his creatures; it is a posture of humility before the majesty of God. This is the biblical meaning of *proskyneō*[11] and this is where authentic worship begins – and without it the wonderful possible of intimacy with God is easily cheapened.[12]

c. They use their voices to praise God (11)

The voice of *the living creatures* has already been heard, representing the animate creation. Now the people of God (represented by the *twenty-four elders*) join creation's chorus, extending the song with their distinctive voice and enriching it with their harmonies. God is worthy of all *glory and honour* and praise because he is the great Creator, to whom they owe their very existence. The praise of which he is worthy is not such that it can be simply contained in the silent privacy of the heart; to be complete it must be expressed. As C. S. Lewis once put it, 'I think we delight to praise what we enjoy because *the praise not merely expresses but completes the enjoyment; it is its appointed consummation*. It is not out of compliment that lovers keep on telling one another how beautiful they are; the delight is

---

[9] BDAG, p. 882, quoted in C. Jack, 'The Proskuneo Myth: When a Kiss is not a Kiss', in D. J. Cohen and M. Parsons (eds.), *In Praise of Worship: An Exploration of Text and Practice* (Eugene: Pickwick Publications, 2010), pp. 84–97. This is also reflected in *NIDNTT*: 'The basic meaning of *proskyneō*, in the opinion of most scholars is to kiss . . . Among the Greeks the vb. is a technical term for the adoration of the gods, meaning to fall down, prostrate oneself, adore on one's knees. Probably it came to have this meaning because in order to kiss the earth (i.e. the earth deity) or the image of a god, one had to cast oneself on the ground' (*NIDNTT*, vol. 2, pp. 875–876).

[10] Jack, 'The Proskuneo Myth', pp. 8–9.

[11] 'Worship entails a response to God which includes bowing before him, figuratively, if not literally, and honouring him in a spirit of reverence and submission' (Jack, 'The Proskuneo Myth', p. 13). 'Worship, do obeisance to, prostrate oneself, do reverence to' (*NIDNTTE*, vol. 2, p. 875).

[12] While the idea of intimacy with God is not implied by the verb *proskyneō*, I think it is suggested by Scripture's frequent use of lover/beloved, bridegroom/bride language for the relationship between God and his people – e.g. Hos. 1 – 3; Eph. 5:22–33; arguably also the Song of Songs.

incomplete till it is expressed.'[13] To praise and delight in God is not to diminish our humanity but to fulfil and enrich it; it is to discover the joy for which we were created.

God's pilgrim people, then, are inspired and enriched in their worship on earth as they reflect on the glorious worship of the angelic choirs of heaven. Such reflection is always important for us, but it is especially so when the dark clouds of suffering gather round us. It is hardly surprising, then, that the clearest exposition of heavenly worship comes in the context of the seven 'seals' of Revelation 6 – 8, which depict the realities of a suffering world (seals 1–4), a suffering church (seal 5) and the suffering of final divine judgment (seals 6–7) before the dawning of the new creation. How can the people of God live and worship in such a world? Revelation 7 tells us.

2. A protected people (Revelation 7:1–8)

Sometimes when registering at a conference, or at a large French campsite, my family has been presented with wrist bands to wear throughout our stay. They are a kind of badge of belonging, demonstrating that we have the right to be on the site and to use its facilities. The staff employed as 'bouncers' on the entrance barriers and around the site can then see the wrist bands and know that they are not to turn us away or trouble us.

The *seal of the living God* (2) functions in a similar (if more dramatic) way in the vision that John *saw* (1) and recorded in Revelation 7. In the vision *four angels* stand in the *four corners of the earth, holding back the four winds of the earth* (1). When released, the four winds will damage the creation (2) and potentially the servants of God as well (3). What hope is there, then, for those who serve God? A fifth angel *having the seal of the living God* (2) cries out to the angels holding back the winds, '*Do not harm the land or the sea or the trees until we put a seal on the foreheads of the servants of our God*' (3). *144,000* people are then *sealed . . . from all the tribes of Israel* (4), and so are protected in the midst of the tsunami of suffering which is about to engulf the world.

So who are these 144,000 and what is the seal? These are among the most hotly disputed questions among interpreters of Revelation and it is beyond the scope of this book to explore all the issues. It is clear that the 144,000 who are sealed are *the servants of our God* (3), but is it only people literally from the tribes of Israel or are all the

[13] C. S. Lewis, *Reflections on the Psalms* (London: Collins, 1977 [1958]), p. 81, emphasis added.

servants of God included whether from Israel or not? We cannot be dogmatic, but at least two observations point towards the broader, more symbolic interpretation. The first is that Revelation 14 also mentions a group of 144,000 who 'follow the Lamb wherever he goes' and are 'purchased from among mankind',[14] which appears to be a clear reference back to Revelation 5:9 in which the Lamb 'purchased for God persons *from every tribe and language and people and nation*'. The second is that the book of Revelation as a whole is given by God 'to show *his servants* what must soon take place'[15] and those servants are located in the (predominantly Gentile) churches of Asia Minor (Rev. 1:4). It seems likely, then, that the 144,000 represent the whole people of God (Jewish and Gentile).[16]

The seal is a sign of ownership by God and protection from his wrath – not unlike the blood of the Passover lamb in Exodus (Exod. 12:22–23). Beyond that, John does not specify exactly what the seal is. However, in the light of wider New Testament theology we can say that the blood of Jesus purchases us for God so that we belong to him and that the gift of his Spirit is the sign and seal of his ownership. 'Now it is God who makes both us and you stand firm in Christ. He anointed us, *set his seal of ownership on us*, and put his Spirit in our hearts as a deposit, *guaranteeing* what is to come.'[17]

The people of God, then, are a protected people, sealed by his Holy Spirit. This is not a guarantee that we will not suffer (after all the fifth seal suggests that God's people may be the particular targets of certain kinds of suffering) but that they will be kept in their suffering. Even the final stages of judgment on the world, which Revelation describes in painful detail, will not deprive them of their eternal destiny, as they are carried through death into glory. The church will not be destroyed; the new creation will not be empty; the worshipping voice of the people of God will not be silenced, for they are purchased with the blood of Christ and sealed by the Holy Spirit. This is our security.

[14] Rev. 14:3–4.

[15] Rev. 1:1, emphasis added.

[16] See Beale, *Temple*, pp. 416–423. In lectures on Revelation available via the Gospel Coalition (<www.thegospelcoalition.org>), D. A. Carson lists several reasons why the 144,000 should be identified with the great multitude from all nations in Rev. 7:9–10. These include: (1) Most agree that at least the number is symbolic; (2) This is the only way to understand the identity of the 144,000 mentioned in Rev. 14; (3) The anomalies in the list of tribes suggest a symbolic meaning (e.g. the absence of Dan and Ephraim and the inclusion of both Joseph and his son Manasseh); (4) The loss of genealogical records in the fall of the temple in AD 70 meant that ancestries could no longer be traced and that the tribal lines were therefore lost by mixed marriages; (5) Passages such as Rom. 2:25–28 and 1 Pet. 2:9 suggest that the distinction between Israel and the Gentiles is no longer valid for defining who the people of God are.

[17] 2 Cor. 1:21–22, emphasis added.

3. A praising people (7:9–17)

My youngest daughter has recently finished her GCSE examinations. For months the family home has been rather subdued as she has kept her head down and persevered with her revision. All of that changed with the completing of her final paper, as crowds of friends arrived and a week of parties and proms ensued. The struggle is over; the celebrations have begun! That is very much the tone of these verses. Beyond all the struggles and suffering of this present life, a great celebration awaits the faithful people of God: they will share forever in the ultimate worship of heaven!

John sees *a great multitude that no one could count, from every nation, tribe, people and language, standing before the throne and before the Lamb* (9). It may seem strange that the crowd that has just been numbered as 144,000 should now be described as uncountable, but it is not unusual for imagery to shift dramatically in Revelation. For example, it is hard to imagine a greater contrast than that between a lion and a lamb, yet Christ is described as both in adjacent verses (Rev. 5:5–6)! The symbolic number 144,000 speaks of the people of God in their completeness, while the uncountable multitude speaks of the people of God in their vastness. The description of their coming from *every nation, tribe, people and language* (9) speaks of them in their diversity, uniting in one people the glorious riches of the whole human family. God's purposes in salvation are not small and concessionary but expansive and generous! He is determined to reach every people-group on earth with the good news of his salvation – and all his worshippers will share the passion of his heart, for they seek his glory above all else. This vast, global crowd no longer toils under the suffering and opposition of a world in rebellion against God. The struggle is over; the celebration is ready to begin. So they stand *before the throne* [of God] *and before the Lamb* (9), poised to worship and rejoice in their deliverance.[18]

a. The joy of the ultimate worshippers (10–12)

Their song is one of celebration, sung not in a restrained whimper but with a *loud* and joyful voice (10). It is not a song of self-congratulation but of praise to God and to the Lamb, knowing that their own achievements have not saved them but only the gracious actions of God in Christ. *Salvation belongs to our God, who sits on the throne, and to the Lamb* (10). As they hear the news of salvation,

---

[18] '"Palm Branches" is an allusion to the festival of Tabernacles . . . a reminder that Israel's continued existence as a nation was traceable ultimately to God's redemption at the Red Sea and victory over the Egyptians' (Beale, *Temple*, p. 428).

the angels of heaven fall on their faces, overwhelmed with joy and adoration.

All the angels were standing round the throne and round the elders and the four living creatures. They fell down on their faces before the throne and worshipped God, saying:
> '*Amen!*
> *Praise and glory*
> *and wisdom and thanks and honour*
> *and power and strength*
> *be to our God for ever and ever.*
> *Amen!*' (11–12)

Too often we rejoice in the wrong things. Our 'joy' in worship is dependent on liking the musical style, unhealthily focused on our favourite preachers or worship leaders, over-influenced by the atmosphere, the lighting, the presence (or absence) of particular friends. It is not so for this great multitude or for their angelic companions. They sing of the plan of God now fulfilled; they sing of the achievement of the Lamb in saving countless millions of people for himself. It is the song of salvation which provides the melody for the ultimate worship of heaven. This is their joy – and if our worship is to be shaped and inspired by their heavenly worship, we must make it our joy too.

b. The story of the ultimate worshippers (13–14)

One of the elders stands up from his position of prostration. He addresses John, asking him about the great crowd of people in white robes. He asks not for his own sake but for John's, like a great teacher, seeking to elicit understanding from their pupil before filling in the gaps. When it becomes clear that John cannot respond (14a), the elder explains: *And he said, 'These are they who have come out of the great tribulation; they have washed their robes and made them white in the blood of the Lamb'* (14b).

The prophet Daniel prophesied 'a time of distress such as has not happened from the beginning of nations until then',[19] to which Jesus referred in Matthew's Gospel (24:21). This is almost certainly the background to *the great tribulation* here. It is a period of great conflict in which God's faithful people are opposed and in which judgment against their opponents begins. To some degree this tribulation continues throughout time, but appears to reach a climax of

---

[19] Dan. 12:1.

intensity at the end of history,[20] as the sixth seal of Revelation 6 suggests (Rev. 6:15–17). The people in this great multitude have *come out of* this period of suffering. They may have come through martyrdom, but if so the martyrs probably represent all God's faithful people who have come through death to glory. Their robes are white because they have washed them *and made them white in the blood of the Lamb* (14b). That is to say, they have persevered in their faith in Christ who loved them and died 'to free them from their sins by his blood'.[21] Blood *stains* clothes, but the blood of Jesus the Lamb washes them white, for his is the blood of sacrifice. Those who are cleansed by his blood are clothed in the radiance of his righteousness – holy in God's sight, 'without blemish and free from accusation'.[22]

c. The future of the ultimate worshippers (15–17)

The tenses of the verbs shift to the future in the middle of verse 15. This may simply be because John is describing a vision that is, in its entirety, future for him, but it seems more likely that the shift is intentional. John's vision moves beyond the process of faithful believers moving through death and into the presence of God, towards a glimpse of God's people enjoying the resurrection life of the new creation. Revelation finishes not with disembodied spirits floating up into an ethereal heaven but with heaven coming down to earth (Rev. 21:1–2). Just as it was the word of God that created in the beginning, that promised redemption and that was incarnated in the person of Christ for us and for our salvation, so it is the word of God that now makes 'everything new' as he comes to dwell in his creation (Rev. 21:3–5). It is not (as our language sometimes suggests) that this new creation life is a shadowy, spiritual continuation of our former 'real' lives; rather, our lives in a fallen world now are (at their best) a pale anticipation of the glorious life to come. It is a life more 'real' than we possess the categories truly to imagine; the kind of life for which we yearn and for which we were created. This is the glorious life that God's renewing word will speak into existence, which we will share with him eternally; a life of ultimate worship.

If this life of ultimate worship is established by the word of God, it is characterized by the presence of God, as our passage goes on to emphasize. The ultimate worshippers will experience his presence as an *intimate presence*, for God will *shelter*, or 'spread his tent over', *them* (15b). They will 'see his face, and his name will be on their

[20] For fuller background see Beale, *Temple*, pp. 433–435.
[21] Rev. 1:5.
[22] Col. 1:22.

foreheads'.[23] It will also be a *providing and protecting presence* so that they will neither hunger nor thirst and the sun will not scorch them (16). It will be a *guiding presence* because *the Lamb at the centre of the throne will be their shepherd* (17a). It seems impossible: a *Lamb* who is a shepherd! Yet this Lamb is the 'Lamb of God, who takes away the sin of the world',[24] 'the good shepherd [who] lays down his life for the sheep'.[25] This good shepherd will *lead them to springs of living water* (17b) – that is to drink deep of the life of God by the Holy Spirit[26] – so that his presence will be a *satisfying presence.* Finally it will be a *healing presence.* God will not pass them a tissue or send them to a doctor but will himself *wipe away every tear from their eyes* (17c). It is a beautiful image of extraordinary tenderness and care as the grief, the losses, the setbacks and disappointments of a lifetime are wiped away in a moment, by the consummate, restoring grace of God in Christ.

The parallel passage in Revelation 22 concludes with the angelic announcement, 'These words are trustworthy and true. The Lord, the God who inspires the prophets, sent his angel to show his servants the things that must soon take place.'[27] This vision of the ultimate worship is not mere wishful thinking; it is completely certain. It is therefore right that our worship now should be inspired and shaped by the ultimate experience of worship that is to come.[28] We will not be disappointed! The word of God which has brought us the good news of the gospel is the same word that will bring renewal to the whole creation. The presence of God we experience in part now by the Spirit is the same presence we will experience then in all his glorious fullness. 'Therefore, since we are receiving a kingdom that cannot be shaken, let us be thankful, and so worship God acceptably with reverence and awe, for our "God is a consuming fire."'[29]

---

[23] Rev. 22:4.
[24] John 1:29.
[25] John 10:11.
[26] Cf. John 4:13–14; 7:37–39.
[27] Rev. 22:6.
[28] 'With the qualification that Christian worship in the Apocalypse means more than singing hymns in church on Sunday, it is correct to assert that "in its innermost meaning, primitive Christian worship was intended to be parallel to the worship of heaven"' (D. Peterson, *Engaging with God* [Leicester: Apollos, 1992], pp. 227–278, quoting G. Delling, *Worship in the New Testament* [ET, London: SCM, 1953], p. 45).
[29] Heb. 12:28–29.

Psalm 100
7. The voice of celebration: A joyful noise

'The prayer preceding all prayers is, "May it be the real I who speaks. May it be the real Thou that I speak to." Infinitely various are the levels from which we pray.'[1] These words from C. S. Lewis remind us of the *double reality* that is required for us to engage with God authentically. True prayer (and therefore true worship, for worship and prayer are closely related) happens when the reality of who I am meets the reality of who God is. A failure to face the reality of who I am tarnishes worship with *hypocrisy* and a failure to face the reality of who God is tarnishes it with *idolatry*.[2] The best antidote to both failures is to learn the practice of worship from the Bible's own repository of songs, prayers and poems: the book of Psalms, which gives expression to the many voices that make up 'the real me' and brings us face to face with the tender majesty of the real God.

Faced with 150 psalms it is hardly surprising that scholars have worked hard to categorize and group them in various ways. Recently much attention has been given to the editorial process of grouping Psalms into the five 'books' identified in our modern Bible translations[3] and of the significance of the placing of the first two psalms for our approach to the whole collection.[4] For our purposes, however, it will be most fruitful to focus on the grouping of the psalms into various 'genres' or types.[5]

[1] C. S. Lewis, *Letters to Malcolm* (London: Geoffrey Bles, 1963/4), p. 109.

[2] The two characteristics of the worship catastrophes we explored in ch. 3.

[3] Book I (Pss 1 – 41); Book II (Pss 42 – 72); Book III (Pss 73 – 89); Book IV (Pss 90 – 106); Book V (Pss 107 – 150).

[4] For a summary see D. M. Howard, Jr, 'Editorial Activity in the Psalter: A State-of-the-field Survey', in J. C. McCann (ed.), *The Shape and Shaping of the Psalter* (Sheffield: Sheffield Academic Press, 1993), pp. 52–70.

[5] See H. Gunkel, *The Psalms: A Form-Critical Introduction*, trans. T. M. Horner (Philadelphia: Fortress, 1967).

Comparing Psalms 98 and 88, for example, it is immediately obvious that we are reading two very different kinds of literature. Psalm 98 is full of confident celebration and feels as if it should be sung with the accompaniment of a full orchestra (or a rock band if you prefer!), while Psalm 88 expresses unrelenting personal agony and feels as if it should be sung in a minor key to the accompaniment of a single violin. The first is clearly a song of joyful praise, the second a heart-rending lament. Of course the distinctions are not always so clear cut, and the definition and identification of the different 'genres' in the Psalms will always be more an art than a science. Nonetheless, Gordon Fee and Douglas Stuart helpfully suggest that we can observe the following wide range of 'genres' of psalms:[6]

- *Laments:* for example, Psalms 3, 22, 31, 42 – 43, 88, 120, 142.
- *Thanksgiving psalms:* for example, Psalms 32, 34, 65, 66, 107, 138.
- *Hymns of praise:* for example, Psalms 8, 33, 104, 145 – 148.
- *Salvation history psalms:* for example, Psalms 78, 105, 106, 135, 136.
- *Psalms of celebration and affirmation:* for example, Psalms 2, 50, 51, 89, 95 – 99, 122, 144.
- *Wisdom psalms:* for example, Psalms 1, 37, 73, 119, 133, 139.
- *Songs of trust:* for example, Psalms 11, 23, 62, 91, 121, 125.

Imagine for a moment that you arrive a few minutes late for your church service one day. As you walk towards the door of the church building you can hear that the service is underway and that the congregation is already singing – and it sounds unusually vibrant. You walk through the door and people are dancing, cymbals are crashing, tambourines are beating, trumpets are blasting, spontaneous applause keeps erupting. How do you respond? Has your church at last woken up to the exuberance of truly biblical worship (after all, there is nothing going on that does not appear somewhere in the psalms!) or has it finally lost its way and surrendered to endless noise and appalling superficiality? For many of us our initial response to that question is likely to be largely emotional or cultural; it is to do with what we like or dislike and what we find comfortable or uncomfortable. However, the analysis of diverse genres within the book of Psalms warns us against a narrowing of our vision for worship on the grounds of our cultural norms or personal preferences. Biblical worship is rich and varied; it is not confined to a single

---

[6] G. D. Fee and D. Stuart, *How to Read the Bible for All Its Worth* (Grand Rapids: Zondervan, 1982), pp. 175–177.

form or style but sings with many voices, reflecting a broad range of human experience and resonating with the whole spectrum of human emotion. Calvin put it memorably. 'I have been wont to call this book not inappropriately, *an anatomy of all parts of the soul*; for there is not an emotion of which any one can be conscious that is not here represented as in a mirror.'[7] It is this rich diversity of genres that makes the book of Psalms such a potent tool in enabling 'the real me' truly to meet 'the real God', to use Lewis' categories again.

I suggest that the hermeneutical tool of genre analysis in the Psalms can be helpfully recast as a way of identifying a glorious diversity of 'voices of worship' which can deeply enrich our experience of worship and move us beyond the deadly turf wars of culture and preference. A truly biblical vision for worship will hear the range of these 'voices of worship' and seek to learn to sing along with them all. Reflecting this commitment, each section of this book will conclude with two chapters expounding a range of psalms which enable us to listen to some of those voices and reflect on how they may deepen and extend our worship as Christians.

We begin with the exuberant voice of celebration in Psalm 100 – a voice we have already heard echoing in the praise of the 'great multitude' before the throne in heaven.[8] This is surely a fitting conclusion to our exploration of the Father's gracious purpose in calling a worshipping community to himself in Christ. The psalm begins with an unapologetic summons to joyful, energetic worship.

1. Worship with joy! (1–2)

> *Shout for joy to the LORD, all the earth.*
> *Worship the LORD with gladness;*
> *come before him with joyful songs.*[9]

This is a loud psalm and a joyful one. *Shout for joy to the LORD* (1), is its opening call, or in the words of the ESV, *make a joyful noise!* This is no dirge, sung with long faces in hushed tones; it is a song of celebration, pulsating with exuberant life and unrestrained delight!

---

[7] J. Calvin, *Commentary on the Psalms*, vol. 1, introduction, quoted by H. Lockyer, 'In Wonder of the Psalms', *Christianity Today* 28 (March 2, 1984), p. 76. Emphasis added.

[8] See Rev. 7:9–10, expounded in ch. 6 of this book.

[9] Given the strength of these introductory statements, it is perhaps surprising that neither the NIV nor the NRSV use exclamation marks. For an alternative approach see ESV.

This call is not limited to Psalm 100, but recurs throughout the book of Psalms.[10] It is also an international psalm, written from the perspective of Israel's faith (3) but with a global vision. The whole creation is claimed for the glory of Yahweh, as *all the earth* (1) is called to joy. So what is the context of all this shouting and noise? How are the nations to find such joy?

The context is clearly the worship of Yahweh (2) and it is in joining in that worship that the nations will find their joy. We have noticed before[11] that there is a breadth of meaning in the word for worship here. It could equally well be translated *serve the LORD with gladness*[12] but the way the verse continues strongly suggests that the *service* envisaged here includes adoring and rejoicing in God.[13] *Worship the LORD with gladness; come before him with joyful songs* (2).

The basic building block of Hebrew poetry is not rhyme or metre but repetition (also known as parallelism). So, two adjacent lines in the poem are not usually saying different things but saying the same thing in different ways. The call to *worship the LORD with gladness* (2a) is therefore explained and developed by the parallel invitation to *come before him with joyful songs* (2b).[14] This is then, inescapably, a psalm which called Israel to exuberant, joyful, noisy worship of the Lord – indeed Michael Wilcock suggests it was used to welcome people to the Jerusalem temple for worship.[15] The psalm makes this call to *all the earth* (1) and it therefore beckons us today to worship with the voice of exuberant celebration! So what is it that calls forth such joy?

2. ... because the Lord is God (3)

In the Bible, worship is never a mere feeling to be worked up; it is *always* a response to what God has revealed of himself. Worship has its reasons. It is not the ephemeral froth on a religious life that vanishes the moment a meeting is over; it *rests* on something secure.

[10] See for example Pss 98:4–6; 95:1–5; 92:1–3; 33:1–5; 47; 66:1–3; 81:1–4; 150.

[11] See ch. 2 of this book, fn. 30.

[12] ESV, see also KJV.

[13] It is worth noting that the *NIDOTTE* article quoted in ch. 2 cites Ps. 100:2 as an example of worship as a 'cultic service'.

[14] 'The parts of a verse in the Psalter cohere by the principle of repetition, restatement, differentiation or progression' (W. A. Vangemeren in his introduction to T. Longman III and D. E. Garland, *The Psalms*, Expositor's Bible Commentary, vol. 5 [rev. ed., Grand Rapids: Zondervan, 2008]. See also pp. 48–50 for an extended analysis.)

[15] M. Wilcock, *The Message of Psalms 73–150*, BST (Leicester: Inter-Varsity Press, 2001), p. 108.

Know that the LORD *is God* (3a). Knowing truth about God and experiencing joy in God are not incompatible opposites; they belong together! If our knowledge of God's truth does not lead to worship and joy, it is not true knowledge but rather the seed of intellectual pride. If the joy in our worship does not arise from what we *know* of God it is not true joy but rather the beginnings of idolatry. Worship has its reasons and this psalm sets out some of the best of them.

The LORD is God. He alone is sovereign, transcendent and almighty. Since he alone is God it follows that he is our Creator who claims us as his own – *it is he who made us, and we are his* (3b). Vehemently though this idea is rejected in contemporary society, this psalm presents it to us as the basis for joy! For this surely is what gives our lives their true significance, dignity and richness. We are not mere accidents of biology eking out a meaningless existence alone in the universe; we are here because God made us and made us for himself. That much is true of every human being: we belong to him because he created us. However, the people of God belong to him twice over! We are his because he made us and his because he redeemed us, rescuing us from our rebellion and restoring us to himself – *we are his people, the sheep of his pasture* (3c). Psalm 95 contains exactly the same sequence of thought.

> Come, let us bow down in worship,
>> let us kneel before the LORD *our Maker*;
> for he is our God
>> and *we are the people of his pasture*,
> the flock under his care.[16]

As Christian readers of this psalm, our minds are inevitably drawn to Christ – the eternal Word of God, through whom all things were made (John 1:1–3) and the good shepherd of his people who laid down his life for the sheep (John 10:11). We belong to Christ both by creation and by salvation and rejoice to be in the flock under his care. If ancient Israel had cause for exuberant praise, we have much more!

This knowledge that the Lord is God and that they belonged, doubly, to him brought a deep sense of security and joy to the people of God as they made their way up to the temple in Jerusalem, with the call to worship ringing in their ears. Then, as they enter through the temple gates, the call comes again in a slightly different form.

---

[16] Ps. 95:6–7, emphasis added.

3. Praise with thankfulness (4)

> *Enter his gates with thanksgiving*
> *and his courts with praise;*
> *give thanks to him and praise his name (4).*

The attitude of our hearts at the point when we come together for corporate worship is enormously important. It is all too easy to come as consumers looking for entertainment, as critics looking to find fault, as cynics looking to see through the motivations of others or as self-absorbed narcissists unwilling to look beyond our own hopes and needs. This psalm challenges all those attitudes. It calls us to come and worship God with thankful hearts, to come to praise him, to make much of him, to enjoy and delight in him!

The language in this verse shifts from that of worship to that of thanksgiving and praise. The distinction should not be pressed too hard, but it is probably best to understand worship as the broader idea, encompassing the *whole* of our response to God in heart, voice and action, and to see praise as the particular expression of that response in word and song. The verse uses a variety of words for this praise, each with its own shade of meaning:

- *Thanksgiving* (4a, c)[17] *(tôdâ / yādâ)* – the acknowledgement of God's goodness.
- *Praise* (4b)[18] – which is often linked with singing or songs of praise. In fact the book of Psalms as a whole takes this word as its name in Hebrew – *tĕhillîm* (praises/songs).
- *Bless* (4d, ESV, lit. 'bless his name')[19] – that is to speak well of him and his goodness.

Giving thanks to God; singing praise to God; speaking well of God: these are what stand at the heart of biblical praise. Notice how God-centred and God-saturated this concept is. There is still a tendency for us in our praise songs to speak well of ourselves and to 'talk up' our praise[20] – an activity which is vacuous and (in the

[17] Heb. *ydh* (acknowledge, give thanks, praise, confess) and *tôdâ* (thanksgiving, thank offering, son of thanksgiving, praise, choir, confession) (*NIDOTTE*, vol. 2, p. 405).

[18] Heb. *tĕhillâ* (praise, renown) (*NIDOTTE*, vol. 1, p. 1035).

[19] Heb. *brk*. 'God blesses human beings by speaking well of them, thereby imparting "blessing" (good things) to them, and so they are "blessed" (*barûk*); human beings bless God by speaking well of him, attributing "blessing" (good qualities) to him, and so he is "blessed" (*barûk*)' (*NIDOTTE*, vol. 1, p. 764).

[20] I am referring to the kind of praise song which describes our praise of God at length but says little if anything about the holiness, goodness and grace of God which should lead us to praise him in the first place.

end) desperately unsatisfying and self-centred. Biblical praise revels in biblical truth; we sing about God as well as to God. As we have seen before, authentic praise has its reasons and the psalm concludes by spelling out some more of them.

4. . . . because the Lord is good (5)

> *For the LORD is good and his love endures forever;*
> *his faithfulness continues through all generations (5).*

Have you ever thought what it would be like if the God who is there were *not* good? Imagine a world in which absolute power is wielded with moral indifference or with evil intent – like the very worst kind of tyrant but with *no* limits as to what they could do. It is the ultimate dystopian vision. This psalm, however, insists that Yahweh – the God who is there – is *good!* Indeed he is the final measure of all goodness and his power is exercised in perfect alignment with that goodness and love. It is little wonder that this is the focus of the psalm's praise, for the goodness of God is surely the most fundamental reason for thankfulness in the whole of creation! In the heart-warming words of Psalm 4, '*You* have put more joy in my heart than they have when their grain and wine abound.'[21] Of course his goodness does not mean that, in a world marred by sin and selfishness, he will never permit painful things to happen. What it means is that his love will never fail and will *endure forever* (5a) and that in his unswerving *faithfulness* (5b) he will fulfil all his promises to his people in *all generations* (5b), never abandoning them but bringing them safely to eternal glory. The New Testament reminds us that it is in Christ that God's promises find their 'yes and amen!'[22] and in him that God's faithfulness is therefore perfectly revealed. The love that *endures forever* is precisely the 'love of God that is in Christ Jesus our Lord' from which we can never be separated![23]

5. Conclusion

There are number of conclusions to be drawn from our exploration of this short psalm.

a. True worship overflows in missional passion

We will develop this idea much more in chapter 14, but it is a neglected

[21] Ps. 4:7 (ESV), emphasis added.
[22] 2 Cor. 1:20.
[23] Rom. 8:35–39.

theme, which surfaces in many psalms and is the launching point for this one. *Shout for joy to the LORD, **all the earth*** (1). Influenced both by a consumerist mindset and an individualistic culture, our approach to worship can easily narrow down to a personal quest for intense spiritual experience. There is much that is good in such a quest, but by itself it is inadequate, as the psalms highlight again and again. True worship arises from the awareness that God's glory and goodness are such that he *must be worshipped* by all his creatures and it therefore overflows into mission, calling *all the earth* to his praise. The true worshipper will never regard it as sufficient only for them – or only for people in their culture circle – to worship the Lord, but will ache with longing for the day when people 'from every nation, tribe, people and language'[24] stand before the throne of God and the Lamb.

b. Knowledge of God and enjoyment of God grow together

The more deeply we buy in to a consumerist attitude, the more likely we are to confuse enjoyment of a particular form of worship with enjoyment of God himself – and this is the case whether our preferences are more contemporary or more traditional. True enjoyment of God does not arise from singing our favourite songs, having music that conforms perfectly to our cultural preferences, or creating a conducive atmosphere. True enjoyment of God arises from deepening knowledge of God – just as the joy of friendship grows as we get to know each other more deeply. As we have seen, both of the calls to jubilant worship in this psalm are grounded in joyful reflection on who God is (3, 5). D. A. Carson makes the point powerfully: 'Those who focus much on God have much for which to praise. Those whose vision is merely terrestrial or self-centred dry up inside like desiccated prunes. God is your praise!'[25]

More specifically, if we are going to worship with true joy, Psalm 100 calls us first *to reflect on what it means for God to be God* (2–3): meditate on his sovereignty; remember he is both your great Creator and your gracious Redeemer; know that you are a human being created to know God and bear his image in the world; take to heart that you were made for him and that he has claimed you for himself in Christ! Second, *it encourages us to cultivate thankfulness for God's goodness* (4–5): remember his goodness and savour it; reflect often and deeply on his love to you in Jesus Christ; recall his faithfulness to you over the years; enjoy the security of knowing he will never abandon you and has a great and glorious future for you.

[24] Rev. 7:9.
[25] D. A. Carson, *For the Love of God*, vol. 1 (Leicester: Inter-Varsity Press, 1998), 6 June.

Perhaps we have allowed too much distance to grow between the teaching ministry of the church and the worshipping life of the church; too great a gulf between theology and doxology. The message of this psalm is that, if we want to worship with authentic joy, we should hold the two together in a continual, creative conversation.

c. Recognize the importance of singing

> Worship the LORD with gladness;
> come before him with **joyful songs** (2).

Without doubt it is possible to give too much emphasis to music and singing within our worship, to the point that in practice 'worship' and 'singing' become virtually equated (however much we may deny this in theory). However, in reaction to this tendency, there is an equal and opposite danger of failing to give to music and singing the honourable place it has within Scripture. Music is a gift of God in creation, which has its place in the earliest chapters of the Bible.[26] Its presence in every known culture testifies to its universal power[27] to reach the depths of the human heart, carry the breadth of human emotion and shape the values of human society. Reggie M. Kidd encourages us to 'think of singing as a language that allows us to embody our love for our Creator. Song is a means he has given us to communicate our deepest affections, to have our thoughts exquisitely shaped, and to have our spirits braved for the boldest of obediences.'[28] Scripture encourages excellence and creativity and even extravagance in music.[29] After an extensive analysis of the biblical material on music Jeremy Begbie, while acknowledging Scripture's warnings about the misuse of music,[30] draws this broadly positive conclusion: 'Perhaps the most important thing to note here is the essentially positive impression of music given in Scripture . . . Overall, we find a warm-hearted acceptance and encouragement of its proper use.'[31]

---

[26] '[Adah's] brother's name was Jubal; he was the father of all who play stringed instruments and pipes' (Gen. 4:21).

[27] 'There have been cultures without counting, cultures without painting, cultures bereft of the wheel or the written word, but never a culture without music' (J. D. Barrow, *The Artful Universe Expanded* [Oxford: Oxford University Press, 2005], ch. 5).

[28] R. M. Kidd, *With One Voice: Discovering Christ's Song in Our Worship* (Grand Rapids: Baker Books, 2005), p. 14.

[29] E.g. Ps. 33:3: 'Sing to him a new song; play skilfully and shout for joy'; and see Ps. 150.

[30] See e.g. Amos 5:23–24; 6:4–6; Isa. 5:11–12.

[31] J. Begbie, *Resounding Truth: Christian Wisdom in the World of Music* (Grand Rapids: Baker Academic, 2007), p. 74.

In Exodus 15, as the Israelites witness God's salvation in the final destruction of their Egyptian oppressors in the Red Sea, they sing the song of Moses and Miriam. In Deuteronomy 32 just before the people enter the Promised Land, Moses teaches them a song. Israel's greatest king (David) was also its most prolific song writer, bequeathing large sections of the book of Psalms to subsequent generations of God's people. The book of Psalms itself is the largest book of the Bible, enabling every movement of the human heart to be brought to God through poetry and song. In Romans 15 Paul can describe his mission to the Gentiles as fulfilling the ancient words of David, 'Therefore I will praise you among the Gentiles; *I will sing the praises of your name*'.[32] The book of Revelation reveals heaven to be a place of singing and of loud, exuberant exclamations of praise (Rev. 5:9–14; 7:9–10). It is hardly surprising, then, to find that – whatever else the early Christians did when they met together – there is no doubt that they *sang* together!

> Do not get drunk on wine, which leads to debauchery. Instead, be filled with the Spirit, speaking to one another with *psalms, hymns, and songs* from the Spirit. *Sing and make music* from your heart to the Lord, always giving thanks to God the Father for everything, in the name of our Lord Jesus Christ.[33]

The encouragement of Psalm 100, then, to *come before [the Lord] with joyful songs* (2) is not an isolated suggestion but rather a short cadence in the epic song of praise which rings through the whole biblical narrative. The power of music, then, is not to be resisted and feared, but responsibly harnessed for the glory and praise of God and the edification of his people. Worship is much more than singing, but singing does have a significant and honourable place within worship.

d. Learn to sing with the exuberant voice of celebration

For reasons of temperament, life situation, preference and culture most of us find that we sing more naturally with some of the 'voices of worship' than with others. This is entirely understandable, and the sheer breadth of genre in the book of Psalms guarantees that all of us can find some psalms in which we feel at home! Nonetheless, our experience will fail to reflect the wonderful breadth of biblical worship if we never step outside what feels comfortable to us to learn

---

[32] Rom. 15:9.
[33] Eph. 5:18–21. See also Col. 3:16; 1 Cor. 14:26.

other less familiar 'voices'. Some may need to learn the voice of lament and take their sorrows and doubts to God with honest vulnerability. Others may need to learn the reverent voice of adoration that stands in awe of the holiness of God.

However, as this chapter comes to a close, I want to emphasize the place of the more exuberant voice of celebration that sounds so clearly through Psalm 100. I write as a restrained Englishman, aware that much in my culture tends to push me towards a stance that is cool, detached and sometimes cynical. I know that we tend to prefer our religion understated, reserved and sophisticated, and are deeply suspicious of anything that could appear over-enthusiastic or even fanatical. I accept that the voice of celebration may sound different on the lips of a reserved Englishman from how it will sound in an African village.[34] Still, I cannot avoid the conclusion that I am out of step with the drumbeat of this psalm if I seek to celebrate God's goodness by singing only dour tunes, with a long face, suppressing all emotion and looking for all the world as if I wished I were somewhere else! Can it really be right to seem more excited to sing 'Mama Mia' or to watch my local team score a goal than to contemplate the abundant goodness and awesome power of God? Is not the goodness of God, revealed (supremely) in Jesus Christ *such good news* that it demands from us vibrant, wholehearted and energetic praise?

Biblical worship has many voices, but there is a place for leaving on one side what others may think of us, filling our minds with the glory and grace of Father, Son and Holy Spirit, giving ourselves without reservation in joyful, exuberant, extravagant praise.

---

[34] Though I think we need to acknowledge that the emerging cultures of the younger generations are less restrained and more at home with exuberant self-expression.

Psalm 99
8. The voice of adoration:
A trembling world

One of the surprises of pastoral ministry is to discover that people are capable of experiencing sharply contrasting emotions in quick succession, even when their situation has not changed significantly. It is not uncommon, for example, for a person to experience raw grief beside the grave of their loved one and, later on the same day as relatives gather for tea after the funeral, for the same person to experience a strong sense of well-being (sometimes almost elation) that rather takes them by surprise (though, of course, this is usually quite short-lived). When my wife and I lost our two sons,[1] friends who visited us sometimes seemed taken aback by the way that the agony of tears would give way to the relief of laughter and 'ordinary' conversation.

In Old Testament history the exile, first of the northern kingdom (Israel) and then of the southern kingdom (Judah), was an immense shock. It appeared that God's promises had failed as the people witnessed their defeat at the hands of their enemies, their expulsion from the Promised Land, the destruction of their cherished temple and the ending of the royal dynasty of David. What would their response be? Would they give way to unbelief and despair, or would they continue to worship the Lord and, if so, what range of moods would that worship encompass? Many scholars believe that it is this 'post-exilic' situation that prompted the compilation of the fourth book of Psalms[2] into the form in which we now have it, giving the people of God resources to respond to the painful, unanswered questions of Psalm 89:38–51. G. H. Wilson says, 'This grouping [ie Pss. 90-106] stands as the "answer" to the problem posed in Ps. 89

---

[1] Our first child Daniel was born prematurely and lived for just thirteen days and a few years later our third child Jonathan was stillborn.

[2] I.e. Pss 90 – 106.

as to the apparent failure of the Davidic covenant with which Books One-Three are primarily concerned.'[3]

It is, of course, difficult to be certain about this kind of analysis – particularly when the first psalm in the collection (Ps. 90) is attributed to Moses, and Psalms 101 and 103 to David, both of whom lived long before the exile! It is nonetheless perfectly possible to accept that some (possibly the majority) of the psalms in Book IV were written before the exile, but that they were brought together within the Psalter at a later date[4] to resource Israel's worship in the aftermath of this period of national discipline and grief.[5] If this is correct, the contrasting moods of this group of psalms is particularly striking. It suggests that among godly Israelites, a response of confident, exuberant faith about the future (David's house may no longer reign, but the Lord reigns still) went hand-in-hand with sober reflection on their experience of divine holiness and judgment. In his comments on Psalm 99, Derek Kidner makes this wider point: 'In this group of Psalms on the Kingship and advent of the Lord, the mood alternates between high festivity and a chastened awe – for God is all that stirs us and all that shames us. Here after the carefree delight of Psalm 98, we recollect how exalted and how holy he is, and how profound is the reverence we owe him.'[6]

So perhaps it is not so surprising that, so soon after exploring the loud celebrations of Psalm 100 we find ourselves entering the quieter more reflective landscape of Psalm 99, with its reverent voice of adoration. Some of us may gravitate more to the voice of celebration and others to the voice of adoration, but by placing these two psalms

[3] G. H. Wilson, *The Editing of the Hebrew Psalter*, Society of Biblical Literature Dissertation Series 76 (Chico: Scholars Press, 1985), p. 215. Quoted in M. E. Tate, *Psalms 51–100*, WBC 20 (Nashville: Thomas Nelson, 2000), p. 531. See also T. Longman III and D. E. Garland, *The Psalms*, Expositor's Bible Commentary, vol. 5 (Grand Rapids: Zondervan, 2008), pp. 687–689.

[4] An imperfect analogy from our own experience might be the way in which Edwards Mote's great hymn, 'My hope is built on nothing less than Jesus' blood and righteousness' (1834), has been brought into the repertoire of many churches today, allowing words formed in the nineteenth century context to find new resonances on twenty-first-century lips.

[5] So I would argue for the authenticity of the titles (see Derek Kidner, *Psalms 1–72*, TOTC [Leicester: Inter-Varsity Press, 1973], pp. 32–33) and therefore accepting Mosaic authorship of Ps. 90 and Davidic authorship of Pss 101 and 103. Furthermore, I suggest that the likely reference to the Ark of the Covenant in Ps. 99:1, 5 most likely points to a pre-exilic author. Nonetheless, if (as seems likely) these psalms are presented to us canonically as resourcing worship in the light of the exile, Tate is surely right that 'the cultic situations for Pss. 93–99 are mostly post-exilic, and these should be considered the primary contexts for their interpretation' (Tate, *Psalms 51–100*, p. 507).

[6] D. Kidner, *Psalms 73–150*, TOTC (Leicester: Inter-Varsity Press, 1975), pp. 353–354.

side by side, the Psalter encourages us to see that both are important and both belong together.

Isaiah's famous vision of 'the Lord, high and exalted, seated on a throne' had its focus in the continuing call of the angelic seraphim, 'Holy, holy, holy, is the LORD Almighty; the whole earth is full of his glory'.[7] As we noted in chapter 6,[8] through the double-repetition of the word 'holy', the seraphim were praising the Lord not only as *most* holy, but as *unimaginably and indescribably* holy. The same threefold assertion of the holiness of the Lord is found in Psalm 99, with its short refrain marking the end of each section: *he/our God is holy* (3, 5, 9). This, then, is clearly the emphasis of this psalm. '*Holy* is a word to emphasize the distance between God and man: not only morally, as between the pure and the polluted, but in the realm of being between the eternal and the creaturely.'[9] Holiness is what makes God, God; it means he is gloriously *other* than us – infinite, eternal, almighty, radiant and pure. His presence is a holy presence which we should not approach lightly but with reverent awe. Psalm 99 calls us to such a response as it reflects, from various angles, on the holiness of God.

1. His holy reign (1–3)

> The LORD reigns,
>   let the nations tremble;
> he sits enthroned between the cherubim,
>   let the earth shake (1).

In the face of the failure of the Davidic dynasty, it was the ancient conviction that the Lord himself reigned which sustained the faith and hope of godly Israelites. Notwithstanding the apparent victory first of Assyria and then of Babylon, the assertion remained that the Lord's reign was supreme and that he was therefore to be feared both within Israel and among the nations (1a). Not only so, but his reign was still established in Jerusalem. This is almost certainly the impli-cation of the phrase *he sits enthroned between the cherubim* (1b). The cherubim are heavenly angelic figures which guard the glory of God (see Gen. 3:24). These figures were represented as statues over-shadowing the lid of the Ark of the Covenant, which was placed within the Most Holy Place of the Jerusalem temple (prior to its destruction). Insofar as it represented his heavenly rule, the ark (and by extension, the temple) was understood to be God's footstool on

[7] Isa. 6:1–3.
[8] See fn. 12.
[9] Kidner, *Psalms 73–150*, p. 354, emphasis original.

earth,[10] the place where his heavenly reign was tangibly expressed on earth; hence the conclusion drawn in verse 2: *Great is the LORD in Zion; he is exalted over all the nations.*

I tend to the view that this psalm was written before the exile. Nonetheless, its positioning in a block of psalms brought together for the use of the post-exilic community[11] is remarkable, given the claims it is making. In addition to the personal suffering and disorientation of national defeat and exile, Israel's crisis was deeply spiritual. They had witnessed the failure of the Davidic dynasty which God had promised would last forever.[12] They had seen the destruction of the temple which the Lord said he had 'consecrated . . . by putting his name there forever'.[13] They had been expelled from the land which the Lord had given to Abram 'and his offspring, forever'.[14] Never did the chasm between their present and their history, between what they experienced and what they had been promised, seem wider. As new covenant believers we look back on their experience from the other side of the cross, resurrection and ascension of Christ, whom we know as the true fulfilment of all these promises. For them, though, that was all, at best, a dimly perceived and distant future. Their only refuge from despair was simple trust that, somehow, God would yet be true to his word and faithful to his promises. For all its sobriety and reverence, it is exactly such trust that this psalm expresses. With magnificent faith, it asserts that the irrevocable nature of Yahweh's covenant relationship with Israel was such that, despite the multiple contradictions of their present experience[15] still his reign touched the earth tangibly in Jerusalem and was established among his people! This small post-exilic community living under the watchful eye of the Persian Empire, was still linked, in the purposes of God, to the Davidic nation state to which so many of the promises had been made, yet which had been swept away at the exile.[16] So strong is this conviction, that the nations are still envisaged seeing clearly in the life of Israel that there is a God who reigns and that his reign is a holy reign, so that they too are summoned to *tremble* and shake before him (1), and to join in reverent *praise* of his *great and awesome name* (3).

---

[10] V. 5, cf. Ps. 132:7–16; 1 Chr. 28:2.

[11] As indicated, for example, by Pss 89:38–52; 106:47.

[12] See 2 Sam. 7:16.

[13] 1 Kgs 9:3.

[14] Gen. 13:15.

[15] And despite the fact that the Ark of the Covenant was never returned to Jerusalem.

[16] I am grateful to James Robson of Wycliffe Hall, Oxford for emphasizing this point in personal correspondence.

Though we live at a different moment in salvation history, we also know what it is to inhabit the space between what is and what has been promised.[17] *The LORD reigns* (1) – and, in his earthly life, Jesus gave us a clear vision of that reign, the kingdom which he had come to inaugurate. It was, unmistakably, a kingdom of righteousness, peace, joy, healing, justice and freedom (see e.g. Matt. 10:7–8). Not only so, but the encouragement of Scripture and the life of the early church both lead us to expect that we will experience at least some measure of these realities now by the power of the Spirit, while we await the kingdom's final consummation when Christ returns.[18] Nonetheless, we experience continuing struggle with sin (Gal. 5:16–18), often we do not see the healing for which we pray (1 Tim. 5:23),[19] sometimes we are disappointed and hurt within our church families (2 Cor. 12:11–21), often we are confused by God's ways in our lives (2 Cor. 1:8–9). Like Israel in the aftermath of the exile, we struggle to see that *the LORD reigns* (1). How do we react? The psalms give us a rich vocabulary of response from which to draw, including the raw honesty of lament which we will explore later in this book. Psalms 99 and 100, however, give us words of robust faith for times of perplexing reality – robust faith in the reign of God and the word of God. Read together, they also remind us that such faith can (and, perhaps, should) be expressed both in exuberant confidence and in reverent reflection.

As we have seen, this psalm calls all the nations to worship Yahweh, not just Israel. Nonetheless, Israel has more reasons to worship him, for they have seen him at work in their history in a quite unique way. Their calling therefore (as it was from the beginning), is to lead the nations in worship of their God, whose holy acts (expressing his holy reign) have been revealed among them.

2. His holy acts (4–5)

I recently had the privilege of meeting James and Ruth Padilla DeBorst, who have been at the heart of missiological thinking in Central and Latin America in recent decades. Ruth reflected memorably on the challenge faced by the previous generation of student evangelists in this region[20] as they sought to communicate

[17] I am grateful to Julian Hardyman of Eden Baptist Church, Cambridge for prompting these reflections in personal correspondence.

[18] For example Rom. 8:1–2 speaks of the Spirit's liberating grace; Gal. 5:22–25 of his transformational work; and Jas 5:13–18 of an ongoing ministry of healing. Jesus' encouragement to prayerful expectancy in John 14:11–14 seems also to push in this direction.

[19] And probably 2 Cor. 12:7–10.

[20] Including her father, the well-known missiologist René Padilla.

the gospel in a situation where the dominant issues (especially among students) were oppression and corruption. A gospel which never explained how personal salvation must be worked out in the pursuit of social righteousness and a concern for justice simply could not gain any traction. However, Scripture revealed a God of justice who was concerned for the plight of the oppressed, in a way which resonated profoundly in their context, opening many doors for the gospel.

This is the God – the God who *loves justice* (4) – who had stepped into Israel's history, liberating them from slavery and oppression. While they were still in their slavery he had promised them, 'I am the LORD, and I will bring you out from under the yoke of the Egyptians. I will free you from being slaves to them, and I will redeem you with an outstretched arm and *with mighty acts of judgment.*'[21] God did what he had promised, asserting his reign over Pharaoh to give Israel justice and establish equity. In the words of Psalm 99:

> *The King is mighty, he loves justice –*
> *you have established equity;*
> *in Jacob* [i.e. for the nation of Israel] *you have done*
> *what is just and right* (4).

It is possible that the reference to God's justice here refers to the justice of God's judgment against Israel in sending them into exile. However, it has often been observed that Book IV of the Psalms is characterized by frequent references to Moses and the exodus,[22] presumably because it was this story that gave them hope in the aftermath of exile. It is therefore better to see verse 4 as referring back to the exodus, reminding the people that God's acts in bringing them salvation were *holy acts* of awesome power and devastating judgment against Egypt. In response, Israel is called to reverent adoration of the holy God, who has shown himself to be *their* God.

> *Exalt the LORD our God;*
> *and worship at his footstool;*
> *he is holy* (5).

Christian readers of this psalm can easily make Israel's praise here their own. We do so, first, realizing that we ourselves stand in the

---

[21] Exod. 6:6.
[22] So much so that Derek Kidner suggests it could be entitled 'an Exodus collection' (Kidner, *Psalms 73-150*, p. 74).

same great story of God's salvation which first called Israel out of slavery in Egypt and has now called us from slavery to sin and Satan through the Lord Jesus Christ (Col. 1:13–14). We do so, second, recognizing that the cross was itself an act of justice and judgment. For 'God put forward' Christ Jesus, his own son, 'as a propitiation by his blood, to be received through faith . . . *so that he might be just and the justifier* of the one who has faith in Jesus';[23] God's justice demanded that human rebellion should be punished and Christ bore that punishment in our place as he was 'pierced for our transgressions'.[24] Not only so, but it is an act of judgment against all the powers of evil which stood against us.

> He forgave us all our sins, having cancelled the charge of our legal indebtedness, which stood against us and condemned us; he has taken it away, nailing it to the cross. And having disarmed the powers and authorities, he made a public spectacle of them, triumphing over them by the cross.[25]

We therefore kneel on the holy ground of Calvary, marvelling at the cross, the true *footstool* (5) of the Lord, where his reign touches the earth in costly grace and, with the voice of reverent adoration, worship the God of holy love, made known to us in Christ.

3. His holy word (6–9)

It is often said that 'actions speak louder than words'. As a cutting challenge against hypocrisy (whether religious or political) it is a rather effective sound bite, but the point can easily be overstated. Actions can easily be ambiguous; frequently they require words to explain their significance. So if I reduce my consumption of red meat, is it a statement of environmental concern, a step towards principled vegetarianism, a change in my personal tastes and preferences, or an act of self-preservation on health grounds? You will only know if I use words to tell you!

Psalm 99 has already acknowledged God's holy reign and seen how that reign is expressed in his holy acts of justice and salvation. Is that the whole picture? No, the full significance of God's holy acts can be understood only as he speaks his holy word. This is the focus of the final section of the psalm, which speaks of God *answering* (6, 8) and *speaking* (7). The holiness of that word is revealed in its being spoken *from the pillar of cloud* (7), the manifestation

[23] Rom. 3:25–26 (ESV), emphasis added.
[24] Isa. 53:5.
[25] Col. 2:13–15.

of God's holy presence among his people. So what is this holy word God speaks and why does it elicit such reverent praise from his people?

a. A word of gracious response (6)

> Moses and Aaron were among his priests,
>   Samuel was among those who called on his name;
> they called on the LORD
>   and he answered them (6).

Although Moses was not a 'priest' in the technical sense, he was one of the great mediators of Scripture (Exod. 32:31–32),[26] and that seems to be the sense in which the word is being used here. These three giants of Old Testament faith all cried out to the Lord on behalf of his people[27] – particularly in times of national failure and sin – and *he answered them* (7); he responded to their intercession and spoke to them. The reference to these three priestly mediators makes it impossible to tie this verse to any one incident (in Moses' case there are many examples of such mediation). What links all the incidents together is that God spoke and though his words of response mixed mercy with judgment, they were words of grace which brought a future to a people who deserved only destruction.

b. A word of holy instruction (7)

> He spoke to them from the pillar of cloud;
>   they kept his statutes and the decrees he gave them (7).

In the case of Moses and Aaron the *pillar of cloud* was literal (e.g. Exod. 33:9). We never read of Samuel seeing the pillar of cloud but the God who spoke to him was the same God, whose presence was holy. The focus in this verse seems to broaden beyond God's response to the particular sins of Israel, to his giving *statutes and decrees* that would govern and shape the whole of their lives. Moses, Aaron and Samuel were models of obedience to those laws, but the laws were given for the whole community. The holy God whose holy reign was expressed in holy acts of justice, redeeming Israel for himself (4–5), intended them to live as a holy people who would shine his light and display his righteousness among the nations (see Gen. 18:18–19; Exod. 19:4–6; Deut. 4:6–8). This was what his word

---

[26] And see ch. 3 of this book.
[27] For Samuel see 1 Sam. 7:5, 8–9; 12:16–18.

of holy instruction revealed to them so clearly – and so comprehensive and holy was its wisdom that it produced awe and wonder in those who heard it (see Exod. 19:16–19; Deut. 4:6–8; Heb. 12:18–21).

c. A word of grace and of discipline (8)

> LORD our God,
> > you answered them;
> > you were to Israel a forgiving God,
> > > though you punished their misdeeds (8).

The focus shifts back to times of national failure and sin when Moses, Aaron and Samuel had interceded on behalf of the people. The Lord's answer was, as we have already seen, one of grace, but it was a grace that mixed mercy with judgment and discipline towards those who resisted his wisdom and rebelled against his rule. Following Israel's worship of the golden calf, the nation was restored but about three thousand died (Exod. 32 – 34; see 32:28). When Miriam and Aaron opposed Moses, Miriam was struck with leprosy and excluded from the camp for seven days, but she was brought back (Num. 12).[28] God's 'answering' word was spoken both to restore his people and to purify them.

The word God speaks is a holy word, revealing his gracious heart, his transforming wisdom and his purifying purposes. It is not to be received coldly as mere information, but received with worship as the holy word of the God who reigns, who acts and who speaks in majestic holiness.

> Exalt [lift up, acknowledge and rejoice in his kingly reign]
> > the LORD our God
> and worship at his holy mountain,
> for the LORD our God is holy (9).

4. Conclusion

> Guard your steps when you go to the house of God. Go near to listen rather than to offer the sacrifice of fools, who do not know that they do wrong.
> > > Do not be quick with your mouth,
> > > > do not be hasty in your heart
> > > > > to utter anything before God.

---

[28] See also Num. 16 and 1 Sam. 8 – 9 for further examples.

> God is in heaven
>> and you are on earth,
>> so let your words be few.
> A dream comes when there are many cares,
>> and many words mark the speech of a fool.

When you make a vow to God, do not delay to fulfil it. He has no pleasure in fools; fulfil your vow. It is better not to make a vow than to make one and not fulfil it. Do not let your mouth lead you into sin. And do not protest to the temple messenger, 'My vow was a mistake.' Why should God be angry at what you say and destroy the work of your hands? Much dreaming and many words are meaningless. Therefore fear God.[29]

It would be sad if these sobering words from the 'teacher' of Ecclesiastes were the whole of the biblical picture on worship. In truth, the New Testament takes us much further, with the glorious invitation to address God as 'Our Father' (Matt. 6:9) and the deep reassurance, given by the Holy Spirit, that we approach him with joy as his dearly loved children, redeemed in Christ (Gal. 4:4–7; Heb. 10:19–25). Nonetheless, the teacher gives us a powerful reminder that we must not lose from our worship the reverent voice of adoration, for God is still God in heaven and we are still his creatures on earth. The reminder that, in worship, our listening to God must come before our speaking to him is particularly important in a culture that gives great value to human self-expression but is slow to stop and listen carefully to divine revelation. Perhaps it would be a good discipline to aim for in our corporate worship, that no words should be spoken or sung to God before we have first heard something of his word to us.

The starting point for worship is not the sentiment of my heart, but the reality of God; and the God who is there is a God of awesome majesty, radiant holiness and all-satisfying glory. The 'worship' that leaps to joy and intimacy with God without ever pausing in trembling reverence before his holiness is at best inadequate and can easily become cheap and superficial. The worship which has learned, by the inner working of the Holy Spirit, to embrace reverent adoration before the holy majesty of God and exuberant celebration of his justifying, life-giving, adopting grace in Christ, is without parallel in its ability to satisfy the human heart.

It is worth pointing out that the reverent voice of adoration does not only take a traditional form, as can sometimes be assumed. I have experienced hymn-singing without a trace of evident spiritual life or

[29] Eccl. 5:1–7.

reverence, and contemporary worship times when the sense of God's holy presence has been almost tangible. Nonetheless, I think there is a particular challenge to the contemporary church to grow in our appreciation of this wonderful, enriching, God-honouring voice of reverent adoration. The form may be liturgical or not; it may be richly traditional or thoroughly contemporary; it may in fact be silent or it may be spoken out (or sung). What matters is a heart that stands in awe of the holy God; a disposition to listen before we speak (or sing); a response that takes us low in order that we may lift him high.

> Worship the LORD in the splendour of his holiness;
> tremble before him, all the earth.[30]

---

[30] Ps. 96:9.

Part 2
Worship and
the supremacy of Christ

Hebrews 9:1 – 10:25
9. All fulfilled

A few weeks ago I spent some days camping with my family in a valley in the Swiss Alps. It was a place of extraordinary beauty, but we did notice the absence of any direct evening sunshine. The reason was obvious enough: we were surrounded by foothills of the great alpine mountains just a few miles to the south, and the shadows of these great hills were blocking out the sun. There was something impressive about their power to bring the cool dusk of evening early to the entire valley floor. Viewed from the right angle and at the right time, it would doubtless have been possible to see how those shadows created an arresting image of the jagged outlines of the higher mountains. However, the next day, as the morning mist lifted, the rising sun began to bathe the snow-clad peaks in brilliant light. We gazed in quiet wonder at the majestic, alpine reality that the previous night had plunged the valley into shade, and having seen that breath-taking reality, all thought of the shadows was quickly dissipated.

The relationship of shadows to the reality of which they are a projection is an image often used in the New Testament to describe the relationship of the Hebrew Scriptures to Christ. For example Paul encourages the Colossian believers, 'Therefore do not let anyone judge you by what you eat or drink, or with regard to a religious festival, a New Moon celebration or a Sabbath day. These are a *shadow* of the things that were to come; the *reality*, however, is found in Christ.'[1] The same image lies at the heart of the argument of Hebrews 9 – 10. *The law is only a **shadow** of the good things that are coming—not the **realities** themselves* (10:1). In the context of Hebrews the focus of attention is specifically on the sacrificial system which lay at the heart of Old Testament worship (here seen as the

[1] Col. 2:16–17, emphasis added.

shadow) and the way in which those sacrifices find their fulfilment in the death of Christ (the reality).

The background to these chapters is the book of Leviticus, which sets out in detail how, through an elaborate sacrificial system, the holy God could live among a fallen and flawed people.

At this stage in its history, the worship of Israel was essentially sacrificial in nature. The opening chapters of Leviticus detail five sacrifices that were to be offered for different purposes and in various ways. They were the whole or burnt offering (1:1–17; 6:8–13), a general act of worship and atonement; the grain offering (2:1–16; 6:14–23), an expression of covenant commitment; the fellowship or peace offering (3:1–17; 6:11–21), a celebratory and communion meal in the presence of God; the sin or purification offering (4:1–5; 6:24–30), which dealt with unintentional sins; and the guilt or reparation offering (5:14–6:7; 7:1–10) which involved making restitution for wrong.[2]

The diversity is impressive, encompassing both offerings which 'expressed the sense human beings have of belonging to God by right [ie by creation]', and those which expressed 'their sense of alienation from God because of their sin and guilt'.[3] These offerings were not human inventions dreamed up in the hope of manipulating the gods; they were God's provision for his people to establish and sustain their relationship with him.[4]

All but one of these offerings was a blood sacrifice[5] and, though there were variations in detail and context, they each followed the same basic ritual. 'The worshipper brought the offering, laid his hand or hands on it and killed it. The priest then applied the blood, burnt some of the flesh and arranged for the consumption of what was left of it . . . By laying his hand(s) on the animal, the offerer was certainly identifying himself with it and "solemnly" designating "the victim as standing for him".'[6] The drama of the ritual pointed inexorably to the principle of substitution: the giving up of the life of an innocent

---

[2] D. Tidball, *The Message of the Cross*, BST (Leicester: Inter-Varsity Press, 2001), p. 75.

[3] J. R. W. Stott, *The Cross of Christ* (Leicester: Inter-Varsity Press, 1986), p. 135.

[4] 'We are to think of the sacrificial system as God-given, not man-made, and of the individual sacrifices not as a human device to placate God but as a means of atonement provided by God himself' (Stott, *Cross of Christ*, p. 138).

[5] The exception being the grain offering which was always offered in association with one of the others.

[6] Stott, *Cross of Christ*, p. 137, who was himself quoting F. D. Kidner, *Sacrifice in the Old Testament* (London: Tyndale Press, 1952), p. 14.

victim offered in place of the life of the guilty worshipper, who was thereby forgiven.[7]

However, even a relatively casual reader of the book of Leviticus cannot help feeling rather overwhelmed by the range and frequency of sacrifices offered – some daily, some weekly, some monthly, some annually and others on particular occasions. The sheer number of animals to be offered must have created a considerable burden on Israel's agrarian economy, but more importantly it left a sense that their job was never really done. The requirement for offerings to be made to make atonement for the priests is also striking,[8] highlighting the difficulty of one set of sinful human beings acting as mediators for a wider set of sinful human beings. Furthermore, there is an obvious problem with the principle of substitution in this context. If 'the life of a creature is in the blood' and 'it is the blood that makes atonement for one's life',[9] the inescapable fact is that the substitution was inadequate, for it was the life of an *animal* that was being offered for the life of a *human being*.

The system of sacrifices was a gracious gift of God to Israel and there is no doubt that it was at the centre of their worship. Comparing sacrifice in Israel with that in the surrounding pagan nations, Derek Tidball writes, 'Unlike those sacrifices, designed to twist the arm of a reluctant deity, the sacrifices of Israel were provisions of God's grace to bestow grace.'[10] Nonetheless, we are left with an inescapable sense that these sacrifices were not themselves the final answer to human sin, but were given instead to point to that final answer. They were a shadow that bore testimony to a greater reality, a symbolically-expressed promise of what God would one day provide. The central message of the book of Hebrews is that, in the coming of Christ, all the dimensions of that promise are fulfilled.

A few months ago I bought a new smartphone. I had been researching the options for some time when, in a phone call with an advisor, I unexpectedly came across a phone that appeared to tick all my boxes. The specification was impressive, the reviews reassuring and the price very competitive. After one more day researching options I made my choice and put in my order. A few days later the phone arrived. To my great satisfaction (and surprise!) the phone lived up to all that the advertisers claimed for it. My boxes were ticked and I was delighted; the promises were all fulfilled. That is

[7] See Lev. 4:20, 26, 31, 35; 5:10, 13, 16, 18; 6:7.

[8] See Lev. 8 – 9 and note 8:34 and 9:7. See also Lev. 16:6.

[9] Lev. 17:11.

[10] D. Tidball, *The Message of Leviticus*, BST (Leicester: Inter-Varsity Press, 2005), p. 36.

something of the mood of Hebrews 9 – 10 – although its subject matter is of course incomparably more significant!

Commentators (even with similar theological viewpoints) offer no consensus on precisely how the argument is structured. The passage is centred on an extended series of contrasts between Christ's sacrifice of himself on the cross and the Old Testament sacrifices that foreshadowed it. The aim throughout is to show how Christ has fulfilled all that was promised. While there are a number of recurring ideas, I suggest it is helpful to see the material as clustering around the following key themes.

1. A cleansed conscience (9:1–14)

Ian McEwan's character Briony in *Atonement* provides a poignant illustration of the difficulty of living with guilt and the need to find atonement. Tortured by the memory of a half-innocent childhood mistake that resulted in Robbie (the lover of her older sister, Cecilia) being falsely imprisoned and finally dying on the beaches of Dunkirk, Briony lays aside her gifts as a writer to train as a nurse in order to treat the wounded. Later in life she tells her story in a novel, but changes the ending such that Robbie and Cecilia are reunited and she has the opportunity to try to make amends. The novel is her attempt to make atonement for her childhood mistake and to give Robbie and Cecilia the happiness for which they longed. At the end of the book Briony (possibly reflecting McEwan's own atheism) writes,

> The problem these fifty-nine years has been this: how can a novelist achieve atonement when, with her absolute power of deciding outcomes, she is also God? There is no one, no entity or higher form that she can appeal to, or be reconciled with, or that can forgive her. There is nothing outside her. In her imagination she has set the limits and the terms. No atonement for God, or novelists, even if they are atheists. It was always an impossible task, and that was precisely the point. The attempt was all.[11]

No atonement, but only a story of 'how guilt redefined the methods of self-torture, threading the beads of details into an eternal loop, a rosary to be fingered for a lifetime'.[12]

The presence of a holy God among his fallen and sinful people highlights still further the need for such atonement and this is a

[11] I. McEwan, *Atonement* (London: Vintage 2007), p. 371.
[12] Ibid., p. 173.

central reason for the sacrificial system, as we have seen. However, while that system prepares the way for a complete answer to the problem of sin, it is only in the sacrifice of Christ that the answer is found. The contrast between the two is made at three levels,[13] which recur in the two halves of the passage:

a. The place where the offering is made (1–5; 11)

The offerings of the *first* [old] *covenant* were made in an *earthly sanctuary* (1), that is, the *tabernacle* (2), while Christ entered *the greater and more perfect tabernacle that is not made with human hands, that is to say, is not a part of this creation* (11), that is, the heavenly tabernacle (see Heb. 9:24). The writer describes the earthly sanctuary in some detail (2–5) but for our purposes, the key thing to notice is the division of the tabernacle into two rooms: *the Holy Place* (2) and *the Most Holy Place* (3), where *the cherubim of the Glory* overshadowed *the atonement cover* on the Ark of the Covenant (5).

b. The nature of the offering itself (6–7; 12)

The regular offerings made in the *outer room* (the Holy Place) are briefly mentioned (6) but the focus is on the offering made in the *inner room* (the Most Holy Place) on the Day of Atonement. This offering is made *only* by *the high priest* and *only once a year*, and *never without blood* [the blood of animals], *which he offered for himself and for the sins the people had committed in ignorance* (7). The offering of Christ, however, is made not with *the blood of goats and calves* (who are innocent, unwilling victims) but with *his own blood* (12), thus securing *eternal redemption*.

c. The approach to God which the offering achieves (8–10; 13–14)

Everything about the Old Testament offerings suggests something that is partial and incomplete: it is made in earth not in heaven, with the blood of animals shed to bear human guilt; it is made each year, yet only once each year; it is made by a priest who must atone for his own sins before atoning for the sins of the people, it provides only the most limited access to the Most Holy Place. The conclusion is inevitable: full access to the presence of God has not been achieved, because a full atonement has not been made.

[13] D. A. Carson makes this point in the fourth of a series of lectures on Hebrews provided for Trinity International University, which are available online via the Resources pages of the Gospel Coalition website <www.thegospelcoalition.org>.

The Holy Spirit was showing by this that the way into the Most Holy Place had not yet been disclosed as long as the first tabernacle was still functioning. This is an illustration for the present time, indicating that the gifts and sacrifices being offered were not able to clear the conscience of the worshipper (8–9).

All that is achieved is a *ceremonial washing* (10). However, the offering of Christ suffers from no such limitations, for it is made in heaven itself and he makes it with his own blood.

The blood of goats and bulls and the ashes of a heifer sprinkled on those who are ceremonially unclean sanctify them so that they are outwardly clean. How much more, then, will the blood of Christ, who through the eternal Spirit offered himself unblemished to God, cleanse our consciences from acts that lead to death so that we may serve [worship] *the living God!* (13–14)

The implication is clearly that full access into the Most Holy Place has now been achieved, but the writer will wait for the end of his argument to draw that climactic conclusion.[14] The emphasis here is that, where the old sacrifices achieved a certain kind of external, ceremonial cleansing, this was only an anticipation of the real cleansing – a cleansing of the conscience – that would come through the cross. It is this cleansing that enables us truly to *serve/worship the living God* (14).

Our lives do not have to be tortured by troubled consciences, and our engagement with God does not need to take place under the cloud of persistent guilt. It is precisely from such things that Christ died to set us free! This is something we may often be reluctant to accept. Some feel that a driven life of overwork and high achievement is somehow needed to make up for the failures of the past. Others assent to the idea of divine forgiveness but secretly believe that it is reluctant, concessionary and half-hearted, and that God is always looking over their shoulders hoping to 'rub their noses' in their failure once again. Others imagine that, by hanging onto a sense of guilt and 'punishing' themselves with it, they will please God by showing their awareness of sin. This passage leads us out of the doors of all these self-made prisons. We please God by receiving with joyful faith what Christ has accomplished – the cleansing of our *consciences* – not by seeking to atone for ourselves through self-punishment of various kinds. Here is a passage to unlock joy within us! The glorious worship (in the fullest sense of the word) Christ died to establish is

[14] See Heb. 10:19–22.

a joyous living of life for his glory, free from the oppressive weight of lingering guilt. All who trust themselves to Christ can find cleansing of conscience through the cross.

2. A new covenant (9:15–28)

Verse 15 is transitional. *For this reason* creates a strong link back to the previous section, while the description of Christ as the *mediator of a new covenant* introduces the next major theme. The argument is simple: the true cleansing of conscience achieved through the cross is the basis for a new kind of relationship with God in which the final inheritance of the new creation is guaranteed. The final verse (28) of the section returns to the same theme of eternal salvation being decisively achieved through the cross, binding the whole of this block of material together. Between these two 'bookends' we have another contrast between the offering of Christ on the cross and various Old Testament sacrifices. This time the focus is on the sprinkling of sacrificial blood in the establishing and operation of the covenant relationship between God and his people.

It is important to understand that the word (*diatheke*), translated as *will* (16–17) in the NIV,[15] is the same word that is translated as *covenant* in the rest of the passage. Both approaches are entirely possible, although the majority of commentators support the approach of the NIV. It is not difficult to see the appeal of this translation since, while it is clearly the case that a *will is in force only when somebody has died* (17) it is not at all obvious that this is the case for a covenant.[16] However, a growing minority of scholars[17] propose that the word does carry the same meaning throughout the passage and that verses 16–17 specifically explain why forgiveness of *the sins committed under the first covenant* (15) could only be achieved through a death. On this understanding, the following verses refer to the Sinai covenant, which was broken through Israel's disobedience:

For where there is a covenant [that has been broken by sin, v. 15], *of necessity the death of the one making the covenant must be*

---

[15] And in fact in most other modern translations. The NASB is the main exception.

[16] William Lane suggests that the reference is to the covenant ratification ceremony sometimes seen in the OT (e.g. Gen 15:9–21) where 'the bloody dismemberment of representative animals signified the violent death of the ratifying party if he proved faithless to his oath' (W. L. Lane, *Hebrews 9-13*, WBC 47B [Waco: Word Books, 1991], p. 242). This may be correct but such ceremonies are by no means universal in covenant making.

[17] See for example P. T. O'Brien, *The Letter to the Hebrews*, PNTC (Nottingham: Apollos, 2010), pp. 328–332, developing an approach by Scot Hahn.

borne. For a covenant becomes valid on the basis of death, since it never is in force when the one making the covenant is alive.[18]

So if the breaking of the covenant carries with it the threat of inevitable death, it is not surprising that the making of the covenant should involve a sacrificial ritual. This was precisely the case at Sinai (Exod. 24:3–8), as the writer points out in verses 18–21. Furthermore, the sprinkling of sacrificial blood was required not only in the establishing of the old covenant but also in its ongoing operation. The following verses recall how, time and again in Leviticus, the priests are instructed to sprinkle blood onto the tabernacle furniture (e.g. Lev. 16:14–19). *In the same way, he sprinkled with the blood both the tabernacle and everything used in its ceremonies. In fact, the law requires that nearly everything be cleansed with blood, and without the shedding of blood there is no forgiveness* (21–22).

If so much sacrificial blood was spilt in the establishment and operation of the old covenant, what about the new covenant? Well, it too required the shedding of blood – not the blood of sacrificial animals but the blood of Christ, the *better sacrifice* (23); and that blood was required not to cleanse an earthly tabernacle that was a mere copy of the heavenly one, but in some sense to cleanse the heavenly sanctuary itself[19] of the pollution brought about by human sin (23). For, as we have already seen (11–12), the sacrifice of Christ was not made on an earthly altar, but in heaven itself: *For Christ did not enter a sanctuary made with human hands, that was only a copy of the true one; he entered heaven itself, now to appear for us in God's presence* (24).

Appearing for us in God's presence takes us back to where we began, with Christ as the *mediator of a new covenant* (15). The chapter concludes with a thrilling exposition of the superiority of this high-priestly ministry he exercises, based on his sacrifice on the cross. Under the old covenant the High Priest had to *enter the Most Holy Place every year* (25): the job was never done, because he entered with *blood that is not his own* (25b) – i.e. the blood of animals. The new covenant, however, is entirely different: *But he* [Christ] *has appeared once for all at the culmination of the ages to do away with sin by the sacrifice of himself* (26b).

[18] This is the translation offered by G. L. Cockerill in *The Epistle to the Hebrews*, NICNT (Grand Rapids: Eerdmans, 2011), p. 403.

[19] O'Brien tries to avoid this tricky idea by suggesting that the cleansing is of believers who are the temple of the Spirit, but surely this is rather to read a Pauline idea into Hebrews. Cockerill suggests that the idea is an act of heavenly consecration which results in 'cleansing the heavenly Sanctuary of the barrier erected by sin' (Cockerill, *Hebrews*, p. 417).

All is fulfilled! The shadows are all dispersed in the dawning of the great reality to which they bore testimony. Jesus comes *at the culmination of the ages* to deal decisively with sin, once and for all, by offering *himself* as the supreme sacrifice. The singular nature of this sacrifice (*Christ was sacrificed once*, 28) is central to the writer's argument and it remains a vital emphasis in truly biblical theology. The cross has dealt with our sin completely and any suggestion of things we must do to add to that achievement flies in the face of this passage and drastically undermines the work of Christ. We have no need to punish ourselves by holding onto our shame; we have no need to prove ourselves by working or giving with a 'martyr mentality'; we have no need to impress God with extravagant claims about the extent of our heart's devotion;[20] we have no need, in our communion services, to offer again to God's glorious majesty the pure, holy and spotless victim (i.e. Christ), as some liturgies propose.[21] For, in offering himself *once* upon the cross, Christ has *done away with sin* (26). The worship he requires is simply that we receive and celebrate what he has done, not that we seek to supplement or repeat it.

It is precisely because his sacrifice has done away with sin that Christ can guarantee our future inheritance, as *the mediator of a new covenant* (15). All is fulfilled; nothing remains to be paid and so we look forward with joy to his appearing *a second time, not to bear sin, but to bring salvation to those who are waiting for him* (28). New covenant faith is therefore confident faith, as the writer himself will conclude later (Heb. 10:19). Some mistake this confidence for arrogance, as if we were claiming to be personally worthy of our inheritance in the new creation. Nothing could be further from the truth. For we do not turn inwards, looking for personal achievement as the basis for eternal hope; rather we turn upwards, looking to the achievement of Christ on the cross, whose work is finished and complete. This is the confidence that should fill our churches with joyful praise and celebration!

3. A perfect sacrifice (10:1–18)

The attempt to fill a hole in the sand at the top of a beach with buckets of sea water is a childhood memory which many people share. It is, of course, a rather frustrating experience, because the water from one bucket usually drains away before the next one has

---

[20] I wonder if I sometimes detect this perceived need in 'worship songs' which make very extravagant claims of devotion to God, while articulating little if anything about the goodness of God which might provoke such devotion.

[21] See the first eucharistic prayer of the Roman Missal.

time to arrive. The longed-for beach pool never actually materializes! Shockingly, the writer of Hebrews speaks of the ministry of the Old Testament high priest in daringly similar terms. As in chapter nine, the focus is on the offerings in the annual Day of Atonement.[22] [The law] *can never by the same sacrifices repeated endlessly year after year, make perfect those who draw near to worship* (1).

How do we know? Because if these sacrifices truly did cleanse the consciences of the worshippers once and for all, they would not need to be offered again and again, year after year (2). Don Carson captures the problem well:

> So, the priest goes in and offers his sacrifice on the Day of Atonement God has ordained, and this is the means by which sins are set aside. Wonderful! And then there's no more Day of Atonement until next year. So the day after the Day of Atonement you go and commit a whole bunch of sins. Who pays for those? When? Next year? What happens to your conscience in the meantime? So after a while, the repetition of the sacrifice becomes a reminder of your sinfulness, but not really an answer to it.[23]

The writer of Hebrews does not hold back from drawing their stark conclusion: *Those sacrifices are an annual reminder of sins. It is impossible for the blood of bulls and goats to take away sins* (3–4).

Against this depressing background, the writer gives his final, climactic exposition of the sufficiency of Christ's sacrifice on the cross.

a. A final offering (5–10)

Centuries earlier in Psalm 40, King David[24] had expressed the understanding that 'animal sacrifices were not really at the heart of what God wanted from his people'.[25] His conclusion had been expressed in surprisingly comprehensive terms, encompassing a broad range of the sacrifices prescribed by Leviticus, and none of this was what God truly desired. Rather he had been had given a *body*[26] which he was to use obediently, to fulfil the will of God. The writer of Hebrews now puts these words into the mouth of Christ, the true

---

[22] For full details, see Lev. 16.

[23] Carson, fourth lecture on Hebrews, <www.thegospelcoalition.org>.

[24] It seems likely that the author of Hebrews is assuming Davidic authorship of Ps. 40 as he puts words in the mouth of the one he believes to be the true Davidic Messiah.

[25] S. K. Stanley in an unpublished PhD thesis, *A New Covenant Hermeneutic: The Use of Scripture in Hebrews 8-10* (University of Sheffield), p. 163. Quoted in O'Brien, *Hebrews*, p. 351.

[26] Hebrews is quoting from the LXX at this point.

Son of David, seeing the sacrifice of *his body* on the cross as the ultimate fulfilment of the *will* of God, of which David had spoken. So Christ *sets aside* (9) the whole system of offerings (which God ultimately did not desire) in order to do precisely that which God did desire: the offering of his body on the cross. *And by that will, we have been made holy through the sacrifice of the body of Jesus Christ once for all* (10).

It was, quite literally, the offering to end all offerings. The final offering, made *once and for all*; and, unlike the annual reminders of sin (3) which had foreshadowed it, this offering did *take away sins* (4) so as to *make us holy* (10).

b. A finished work (11–14)

The image shifts away from the annual Day of Atonement to the pattern of daily sacrifices made by the priests in the tabernacle. The focus, though, is still on the continuing, repetitive nature of their priestly work. The offerings they make have to be made day after day and, though they are prescribed in the first place by God himself, they *can never take away sins* (11b). Our eyes are drawn to a particular characteristic of the priest as they carry out their ceaseless duties: they are always standing because their work is never done.

However, returning to words he used in the opening of the letter (Heb. 1:3), the writer insists that Christ's priestly work is finished! He is not standing, but has *sat down at the right hand of God* (12), the completion of his work so certain that he now *waits* for the final defeat of all *his enemies* (13). His sacrifice is an effective sacrifice, *making perfect forever those who are being made holy* (14).

c. A forgiven people (15–18)

Having reached the triumphant conclusion of verse 14, the writer is able to return to Jeremiah's language of the new covenant (Jer. 31:31–34), introduced in chapter 8, for all that Jeremiah had promised is now fulfilled in the sacrifice of Christ. The new covenant promise was of a people sanctified for God, a people of joyful obedience upon whose hearts God's law was written (15–16) because[27] they were first and foremost a forgiven people (17).

In the light of such forgiveness, no more sacrifices for sin are required. *And where these have been forgiven, sacrifice for sin is no longer necessary* (18). In Christ, all is fulfilled!

---

[27] 'In Jeremiah 31, the introductory *For* shows that the basis of the preceding promises is the assurance of a decisive cleansing from sin' (O'Brien, *Hebrews*, p. 358).

4. A confident access (10:19–25)

Buckingham Palace is unquestionably one of the treasures of London. From a royalist perspective at least, it is a constant, physical reminder of the reign of the sovereign and of their life at the heart of the capital city. Groups of tourists are always to be found gathered around its gates, enjoying the tightly drawn symmetry of its architecture and (perhaps) imagining something of its life. Since 1993, tourists have been able to pay for an opportunity to go into the palace and see some of its treasures for themselves, narrowing slightly the perceived distance between royalty and the people. Of course what many would really love is the opportunity to enter the royal apartments and see what the life of the royal family is actually like. However, such access is (necessarily) denied to the population at large.

The writer of Hebrews describes Old Testament worship in very similar terms. The provision of the tabernacle was a constant, physical reminder of the reign of Yahweh and of his life at the heart of the community of his people. The sacrificial system, which dominated their worship, gave them an external, ceremonial cleansing from sin and a certain kind of access into the place of his dwelling among them. Nevertheless, they were denied access into the most significant part of the tabernacle: the Most Holy Place of his immediate presence. Old Testament worship could go so far, but it could go no further. It offered no final cleansing of the conscience from sin and therefore no access to this Most Holy Place.

However, through offering himself as a sacrifice on the cross, Christ has changed everything, fulfilling all that the structures of Old Testament worship were pointing towards. The perfect offering has been made; the new covenant has been established and sealed; the cleansing of conscience has finally been achieved. A way into the Most Holy Place of God's presence has therefore been opened and a sinful humanity is invited to draw near to God through the cross:

Therefore, brothers and sisters, since we have confidence to enter the Most Holy Place by the blood of Jesus, by a new and living way opened for us through the curtain, that is, his body, and since we have a great priest over the house of God, let us draw near to God with a sincere heart and with the full assurance that faith brings, having our hearts sprinkled to cleanse us from a guilty conscience and having our bodies washed with pure water (19–22).

This perspective necessarily transforms our understanding of worship. If Old Testament worship was a response to the word which God revealed in the giving of the law, New Testament worship is a response to the word of the gospel which God has revealed in Jesus his Son (Heb. 1:1–4). If Old Testament worshippers encountered the reality of God's presence in the tabernacle where he lived among them, New Testament worshippers encounter his presence in Christ, the new temple, by the Holy Spirit whom he gives (John 2:19–22; 1 Pet. 2:4–5). If Old Testament worship was centred on the offering of sacrifices to God, New Testament worship is centred on celebrating the sacrifice he has made for us in Christ. If Old Testament worship kept us at a distance from the presence of God, New Testament worship invites us to come near.

We can draw three conclusions:[28]

a. New Testament worship is intimate and experiential (22)

That is the inescapable implication of verse 22: we are urged to *draw near to God* and to do so with confident *assurance* because we know that, having made the perfect sacrifice for sin, Christ has cleansed us completely. We have noted with some concern the trend in some circles for the idea of worship to be reduced to the pursuit of intimate communion with God,[29] but it is crucial that we do not overreact and lose this particular treasure which Christ died to give us. The language is deeply experiential: it is inconceivable that we would *draw near to God* and think we had just watched an entertaining show, or gone through a religious ritual. To *draw near to God* is to engage with the holiness of his presence, the richness of his grace, the greatness of his power and the fullness of his love. My own experience of worship – whether corporate or individual – is deeply affected by the extent to which I embrace the expectation of drawing near to God through Christ. Without such an expectation our churches are little more than religious clubs; with it they become supernatural communities of grace.

b. New Testament worship is eschatological (23)

Let us hold unswervingly to the hope we profess, for he who promised is faithful (23).

However great the joys of our present access to God, Christian worship is characterized by longing as well as satisfaction. The New Testament calls that longing *hope* (23). We long for the 'face to face' communion that is promised in the new creation (Rev. 22:4). We long to see the enemies of Christ finally subdued beneath his feet (Heb.

---

[28] Drawn from the three imperatives (*let us . . .*) of vv. 22–25.
[29] See ch. 8 of this book.

2:8; 10:13). We long for the renewal of all things as heaven comes to earth (Rev. 21:1–5). We long for the wiping away of tears and the end of suffering (Rev. 21:4). We have seen that this hope is guaranteed to us in the new covenant through the cross (Heb. 9:15, 28), for *he who promised is* indeed *faithful* (23). New Testament worship is not focused on the small world of our personal wounds, fears or aspirations, but lifts our eyes to our promised inheritance, nurturing our churches as communities of hope and strengthening our resolve to live distinctive lives as citizens of heaven (Phil. 3:20–21).

c. New Testament worship is communal (24–25)

Let us consider how we may spur one another on toward love and good deeds, not giving up meeting together, as some are in the habit of doing, but encouraging one another – and all the more as you see the Day approaching.

The communal emphasis that is implicit in the plural form of each of these commands (*let us* draw near . . . hold unswervingly . . . *spur one another on*, 22–24) becomes explicit in the last of them. The text envisages a close connection between our gatherings (*meeting together*, 25) and the obedience of our lives (*love and good deeds*, 24) rather than driving a wedge between them. We do not meet only to seek an enhanced experience of personal communion with God; we come to worship God together so as to encourage each other to go and worship him in the whole of our lives. This connection is so important that we will return to it in both chapters 11 and 18.

Colossians 1:15–23
10. All for Jesus

'Therefore God exalted him . . .'[1] These majestic words about Christ, from the second chapter of Paul's letter to the Philippians, establish the link between the last chapter and this one. The phrase functions as a 'hinge' between the two sections of what many consider to have been one of the hymns of the early church's worship.[2] The preceding verses (Phil. 2:5–8) speak of his perfect obedience to the Father, not using his equality with God for his own advantage, but taking on a human nature and obediently humbling himself even to the point of death on a cross. The subsequent verses tell us that, *because* Jesus thus fulfilled the promise of salvation set out in the Old Testament, God exalted him, giving him 'the name that is above every name'.[3] As a result 'every tongue' 'in heaven and on earth and under the earth' will worship and confess him as Lord.[4] All is fulfilled by Christ; therefore all will worship Christ. This, however, does not represent the discovery of a new purpose for creation, but rather the restoration of its original purpose, as we shall see in Colossians 1.

In the scholarly community, vigorous debate continues regarding the situation in Colossae that Paul's letter addresses.[5] It seems evident that there was some kind of threat to the church posed by

---

[1] Phil. 2:9.

[2] It should be noted, however, that not all are persuaded that this is the case, e.g. G. D. Fee, *Philippians*, IVPNTC (Leicester: Inter-Varsity Press, 1999), p. 90. Even if it is a hymn, it does not automatically follow that Paul was not its author – he would not, after all, be the only theologian of the church to write in both prose and poetry!

[3] Phil. 2:9b. Peter Lewis quotes P. T. O'Brien, '"It is not the name Jesus but the name that belongs to Jesus that is meant" . . . He is *Yahweh-Jesus*, he is *the Lord Jesus*' (P. H. Lewis, *The Glory of Christ* [London: Hodder & Stoughton, 1992], p. 236).

[4] Phil. 2:10–11.

[5] I am assuming Pauline authorship of Colossians. For a thoughtful defence see D. J. Moo, *The Letters to the Colossians and to Philemon*, PNTC (Nottingham: Apollos, 2008), pp. 28–41.

people who sought to 'deceive' the believers by 'fine-sounding arguments'.[6] but there is little sign of consensus on who they were[7] or
exactly what their message was. Nonetheless, the emphasis within
the letter on 'filling' and 'fullness' (e.g. 1:9, 19; 2:9–10) does suggest
that they were promoting their particular programme of speculation
and discipline as the key to spiritual fulfilment. Whatever the precise
details of their programme, Paul clearly detected in their message a
threat to the believers' confidence in the sufficiency and finality of
Christ. The words of Colossians 1:15–20 represent the highwater
mark in his response to that threat, in this great exposition of the
supremacy of Christ.

Like the passage quoted above from Philippians, many have seen
these verses as a hymn from the worship of the early church (or
possibly the fragments of a hymn edited by Paul for polemic effect).
A number of structural and stylistic arguments are put forward in
support of this suggestion, though it has also been the subject of
rigorous critique.[8] What is clear, however, is that the verses are
written in an 'exalted style'[9] which makes them stand out from the
surrounding context. The identification of Christ first as *the firstborn
over all creation* (15) and second as *the firstborn from among the
dead* (18b) help us identify the start of the two major sections
taking us from the creation to new creation, from the beginning of
history to the climax of history, with verses 17–18a forming a 'bridge'
between the two.[10]

1. All creation exists for the glory of Jesus (15–16)

Less than half a mile from our church building in Southampton, a
city centre park has a statue of Isaac Watts, one of the best-loved
English hymn writers.[11] On the north side of the statute the inscription

[6] Col. 2:4, and see Col. 2:8.

[7] There seems to be cautious support for the proposal by Clinton Arnold of some
kind of syncretistic blend of traditional Jewish thinking with mystical local (Phrygian)
folk religion. See C. Arnold, *The Colossian Syncretism: The Interface between Christianity and Folk Belief in Colosse*, WUNT 77 (Tubingen: Mohr Siebeck, 1995; repr.,
Grand Rapids: Baker, 1996).

[8] See J. F. Balchin, 'Colossians 1:15-20: An Early Christian Hymn? The Arguments
from Style', *Vox Evangelica* 15 (1985), pp. 65–94.

[9] Balchin, ibid., p. 66, though, as he notes, this need imply nothing against Pauline
authorship.

[10] This is the structure suggested in Moo (*Colossians*, p. 116), which is very close
to the chiasmus proposed by N. T. Wright in *The Climax of the Covenant*
(Minneapolis: Fortress, 1992), pp. 99–106.

[11] The hundreds of hymns he wrote include 'When I survey the wondrous cross';
'Jesus shall reign where're the sun'; 'Joy to the world' and 'O God our help in ages
past'.

stone begins, 'AD 1861 ERECTED BY VOLUNTARY CONTRIBUTIONS IN MEMORY OF ISAAC WATTS, A NATIVE OF SOUTHAMPTON, BORN 1674, DIED 1748.' The surrounding park was subsequently named after him and, from the large clock tower overlooking the park (and the whole city centre), the tune of his hymn 'O God, our help in ages past' chimes out three times each day. It is our city's way of honouring one of its most famous sons in the use of a prominent public space and in the ongoing rhythm of its life.

When it comes to honouring Jesus, a memorial statue, a park and a clock chime will in no way suffice! The assertion of this section of our passage is that the whole of creation exists to give him glory. Consistent with the 'exalted style' of the whole passage, these verses are carefully structured with two titles for Christ (*the image of the invisible God, the firstborn over all creation*, 15) followed by an explanatory paragraph (*for . . .*) in which three prepositions (*in him . . . through him . . . to/for him*, 16) are used to describe his role in creation and his reward from creation. A similar structure is repeated in the second section, as we shall see.

a. His status over creation (15)

The Son is the image of the invisible God, the firstborn over all creation.

The most obvious background to Jesus as *the image of the invisible God* is the creation of 'mankind . . . in the image of God'[12] in Genesis 1. The point, however, is not only that Jesus is the perfect human being who bears the flawless image of God (though this is true) but that he *is* (eternally) the image of God after which we were ourselves fashioned.[13] Jewish tradition frequently identified the 'image of God' in Genesis 1 with the 'wisdom' or 'word' of God,[14] and it is likely that this is also in the background here. The early Christians, though, had come to recognize that the eternal wisdom and word of God were not merely abstract entities but were found in the person of Christ.[15] This is important, but the emphasis on God's invisibility suggests Paul's line of thought is moving beyond creation to incarnation. 'No one has ever seen God'[16] but Christ came to make him

---

[12] Gen. 1:27.

[13] Christian Stettler distinguishes between Christ who *is* the image of God and human beings who are created *according to* or *in* that image. *Der Kolosserhymnas: Untersuchungen zu Form, traditions-geschichtlichen Hintergrund un Aussage von Kol 1, 15-20*, WUNT 2.131 (Tübingen: Mohr Siebeck, 2000), pp. 104–110, quoted in Moo, *Colossians*, p. 117.

[14] See Moo, *Colossians*, p. 118.

[15] See also John 1:1–18; Heb. 1:1–5; 1 Cor. 1:18–31.

[16] John 1:18.

visible within his creation: 'The Word became *flesh* and made his dwelling among us.'[17] He is, therefore, the ultimate representative of God within creation.

He is also *the firstborn over all creation*, which is not to say that Christ was simply the oldest member of the human family, created by God before the rest of us, for he shares the eternality of God – he is *before all things* (17).[18] In the OT the title 'firstborn' was not only used literally but also figuratively as a title of honour and supremacy,[19] and it is in that sense that Paul uses it here: Christ stands supreme and sovereign over the whole of creation.

b. His role in creation (16a)

*For **in him** all things were created: things in heaven and on earth, visible and invisible, whether thrones or powers or rulers or authorities; all things have been created **through him** and for him.*

This paragraph provides Paul's explanation (note, *For . . .*) of Christ's exalted status within creation. Some commentators take the ideas of creation being *in him* and *through him* as basically parallel, but it is probably better to distinguish them. To say that *all things were created in him* is to say that nothing was created apart from him or independently of him;[20] he is the wisdom that gives to all creation[21] its fundamental unity, order and coherence. To say that *all things have been created through him* is to celebrate his agency within the original act of creation. He was the Word God spoke which brought the universe into being; the One 'through whom all things were made'.[22]

Our own laws[23] seek to preserve the right of those who design and create new products or works of art to be identified and honoured appropriately. How much more, then, should Christ, the author and agent of creation, be honoured as supreme and sovereign over that creation? The same laws also seek to enable innovators to receive a reward from their work, and this too is paralleled here in the final phrase of the verse.

---

[17] John 1:14.

[18] This was the claim of the Arian heresy, which asserted of Christ that 'there was once when he was not'. It was in response to this heresy that the church fathers formulated the Nicene Creed in the fourth century.

[19] For example in Ps. 89:27, reflected also in its usage in Heb. 1:6.

[20] Cf. John 1:3.

[21] The universality of the claim is underlined by the listing of *things in heaven and on earth, visible and invisible*.

[22] John 1:3. Cf. Prov. 9; Ps. 104:24.

[23] Of patent, copyright and intellectual property.

c. His reward from creation (16b)

To say of Christ that *all things have been created through him **and for him*** [lit. *to him*] is to acknowledge that the whole of creation finds its goal in him[24] and exists to bring him glory. We enjoy creation most truly when we turn our enjoyment to praise of Christ to whom it owes its existence and when we covenant to use its resources with care. We understand ourselves most truly when we realize that we are beloved creations, fashioned in the wisdom of Christ, formed through the word of Christ and created for the pleasure and glory of Christ. We explore our creativity most meaningfully when we receive it as his gift to us and use it for his pleasure to express his truth and goodness and magnify his grace. Our work is rescued from futility when we remember that, in all things, 'it is the Lord Christ we are serving'.[25] All of creation is *for him.*

Commentators have always found verses 17–18a something of a puzzle. They seem to belong to neither of the main sections[26] but have strong links to both. Furthermore, at first glance they appear to repeat what is said elsewhere and add relatively little to the overall content. Douglas Moo suggests they are best seen a 'brief intermediary strophe between the two larger strophes'[27] and N. T. Wright sees them as the central segment of a larger chiastic structure.[28] What seems certain is that they recapitulate (and develop) what has been said about creation in the first section and at the same time pave the way for the new creation/redemption perspective which makes the second section. We are therefore best to see them as transitional.

He is before all things, and in him all things hold together. And he is the head of the body, the church.

The eternal pre-existence of the person of Christ is implied in the words *he is before all things.*[29] This reflects his status as the *image of the invisible God and the firstborn over all creation* (15). The

---

[24] Cf. Eph. 1:10.

[25] Col. 3:24.

[26] Though some suggest that the section break should be at the end of v. 17, with v. 18a belonging to the second section (though this rather disrupts the structural parallelism of the two strophes).

[27] Moo, *Colossians*, p. 124.

[28] Wright, *Climax of the Covenant*, pp. 99–106. A chiastic structure presents ideas in a symmetrical fashion. The simplest form takes two ideas, A and B and presents them as A,B,B'A'. If a there is a third idea, C, in the middle of the chiasm (A,B,C,C'B'A'), C is often thought to be the key to the whole unit.

[29] *Pace* J. D. Dunn, *Christology in the Making* (Grand Rapids: Eerdmans, 1996), p. 89; see the rebuttals in Wright, *Climax of the Covenant*, pp. 116–117, and Moo, *Colossians*, pp. 124f.

assertion that *in him all things hold together* reflects the view that *in him all things were created* (16). At the same time it extends this idea beyond the original act of creation to a wider theology of Christ's ongoing ordering and upholding of the whole of created reality. Of course this doesn't mean that now we know about the Higgs boson particle there's no room left for Jesus. What it means is that *he* knew about the Higgs boson long before Peter Higgs was even born, because it was his idea! The world is sustained moment to moment by Christ, the eternal Wisdom and Word of God, and this is the basis for its inherent order and predictability. This is what makes science possible; it is also what makes true science *worship*, for it is 'reading the mind of God'.[30]

What is striking, however, is the absence of any repetition of the idea that all things are created *for* (or *to*) *Christ*. This is the first hint that the ideal pattern of creation has been broken; that the universe which was made to be oriented towards Christ has been led away from him. The next section is predicated on the reality that, as a consequence of human sin, the creation has been alienated from Christ and needs to be reconciled to him. While it remains true that *all things hold together*[31] (17) in Christ,[32] and that he is ultimately sovereign over all things, Scripture does witness to a partial breaking down of this order such that the uniting of 'all things in heaven and on earth in Christ'[33] is a description of future promise, not of present reality. So the creation, which was formed to bear testimony to the glory and supremacy of Christ, has been marred and spoilt as his reign is challenged and his glory overlooked. Is there, then, any hope for the future?

Paul insists both that there is hope and that this hope can be seen in the church of Christ. *He* [Christ] *is the head of the body, the church* (18a). In other words, there is a community which delights in the supremacy of Christ and looks to him as the source of their health and nourishment[34] and that community is the church! This

---

[30] See e.g. P. Duce, *Reading the Mind of God: Interpretation in Science and Theology* (Leicester: Apollos, 1998).

[31] This may suggest that Moo (*Colossians*, p. 125) is right to propose that this is the centre of the whole of what he calls 'the hymn' (i.e. Col. 1:15–20), although he does not develop the argument in quite the way I am suggesting.

[32] For he still sustains 'all things by his powerful word' (Heb. 1:3).

[33] Eph. 1:10.

[34] Eph. 4:16. The idea of 'headship' has been the subject of much scholarly debate – not least because of implications for the debate about gender and ministry. Moo (*Colossians*, p. 128), who takes the complementarian view, maintains that 'in the ancient world, the head was conceived to be the governing member of the body, that which both controlled it and provided for its life and sustenance'. A. C. Perriman, *Speaking of Women* (Leicester: Apollos, 1998) argues that the image is, at heart, about social pre-eminence but does not always imply hierarchical authority.

first dawning of hope opens the way for the celebration of hope in the second major section.

2. All creation is to be reconciled for the glory of Jesus (18b–20)

Just a few hundred metres from the statue of Isaac Watts mentioned above, stands another monument: the Southampton Cenotaph. Inscribed on the monument are the names of nearly two thousand of the city's people who fell during active service in the First World War. In recent years a glass wall has been added, recording the names of those who fell in the Second World War and other subsequent conflicts. The monument records the gratitude of the city for those who gave their lives trying to restore a world order that had been shattered through international conflicts and poisonous ideologies, and its commitment to honouring their memory.

The second section of our passage honours Christ, who gave his life to restore the order not just of one civilization at a particular point in history, but of the entire universe. However, the 'monument' is not a statue of stone but the whole of the new creation, and it exists not to remember the dead but to celebrate the victory of the living Christ who is the *firstborn from among the dead* (18b). The structure of these verses mirrors closely that of the first section.

a. His status over the new creation (18b)

He is the beginning and the firstborn from among the dead, so that in everything he might have the supremacy.

As in the first section, two linked titles express the status of Christ over the new creation. He is *the beginning and the firstborn from among the dead.* The word 'dead' confirms our analysis of the transitional section: Paul is now addressing creation in its fallenness rather than its ideal state, for in Scripture death is the consequence and penalty of sin. Through his death and resurrection, however, Christ has broken through death and into life. Moreover, his victory over death has opened the way to life not only to himself but (in some sense) to the whole of creation. *He is the beginning* not only in the sense that he is the first to enter the new creation, but also that he is the founder of the new creation.[35] Similarly, he is the *firstborn from the dead* both in the sense that he was the first to rise and that he is supreme over the new creation which that resurrection has inaugurated.

[35] See Moo, *Colossians*, p. 129, quoting Gen. 49:3 in the LXX in which *beginning* (*archē*) alongside *firstborn* carries the sense of 'founder'.

In Christ, the great work of restoration has been accomplished! The Christ-oriented world order built into creation itself, which was shattered by human sin, is (in principle) now re-established *so that in everything he* [i.e. Christ] *might have the supremacy* again (18). Of course the full realization of this restored world order awaits his second coming in glory, but in the resurrection of Christ from the dead, the decisive victory has been won.

b. His role in the new creation (19–20)

For God was pleased to have all his fullness dwell **in him**, *and* **through him** *to reconcile* **to himself** [lit. 'to him'] *all things, whether things on earth or things in heaven, by making peace through his blood, shed on the cross.*

As in the first section, this is clearly an explanation (*For . . .*) of the status of Christ in the new creation and it is structured around the same set of prepositions used in verse 16.[36] The argument begins with an astonishing claim about Christ: namely that *God in all his fullness was pleased to dwell* **in him** (19).[37] The present tense in Colossians 2:9 makes it clear that this 'dwelling' was not just temporary but remains a continuing reality. 'All the attributes and activities of God – his spirit, word, wisdom and glory are perfectly displayed in Christ'[38] – and this was a matter of divine pleasure and election. It is hard to imagine how Paul could have stated a higher Christology than this! In all probability the slightly unusual phrasing he uses (lit. *all the fullness was pleased . . .*) was calculated to defeat the false teachers in Colossae on their own turf. For them, spiritual 'fullness' came by means of following their particular programme and Paul saw how this fatally undermined confidence in the sufficiency of Christ. For Paul, spiritual 'fullness' was found solely in Christ, since all the fullness [of God] was pleased to live in him (19).

This is not, however, merely an abstract statement about the deity of Christ; it is part of a continuing argument. 'In Jesus Christ all the resources of God for man's salvation are brought to a point: and that point is the human flesh of Jesus.'[39] God comes to his broken world in the person of Christ precisely to bring salvation through him, ending its alienation. The reconciliation is achieved at great cost, for

[36] The Greek words *eis auton* , which occur in both v. 16 and v. 20, can mean either *to him* or *for him.*

[37] This translation of the slightly difficult phrase in the original is supported by both Moo (*Colossians*, p. 132) and in P. T. O'Brien, *Colossians, Philemon*, WBC 44 (Waco: Word Books, 1982), p. 51.

[38] O'Brien, *Colossians*, p. 53, who cites F. F. Bruce at this point.

[39] Lewis, *Glory of Christ*, p. 248.

Christ makes *peace through his blood, shed on the cross* (20b). God in all his fullness hangs on a Roman cross, suffocating in appalling agony: that is the shocking reality at the heart of these verses. In response to the alienation of the creation that arises from human sin, God comes not to destroy the creation but to restore it by taking its alienation onto himself, as he carried our sins to the cross, in Christ.

It is tempting to narrow the scope of these verses to more familiar categories, so that the reconciliation is understood only to be that of guilty sinners to their Creator.[40] Others boldly insist that Paul here is proclaiming universal salvation.[41] There is a middle way, explained by Paul himself in Romans 8:18–25. In the beginning God commissioned human beings to rule over earth on his behalf and with his wisdom such that they would flourish along with the whole creation. The alienation of human beings from God because of their rebellion against him therefore had consequences for creation, which Paul pictures as 'groaning' as it languishes under the weight of human failure, and longing for us to take our true place once again (Rom. 8:22). So the alienation of creation is a product of our own alienation from God. It follows that our reconciliation to God will have positive consequences for the whole of creation, which will be fully realized when Christ returns to make all things new and welcomes his redeemed people to share in his everlasting reign of justice and right-eousness (Rev. 21:5; 22:1–5). In other words, while Paul is not speaking about universal salvation, he really is speaking about the reconcili-ation of the whole created order. Nonetheless, it is the reconciliation of sinful humanity through the cross that stands at the heart of this cosmic reconciliation and makes it possible.

Francis Schaeffer offered what remains one of the most helpful ways of expressing the scope of Paul's vision here. In his book *Pollution and the Death of Man* he spoke of a fourfold alienation that arises from the fall in Genesis 3:

- *Vertical alienation* (of human beings from God, which he under-stands as the starting point).
- *Cosmic alienation* (the whole of the creation being led away from its God-given order).
- *Inward alienation* (our failure to understand ourselves properly, with all the associated psychological implications of that failure).
- *Horizontal alienation* (in which human beings are divided from each other).

[40] Cf. 2 Cor. 5:16–22. See I. H. Marshall, 'The meaning of reconciliation', in R. A. Guelich (ed.), *Unity and Diversity in New Testament Theology: Essays in Honour of George E. Ladd* (Grand Rapids: Eerdmans, 1978), pp. 126–127.

[41] This interpretation began with Origen but continues to have a strong appeal.

The ending of our vertical alienation through the reconciliation accomplished at the cross therefore stands at the heart of the gospel, but that reconciliation then has implications for addressing all of the other 'alienations'. Moreover, Schaeffer was insistent that, while a 'complete healing of all of them' must await Christ's return, nonetheless 'upon the basis of the work of Christ, substantial healing can be a reality here and now'.[42]

c. His reward from the new creation

The NIV follows most translations in assuming that Paul is speaking of *God* reconciling all things *to himself* in Christ in verse 20. However, I think Moo is probably correct to argue that both the Christological orientation of these verses as a whole and the choice of Greek pronoun here point to the reconciliation envisaged being specifically *to Christ*[43] (though of course it remains true that 'God was reconciling the world to himself in Christ'[44]). If so, verse 20 corresponds very closely to the conclusion of verse 16: just as *all things have been created through him and for/to him* [i.e. Christ] (16), so the achievement of the cross is *through him to reconcile to himself* [i.e. Christ] *all things* (20). So the new creation exists for the glory of Christ, just as the original creation was called into being for him. In other words, the Christ-oriented shape of reality which was built into the original creation is restored, through the cross, in the new creation.

The challenge for us is that Paul believes that this Christ-centred life of the new creation should already be partially visible in the community of the church.

3. We are reconciled now for the glory of Jesus (21–23)

Nearly twenty-seven years ago in a rather unremarkable house in Bedford I asked Alison to marry me and happily, she agreed! Immediately our lives began to change, even though it was nearly twenty months before we were able to get married. Our spare time was spent preparing for the wedding, any spare money was saved so that we would be able to set up a home, we began to be viewed more as a couple within our families and circle of friends and, most important of all, we had to learn more about each other's aspirations, preferences and way of doing things as we prepared to share life

---

[42] F. A. Schaeffer and U. Middelmann, *Pollution and the Death of Man* (Leicester: Crossway, 1992), p. 67.
[43] Moo, *Colossians*, pp. 133–134.
[44] 2 Cor. 5:19.

together. The marriage was still to come, but everything about our lives in the present was shaped by that future reality.

Paul's vision of the Christian life is cast in very similar terms. The complete reconciliation of all things in Christ is still to come, but everything in our lives now is to be shaped by that future reality. As we have seen, the church is *already* the community which celebrates the supremacy of Christ, acknowledging him as its true head. It is thus a prophetic community whose present life is to demonstrate something of the reality of the coming new creation. This is the basic thrust of the final section of our passage. The reconciliation to Christ which will embrace the whole of creation when he returns, has already been accomplished for the believers in Colossae. They can therefore look forward to his coming with joyful confidence. *Once you were alienated from God and were enemies in your minds because of your evil behaviour. But now he has reconciled you by Christ's physical body through death to present you holy in his sight, without blemish and free from accusation* (21–22).

However, there is a more cautious note to be sounded too. As we have seen, the programme the false teachers at Colossae were proposing was, in effect, an alternative to unreserved confidence in Christ and the gospel. Their message, if accepted, could prove disastrous to the believers, threatening their final salvation. Paul therefore warns them *not* to *move from the hope held out in the gospel* (23) but to *continue in the faith, stable and steadfast* (23, ESV). It is through such warnings that God, in his grace, keeps his people secure in eternal life, but we should acknowledge the reality of these warnings, nonetheless.

4. Conclusion: worship as the celebration of the supremacy of Christ

To summarize, this great passage establishes that the whole creation was made in Christ, through Christ *and for Christ* (that is, for his glory). Not only so, but in the face of human sin which has dislocated the creation itself and led it away from its Christ-honouring purpose, God has acted in Christ to restore it to its original destiny. He has thus demonstrated his absolute commitment to the glory of his Son, determining that *in everything he might have the supremacy* (18). So we can be confident that the universe is moving towards a future in which the shape of reality itself is profoundly, explicitly and joyfully oriented towards Christ. The particular delight of truly Christian worship, therefore, is to experience the satisfaction of that Christ-saturated future in the middle of time, as our hearts rejoice in him and our lives make visible his radiant goodness and restoring grace.

145

In the light of this clear revelation of God's absolute commitment to the supremacy of his Son, it must follow that a celebration of that supremacy will stand at the heart of all truly Christian worship. As we saw at the end of chapter 5, we are not just theists, we are (trinitarian) Christians! We are very prone to making other things supreme in our worship – by our celebrity subculture, our inflexible traditions or the baptizing of our musical preferences – but this passage provides the strongest possible challenge to such idolatries. We are far from sure that both Philippians 2 and Colossians 1 were used as early Christian hymns, but if they were they set the bar exceedingly high for what authentically Christ-centred, congregational worship should be like. In any case, it is unthinkable that the Christ-oriented world view they express should not profoundly colour Christian worship (in all its forms).

How then can we envisage Christian worship as a celebration of the supremacy of Christ?

a. We celebrate his supremacy in creation

Evangelical Christians have not always been known for a positive view of creation but have been caricatured (with some justification) as being suspicious of the arts, lacking care for creation and having a narrow, pietistic vision of discipleship. Such attitudes are increasingly being challenged by voices within the evangelical community[45] and rightly so. For to be a Christian is to recognize the supremacy of Christ over creation in its entirety: all of it is created *in and through him* and all of it is created *for/to him*. We can therefore embrace the idea that the creation is a revelation of his glory, which causes us to wonder and leads us to worship its Creator. We can embrace our creativity as his gift to us, using it to explore and express our humanity as those fashioned after him and to give him fresh, living expressions of the praise of which he is worthy. We can embrace our curiosity about creation, using the skills of observation and analysis to understand it more fully, and turning our exploration into praise of Christ whose wisdom formed and sustains it all. We can bring him the world in its brokenness, knowing that he has compassion on all that he has made and remains sovereign over it all.

The implication for our congregational worship is that we should resist the tendency for our meetings to become a hermetically sealed subculture of their own. We worship Christ who is supreme in all

---

[45] John Stott's ministry was a fine example of a challenging voice of this kind and his legacy continues to exercise a similar influence through figures like Mark Greene in the London Institute for Contemporary Christianity and Christopher Wright in the Langham Partnership.

creation and actively engaged in the world he has made. The wealth of creation's resources can therefore be used to enrich our worship, through appropriate use of the arts, responsible employment of technology and an open-hearted openness to a broad range of cultural expressions. The needs of an alienated creation should also be addressed in our prayers of lament and intercession, and in our exposition of Scripture. Christian worship should feel less like a step into another, alien world and more like a prophetic engagement with this world, for this world belongs to Christ and he claims it as his own.

b. We celebrate his supremacy in new creation

While Christians are called to engage constructively with creation, we are also called to be realistic about our fallenness and the consequent alienation of creation. Our deepest joy, therefore is to celebrate the work of Christ to establish a new creation, through the reconciliation of all things to himself by his cross and resurrection. We are called to responsible citizenship in the world as it is, while knowing that our true citizenship is in heaven; we are new creation people, people of hope, gospel people.

Too often we understand this gospel in exclusively therapeutic terms: Jesus has answered our 'sin problem' and given us eternal life. This is gloriously true, of course, but its perspective is too narrow. The ultimate motivation for the whole plan of salvation is the glory of Christ. *He is the beginning and the firstborn from among that dead, so that in everything he might have the supremacy* (18)! So, while we delight to thank him for all he has done for us, Christian worship goes further. We praise him for his victory over evil, his ascension to glory and his enthronement as king, and we do so not only because of the benefits to us but because we are learning to delight in what God delights in: namely the manifestation of the majesty and supremacy of his Son! Christian worship does not lead us to turn in on ourselves, but to look up to Christ who is coming to claim all things for himself.

c. We celebrate his supremacy in transformational living

Christians are not to be stuck in the past, for we belong to the future and in that future the supremacy of Christ will be clear for all to see. Colossians invites us to live in the present as those whose lives are already being transformed by the future – and that transformation impacts the whole of life. In the words of Douglas Moo: 'This intention [the reconciliation of all things] will be finally accomplished only when Christ returns in glory to establish the kingdom

147

in its final form (cf 1:22b; 3:4). But God invites human beings in the present time both to participate in this reconciliation and to be agents through whom God's work of reconciliation can begin to be carried out.'[46] It is to this perspective of whole-life worship that we turn in the next chapter.

[46] Moo, *Colossians*, p. 138.

Romans 12
11. All of life

Years ago I heard a preacher say something like this. 'You know, I pity those accountants, working themselves to the bone, all for the sake of riches that will not last. I pity them. *I'm* working for the King of kings, helping men and women find *eternal* life in Christ!' At the time I found his rhetoric rather stirring, and wanted to cheer him; these days I'm not so sure. Why are accountants always singled out by preachers? Do all accountants work only for money? Is it not possible for an accountant to work for Jesus? Do accountants not fulfil a rather important function of helping preserve integrity and justice in the economy (at least in principle)? If so, is God not rather concerned about matters of integrity and justice? As we have seen, Colossians 1 teaches us that creation belongs to Jesus; he is its source, its sustenance and its goal. The call to live and work in creation, in a manner which reflects the wisdom, righteousness and justice of God, was his call. So surely it *is possible* to be an accountant who works for Jesus – and so can an entrepreneur, a cleaner, a home-maker or teacher! The surprise of Romans 12, though, is that this is a question of worship. *Therefore, I urge you, brothers and sisters, in view of God's mercy, to offer your bodies as a living sacrifice, holy and pleasing to God – this is your **true and proper worship*** (1).

This verse marks a major turning point in the book of Romans, as Paul sets out a whole series of practical and ethical instructions, following his magisterial exposition of the gospel (Rom. 1:1, 16) in the first eleven chapters. Indeed, we should probably see verses 1 and 2 as a kind of heading for the whole section from 12:1 to 15:13, such that the instruction he gives here for many different areas of life all falls within the overall rubric of *true and proper worship* (1). The implication is clear, then, that the worship which springs from the gospel truly is whole-life worship.

Several of Paul's letters[1] follow a similar pattern, beginning with doctrinal instruction and concluding with instruction for Christian living. However, it is very important that we avoid a radical separation between the two, because for Paul they belonged together. In his 'theological vision',[2] doctrinal instruction which has no ethical and behavioural implications is mere religion, while ethical instruction which has no foundation in the gospel is mere legalism. If the gospel is believed truly, it will also be obeyed transformingly.[3] The link is evident in the opening 'therefore' of our passage.

Nonetheless, there is another connection which is sometimes overlooked, namely the doxology of Romans 11:33–36[4] in which God is praised for the majestic mystery of the gospel. For Paul, the link between understanding and obedience is praise: praise which magnifies God, lifts our hearts to him in joyful adoration and so motivates us to obedience. It is a link which we ignore at our peril.

1. Transformed worship (1–2)

It is hardly surprising that Paul's exposition of the gospel is followed by a call to worship, because throughout the Old Testament, God saves people in order that they may worship him.[5] The strong link between worship and sacrifice that we observed in the Old Testament[6] is still present in Paul's understanding, but it has been radically transformed by the coming of Christ, 'whom God put forward as a propitiation by his [sacrificial] blood'.[7] Since this final sacrifice for sin has been offered, no further sacrifice for sin remains to be made (see Heb. 10:10, 18). Rather, an altogether new kind of sacrifice is to be made: a sacrifice made not as a rite in a temple but as an act of thankfulness in the spaces of everyday life; a sacrifice made not to seek the mercy of God, but to celebrate the mercy of God already given in Christ; a sacrifice not of a helpless animal put to death, but of the ongoing life of the devoted Christian disciple, lived for the pleasure of their Lord.

---

[1] See also Galatians, Ephesians and Colossians.

[2] The phrase 'theological vision' is taken from T. Keller, *Center Church* (Grand Rapids: Zondervan, 2012), pp. 13–25, and describes his commitment to teasing out the rich implications of the gospel for the practice of Christian living and Christian ministry in any given culture or context.

[3] Cf. 'the obedience of faith', Rom. 1:5 (ESV).

[4] I am grateful to the late Bob Horn, my former boss in UCCF, for pointing this out to me.

[5] See ch. 2 of this book for a development of this theme.

[6] This link is the focus of ch. 9 of this book.

[7] Rom. 3:25 (ESV).

Therefore, I urge you, brothers and sisters, in view of God's mercy, to offer your bodies as a living sacrifice, holy and pleasing to God – this is your true and proper worship. Do not conform to the pattern of this world, but be transformed by the renewing of your mind. Then you will be able to test and approve what God's will is – his good, pleasing and perfect will (1–2).

The phrase 'true and proper worship' at the heart of these verses, translates the Greek phrase, *logikēn latreian*,[8] which is expressed in a number of ways in English translations.[9] The Stoic school of Greek philosophy gave an elevated status to reason, seeing it as that which God and human beings shared in common. The only worship that was deemed appropriate, therefore, was 'rational (*logikē*) worship'. Jewish thinkers such as Philo used this idea to stress the inner, spiritual attitude that was essential in offering acceptable sacrifices to God, while others emphasized moral obedience and purity. However, standing where it does at this point in Romans, and with the encouragement to keep *God's mercy* in view, it is hard to disagree with Peterson and Cranfield that for Paul the phrase means 'reasonable worship' in the sense of 'the worship which is consonant with the truth of the gospel'.[10] Romans has, after all, spoken of the God who gave his Son as a sacrifice for our sins, so what 'worship' would 'make sense' better than to offer our bodies as sacrifices to him? Alongside this, nonetheless, the emphasis on the inner *renewing of our minds* (2) suggests that we should not lose the importance to authentic worship of the inner transformation that the gospel brings about.[11]

a. A responsive sacrifice

We would fly in the face of the whole of Romans if we were to understand this *offering of* [our] *bodies* as a means of gaining the favour of God. The sacrifice of which Paul is speaking is a response to the gospel of grace, not an alternative to it! That is why Paul makes his appeal to us *in view of God's mercy* (1). A central characteristic of biblical worship is its responsive nature. God is always the prime

[8] *logikē* can mean reasonable or spiritual; *latreia* is worship or service (usually associated with offering sacrifices in the temple).

[9] 'Spiritual worship' (ESV, NRSV); 'reasonable service' (KJV); 'truly the way to worship him' (NLT).

[10] C. E. B. Cranfield, *A Critical and Exegetical Commentary on the Epistle to the Romans*, ICC, vol. II (Edinburgh: T&T Clark, 1957), p. 605; D. Peterson, *Engaging with God* (Leicester: Apollos, 1992), p. 176.

[11] See D. J. Moo, *The Epistle to the Romans*, NICNT (Grand Rapids: Eerdmans 1996), pp. 751–753.

mover, taking the initiative as he reveals himself in his saving actions and in his word through which he interprets those actions to us. We move in response to what he has done, falling before him in praise and adoration and rising to serve him in grateful, sacrificial obedience.

b. A living, bodily sacrifice

The sacrifices of the Old Testament were dead sacrifices: an animal's life had been forfeited for the life of the worshipper. In the light of the cross, New Testament worship needs no further dead sacrifices but calls rather for the *living sacrifices* of our bodies offered up for the ongoing service of God. There was an inescapable physicality about Old Testament sacrifices – the real bodies of real animals slaughtered on real altars, their real blood shed, poured out and sprinkled – and this physicality[12] is reflected in Paul's language here. We are not called only to offer our 'lives' in some vague, spiritual sense, but to offer our *bodies*. Contrary to the Stoic philosophers, New Testament worship is not limited to a person's interior world; it is not about mere sentiment or intention. Rather it concerns concrete action in the tangible, visible sphere of everyday living. Christian worship, then, is to be expressed not only in the gathering of the Christian church, but in the cultivating of fields, the administration of government, the nurturing of families, the practical support of the vulnerable, the making of art, the responsible creation of wealth, the pursuit of justice and the enhancing of human flourishing. As Martin Luther wrote about believers, 'Even their seemingly secular works are a worship of God and an obedience well-pleasing to God.'[13]

c. A holy sacrifice

What exactly is it that transforms work (whether paid or not) into worship? How is the work of a Christian to be different from that of their unbelieving colleagues? Is it simply about not taking paper clips from the office to be used at home or not using bad language in the staff room or not quietly 'clocking off' before the working day is finished? These concerns are not unimportant, but the biblical vision is far more radical. The book of Leviticus insists that animals brought for sacrifice must be 'with no defects' and then offered to

---

[12] I am grateful to Graham Kendrick for emphasizing this point to me in personal conversation.
[13] Quoted in T. Keller, *Every Good Endeavour* (London: Hodder & Stoughton, 2012), p. 73.

the Lord by fire as 'a pleasing aroma to the LORD'.[14] The sacrifices of New Testament worship similarly are to be offered as *holy and pleasing to God* (1). Our lives are to be 'set apart' for God – motivated by different values, guided by different wisdom and shaped by different goals from those which are prevalent in the surrounding culture.

Christians should not be half-hearted at work because they would prefer to spend all their days in a worship meeting at church; rather their desire to worship will permeate every sphere of their lives. A Christian's life choices (including career choices) will therefore be shaped more by the desire to use their God-given gifts to the optimum in the cause of human flourishing, than by the desire merely to gain more money or status. In their attitude to people (whether colleagues, stakeholders or customers) they will seek to be fair, balancing truth and grace. They will seek to work well, even when no one can see them, because they desire to work for the pleasure of God (Col. 3:22–25).

How do our everyday lives become holy and pleasing to God? To imagine that it is a question merely of obeying laws would be to contradict the essential thrust of the book of Romans, which has exposed the limitations of the law (Rom. 8:3) and expounded the 'new way of . . . the Spirit' (Rom. 7:6; 8:4). Paul's response is to set out both a negative and a positive instruction (2). First, the negative instruction is to resist being *conformed to the pattern of this world*. The call to holiness involves an active determination to resist the shaping influences of a world in rebellion against God – not just its outward behaviours, but its values, its idolatries and its attitudes too. Second, the positive instruction is to *be transformed by the renewing of your mind. Then you will be able to test and approve what God's will is – his good, pleasing and perfect will* (2b). Transformed living comes out of transformed thinking – Christians need to pay close attention to the life of the mind. Nonetheless, Paul is not talking about a merely intellectual process, but about the work of the Holy Spirit. The point is explained in the first half of Romans 8, in which he writes, 'Those who live according to the flesh have their minds set on what the flesh desires; but those who live in accordance with the Spirit have their minds set on what the Spirit desires.'[15] In other words, the indwelling Spirit of God brings about a transformation at the core of our beings – he changes our *desires* to bring them into line with his own desires, so that we are able (increasingly) to perceive the will of God because our own desires are a reflection of his.

[14] See Lev. 1:3–9.
[15] Rom. 8:5.

However, the paradox is that Paul is *commanding us* to be transformed through this renewing of our minds, though that renewing is in fact the work of the Spirit! Clearly then, it is not an automatic process. The Spirit is always at work to transform our desires, but we are responsible to nurture a responsive sensitivity to his inner testimony so as to experience a continuing[16] transformation of our lives. So, far from leading us away from the disciplines of the Christian life (regular Bible reading, prayer, congregational worship, etc.), a commitment to whole-life worship depends critically on such disciplines and the close walk with God they help to foster.

If we are right to see these two verses as providing a kind of heading for the whole of 12:1 to 15:13[17] it follows that the God-honouring masterpiece of Christian worship is to be painted on the broadest of canvasses. We offer *true and proper* worship by our attitude to those who may regard us as enemies (12:17–21); by a submissive attitude to government and a commitment to responsible citizenship (13:1–6); by loving our neighbours (13:8–10) and living in self-control (13:11–14); by accepting believers with whom we may disagree and seeking to live in the kind of unity that honours God and commends the gospel (14:1 – 15:13). However, in the remainder of chapter 12, we are reminded that the worshipping life is not a solitary life, but one lived as part of a community of love (the local church) which encourages, inspires and resources us to overflow in love to others, even in the context of a hostile world.[18]

2. Transformed attitudes (3–8)

I distinctly remember a car journey I made as a young hospital management trainee, with a senior manager from our region. Two other trainees were also in the car and one of them was questioning the right of managers to require staff whom they managed to act in particular ways. Our senior colleague (whose academic background was in philosophy) responded by suggesting that, while it was not appropriate for managers to require staff to change their underlying beliefs and attitudes, it was acceptable to expect them to change their behaviour. The contrast with Paul's approach to how people can be

---

[16] The present tense of the verb implies a continuing, ongoing process (Moo, *Romans*, p. 756).

[17] See Moo, *Romans*, p. 748.

[18] Neil Hudson from the London Institute for Contemporary Christianity (LICC) argues that local churches need to come to terms with two fundamental truths: (1) Jesus is Lord of all; (2) Making whole-life missionary disciples is the core vocation of the church (N. Hudson, *Imagine Church* [Nottingham: Inter-Varsity Press, 2012], pp. 36–38).

changed could hardly be sharper. The change he looks for is 'inside-out' change, not merely outward conformity to behavioural norms. It is hardly surprising, then, that he begins his portrait of whole-life worship[19] by addressing our attitudes.

a. Our attitude to self (3)

For by the grace given me I say to every one of you: do not think of yourself more highly than you ought, but rather think of yourself with sober judgment, in accordance with the faith God has distributed to each of you (3).

Sober judgment is not the same thing as self-deprecation, as if Paul were making a virtue of having a low self-esteem. Personally I am very familiar with the temptation to say something negative about myself, hoping that it will deny someone else the opportunity to be critical of me by 'getting in there' first! However, such patterns of behaviour damage relationships, constrain personal growth and (most importantly) fail to honour the Holy Spirit for his work in our lives.

Sober judgment rather, is the attitude to ourselves that arises from the gospel itself. This is probably[20] the point of verse 3b which is captured well by the New Living Translation: *Don't think you are better than you really are. Be honest in your evaluation of yourselves,* **measuring yourselves by the faith** *God has given us.* The gospel itself provides 'the measure' by which we come to a *sober* evaluation of ourselves, for it faces us squarely both with the reality of our moral failure and with the inestimable love of God for us. We are both incapable of pleasing God by ourselves and, at the same time, moulded by the Spirit to be his workmanship and do his works (Eph. 2:10). We are both deserving of God's wrath and yet promised a share in his glory! When we view ourselves in this light, our pride is undercut and we realize that we have no right to feel superior to anybody. At the same time we are freed to recognize the grace of God at work in us and experience joy as we use the gifts he has given us.

b. Our attitude to other Christians (4–5)

If we are honest, most pastors are probably afraid of conflicts about music. I write as a musician but I have to acknowledge that we

---

[19] The 'for' at the beginning of v. 3 suggests a strong link to the previous two verses.

[20] 'It is that faith which believers have in common as fellow members of the body of Christ that Paul here highlights as the standard against which each of us is to estimate himself' (Moo, *Romans*, p. 761).

musicians are sometimes a rather prickly breed. All too easily we allow petty rivalries, personal pride, feelings of insecurity and preferences about musical style to foster deep fissures in the unity of the local church which can be very difficult for other leaders to deal with. In this passage on whole-life worship Paul challenges such attitudes very directly. When worship is authentic, it transforms our relationships with others in the church, leading us to repent deeply of the kinds of squabbles and competitiveness that too often accompany this wonderful ministry of music (and other ministries too, of course).

It is possible that Paul was particularly thinking here about the tensions between Gentile and Jewish Christians that appeared to be such a problem in the church of Rome.[21] Nonetheless, he makes no explicit mention of that conflict here and it may be that he is simply addressing the difficulties that can arise in any church situation. His argument is based on the analogy between the church and the human body which occurs frequently in his writing, in various forms. The human body is made up of various parts (*members*) each of which has a different function but all of which belong together in the *one body* (4). So in Christ, we are united as many members within one body and therefore *each member belongs to all the others* (5b). We are all saved by the same gospel (for we are *in Christ*) and we are all united in the one Saviour, therefore none of us has any right to claim superiority over the others. Rather, for all our diversity, we belong together, for we belong to one another in Christ.

It is a helpful exercise to look around our church congregation, to observe its diversity and then to challenge our hearts. Are we glad that some are from different countries from our own, that some have different social backgrounds from ours, that some belong to a different generation with a different dress code and cultural identity? Is the diversity which Christ has built into his church a joy to us or a nuisance? Do we feel threatened by people who are not like us or are we ready to embrace them? The gospel teaches us that we *belong* to each other and this is what should determine our attitudes and relationships.

c. Our attitude to gifts (6–8)

The nurturing of unity in the context of diversity is also a challenge in the light of differences in the gifts individuals possess. In

---

[21] John Stott was certainly right to say that Paul's 'assertion that we are "one body in Christ" will have had enormous implications for the multi-ethnic Christian community in Rome' (J. R .W. Stott, *The Message of Romans*, BST [Leicester: InterVarsity Press, 1994], p. 326).

1 Corinthians 12 (which parallels these verses in many ways and to which we will return in a later chapter) Paul illustrates the problem by highlighting the tendency of some to regard their gifts too highly (1 Cor. 12:21–24), while others may undervalue theirs (1 Cor. 12:14–20). Both attitudes are challenged by the gospel, which teaches us that the only thing any of us deserve from God is his wrath[22] and that all the gifts he gives his church are therefore gifts of his grace. So Paul reminds us that *we have different gifts, according to the grace given to each of us* (6a) and this gospel perspective must determine our attitudes to the use of gifts in the church.

It is hard to be certain exactly how Paul wants us to work out this principle, since the syntax of verses 6b–8 is unclear.[23] However, it seems most likely that he is encouraging the development of appropriate attitudes in relation to the use of these gifts.

(i) Use your gifts humbly (6b)

The gift of prophecy,[24] he says, should be used *in accordance with your faith* (6b). This could mean that the prophet should speak 'only so long as he is sure of his inspiration',[25] or that what the prophet says should be 'in agreement with the faith'[26] or simply that the gift should be used with the humility of spirit that the gospel itself engenders, so that appropriate testing is welcomed and encouraged.[27] I lean to the third of these options, but all of them highlight the danger of the prophetic gift being used in a self-aggrandizing or undisciplined way, and encourage rather an attitude of humility and submission.

(ii) Use your gifts willingly (7–8a)

The instruction to those with gifts of service, teaching and encouragement is rather simple: if you have the gifts then use them! These gifts may seem a little less glamourous than the prophetic gift, but

[22] See the comprehensive argument of Rom. 1:18 – 3:20.

[23] The imperative sense of these verses reflected in most English translations (e.g. NIV, ESV, NLT) may be implied in the original, but is not actually reflected in any of the verbs. The NRSV may be right, then, to allow the verb which begins v. 6 (*We have gifts . . .*) to govern the whole sentence so that Paul is simply giving a list of gifts to illustrate his point about diversity in the body. Nonetheless, the words used to qualify the final three gifts (*generously . . . diligently . . . cheerfully*) seem to suggest that he is not just listing gifts but encouraging their appropriate use, as most translations suggest.

[24] Which we explore in more detail in ch. 16.

[25] Stott, *Romans*, p. 327.

[26] Ibid., noting that in this verse faith carries the definite article, though Moo notes that this objective use of 'faith' is rare in Paul – especially in his earlier letters (Moo, *Romans*, pp. 765–766).

[27] See 1 Cor. 14:29–31.

they are no less significant to the health of the body. Neil Hudson includes a striking section on these gifts entitled 'Whole life Coffee Rotas'[28] in which he points out that 'what we do in church often has much potential to help us develop transferable skills, transferable perspectives and transferable attitudes for our mission on the front-line'.[29] A willing, godly, people-centred attitude to our apparently 'mundane' acts of service in church can be very transformative for how we use our gifts in all of life.

(iii) Use your gifts passionately

Three words are used to qualify the encouragement to use each of the final three gifts in this list. *If it is giving, then give* **generously***; if it is to lead, do it* **diligently***; if it is to show mercy, do it* **cheerfully** (8b). Since Christ has given himself unreservedly for us, the *worship that makes sense* is to give ourselves unreservedly for him and his people, using the gifts he has given us with energy, drive and commitment.

Humility, willingness and passion. What a wonderful combination of attitudes to govern our use of gifts within the church. Passion that gives us energy and drive; willingness that helps us value the gifts God has given us and persevere in using them well; humility that keeps us from taking ourselves too seriously and nurtures a desire to receive from the ministry of others as well as to give through the use of our own gifts. When used in this way these gifts enrich the worship of the church profoundly; when these attitudes are replaced with the contrasting attitudes of pride, reluctance and half-heartedness, the authenticity of our worship is undermined.

3. Transformed relationships (9–21)

'After we have done our best to communicate to a lost world, still we must never forget that the final apologetic which Jesus gives is the observable love of true Christians for true Christians.'[30] These well-known words of Francis Schaeffer remain as pertinent today as they were when they were written, decades ago. It is the nature of God to love and those who claim to be his people are called to reflect that love. It is in the central gospel events of the incarnation, sacrificial death and resurrection of Christ that the divine love is most fully revealed (John 3:16; Rom. 5:8; Rom. 8:32–39) and there can therefore be no authentic response to the gospel that is not made

---

[28] Hudson, *Imagine Church*, pp. 146–149.

[29] Ibid., p. 148.

[30] F. A. Schaeffer, *The Mark of the Christian* (Downers Grove: InterVarsity Press, 1970), p. 17.

visible in a transformed life of Christian love (1 John 4:7–12). It is hardly surprising, then, that Paul's exposition of whole-life worship now focuses on the call to transformed relationships of love: *love must be sincere* (9).

a. Love in the community of the church (9–16)

Sincere love is love without pretence; love without acting. It is **discerning** love which desires the best for others and seeks to see them increasingly free from sin: *hate what is evil; cling to what is good* (9). It is also a **heartfelt** love in which we are deeply *devoted to one another* (10a), an attitude more usually associated with our devotion to God, but here extended to his people. It is a **respectful** love in which we *outdo one another in showing honour* (10b, NRSV), delighting in the flourishing of others rather than seeking the limelight for ourselves.

It is impossible to be certain whether there was a particular flow of thought in Paul's mind in these verses, but it may be helpful to see verses 11–16 as exploring some of the things that *sincere love* produces in the church. These include a nurturing in one another of **passionate service** which is zealous for God, fired up by his Spirit and seeking the glory of Christ (11). A community of sincere love is also a community in which we find strength from each other to pursue the Christian life with **perseverance**, rejoicing in the hope of glory, while bearing with the painful realities of life and supporting one another in prayer (12). As a pastor I frequently have people tell me that it was the love and prayers of the Christian church that kept them going through a bereavement, a crisis at work, a major illness or a trauma in their family. Sincere love also expresses itself in **practical help** – meals for a family just after a child is born, debt advice in a situation of financial hardship, the sharing of wisdom for people trying to navigate the challenges of a new marriage, a rebellious child, an unwanted singleness – and a willingness to *practise hospitality* (13) as we welcome people into our homes.

The principle of **non-retaliation** in verse 14 appears to take us outside the Christian community. However, the plural forms remind us that these words are addressed not so much to the individual as to the church family. When a church is characterized by relationships of *sincere love* it is enabled also to show love to those who may be opposed to its work. *Sincere love* also opens up a **deep sharing** in each other's lives (15). 'Love never stands aloof from other people's joys or pains. Love identifies with them, sings with them and suffers with them. Love enters deeply into their experiences and their emotions, their laughter and their tears, and feels solidarity with them, whatever their mood.'[31] Finally *sincere love* fosters **unity with all of God's people**. The emphasis on the renewal of our minds comes through again in verse 16, which Douglas Moo translates more literally, 'Think the same thing towards each other; don't think highly of yourself, but associate with the lowly; do not become proud in your own estimation.'[32] Sincere love reaches across the boundaries of social status, age, ethnicity and background, to embrace all whom God himself has embraced.

I have often heard people talk about the 'worship wars' that have threatened the unity of their churches, as people squabble over who plays which instruments when, which styles of worship are most appropriate and whether the band or the organ are too quiet or too loud. In the light of this passage it is clear that the term 'worship wars' is an oxymoron. There is no authentic worship without sincere love, which seeks to preserve the unity of God's people.

It must be significant that this classic passage on whole-life worship begins its exposition of that theme *in the life of the church community*. Whole-life worship is not true to its name if it does not include our life and service in the church. This, however, is just the beginning. Paul's focus now moves the discussion about worship outside the church and into the whole of the community.

b. Love in the wider community (17–21)

Christians in the West today often feel themselves to be under increasing pressure from an aggressive secularism that is cynical and intolerant.[33] In such a context our stance towards wider society can easily become defensive or even hostile. However, according to Paul, whole-life worship involves a commitment to cultivate a stance of *sincere love* not only in the church but also towards the wider world, even when it is putting us under pressure. He in no way ignores the realities of persecution, but still maintains a remarkably positive stance towards community engagement, encouraging us to believe that, rather than being *overcome by evil* we should work to *overcome evil with good* (21).

First he returns to the principle of non-retaliation in verse 17a. However, whole-life worship is not limited to what we will not do (i.e. retaliate); it has its own positive agenda. *Be careful to do what*

---

[31] Stott, *Romans*, p. 333.

[32] Moo, *Romans*, p. 770.

[33] For a helpful analysis of the extent to which this feeling is justified in the UK see the 'Clearing the Ground' report produced by an All-Party Parliamentary Group, facilitated by the Evangelical Alliance (Christians in Parliament, 2012; < http://www.eauk.org/current-affairs/publications/upload/Clearing-the-ground.pdf>).

is right in the eyes of everyone. If it is possible, as far as it depends on you, live at peace with everyone (17b–18). Even when they are under pressure, Christians should not expect trouble at every turn, still less provoke it. Rather they should seek to live in peace with their neighbours and aim always to do good[34] 'so that in every way they will make the teaching about God our Saviour attractive'.[35]

For a third time, Paul returns to the principle of non-retaliation in verse 19, rooting it this time in his confidence that matters of vengeance can safely be left in the hands of God. This time he balances the call not to retaliate with a positive call intentionally to express kindness to those who oppose us, with the aim of heaping onto their heads 'the burning pangs of shame' in the hope that it will lead them to repentance.[36] *If your enemy is hungry, feed him; if he is thirsty, give him something to drink. In doing this, you will heap burning coals on his head* (20).

4. Conclusion

To see the full scope of Paul's argument here we would need to read on through the next few chapters of Romans. Nonetheless, we have explored enough to conclude that, for him, authentic worship is whole-life worship.

a. Whole-life worship: a challenging perspective

It is a challenging perspective because it is much easier to spend an hour on Sunday morning saying or singing words to glorify God, than it is to live the whole of life to his glory for seven days each week. The perspective of whole-life worship need not throw cold water on the riches of congregational worship, but it does challenge us to live lives of integrity in which the words we say to God are matched by the lives we lead for God. The writer to the Hebrews makes the link clearly: 'Through Jesus, therefore, let us continually offer to God a sacrifice of praise – the fruit of lips that openly profess his name. *And* do not forget to do good and to share with others, for with such *sacrifices* God is pleased.'[37]

How can we celebrate the love of God in song if we are failing to love his people? How can we sing of his kingly authority if we are

---

[34] Some have objected that Paul would not be concerned about what is *right in the eyes* of unbelievers. Nonetheless, he is simply reflecting similar teaching from Jesus and from the apostle Peter; see Matt. 5:16 and 1 Pet. 2:12.

[35] Titus 2:10.

[36] Moo, *Romans*, p. 789.

[37] Heb. 13:15–16, emphasis added.

living in conscious disobedience to his voice? How can we claim to be offering our lives to him if we live as practical atheists in our homes, our workplaces or our communities? A friend of mine often finishes church services with the song, 'Come, now is the time to worship'[38] because, at the close of a service, the work of worship has only just begun!

b. Whole-life worship: a liberating perspective

It is very hard to avoid living our lives under a dark cloud of guilt and shame if we believe that God is only really interested in church services, quiet times and evangelism, because the reality is that most of us cannot spend most of our lives engaged in those things. Perhaps our perspective is wrong. What if we can worship God by doing the cleaning well? What if we can worship God by researching the world he has made? What if we can worship God by being involved in politics? What if we can worship God by giving thanks for good food or a good night's sleep? What if he can find pleasure in a completed set of accounts as well as in a passionately expressed worship song? A whole-life view of worship is deeply liberating, bringing new significance, direction and joy to every aspect of our human existence.

c. Whole-life worship: a neglected perspective

Over the years I have had many opportunities to lead congregations in praise and worship – due in part to my love of music. In that context I confess I have sometimes become a little weary of people urging me not to forget that 'worship is about the whole of life'. Sometimes it has seemed little more than an empty mantra and some-times it has seemed to provide justification for a rather suspicious attitude towards any kind of musical or emotional engagement with God. What is rare, however, is a serious commitment to establishing the links between the worship of the church gathered together and the worship of the church scattered in the world. This seems to me to be crucial and it is in that sense that I suggest that the perspective of whole-life worship has been rather neglected.[39] I am indebted both to the London Institute for Contemporary Christianity, who produce many resources in this area, and to

---

[38] Brian Doerksen (Vineyard Songs, 1998).

[39] For a more detailed exploration of this issue see especially the table in N. Hudson, *Imagine Church*, pp. 144–145. There is also a wealth of resources available under the Imagine Church section of the LICC website: <www.licc.org.uk/resources/resources-2/imagine-church/>.

Graham Kendrick for stimulating my thinking on how we might we make such links.[40]

(i) Keeping a 'whole life' perspective in our preaching

Those of us who work full time in churches will always tend to default towards sermons in which the application is oriented toward the life of the church, the vision of the church or serving in the church. It will therefore take determined effort to strike the right balance. In the last year I have benefitted greatly by spending some evenings with a group of business people from our church, listening in as they have spoken about the challenges of being a Christian in their workplace. Drawing illustrations from or making applications about current issues in the news will also help keep the connection live.

(ii) Re-imagining the role of the 'worship leader'

I very much like the perspective of the well-known worship leader, Graham Kendrick, who often poses this question when training other leaders: 'What if you were to imagine your role not just as leading this time of worship in your local church, but equipping people to be whole-life worshippers, who can sustain their own spiritual lives through the rest of the week?' This is a very helpful question for any of us involved in worship leading to use to evaluate our ministry. For some this may lead to a re-balancing of the songs we choose, with more songs that declare objective, life-transforming truth alongside those which express personal response – both are needed. Neil Hudson suggests that we need to avoid the suggestion that a prerequisite for healthy 'worship' is to 'leave everything we have been involved with this week behind . . . and just concentrate on Jesus'.[41] Perhaps images of our town or city, our workplaces and communities could sometimes be projected behind song words, where that is appropriate.[42]

(iii) Maintaining a strong commitment to intercessory prayer in our services

We can tell people as much as we like that 'worship is about the whole of life' but if our congregations can sit through a ninety-minute 'worship' service without any prayer for the needs of the world[43] we cannot expect them to believe us! Such prayers need to be fresh

---

[40] I am indebted to Graham Kendrick for helping me think through much of this material in personal conversation. I take full responsibility for the content, but wish to record my gratitude for his stimulus and encouragement.

[41] Hudson, *Imagine Church*, p. 144.

[42] Ibid., p. 145.

[43] Such as that encouraged in 1 Tim. 2:1–7.

in their presentation, thoughtful in their content and engaging in their delivery, but they are a very important part of the rhythm of congregational worship.

(iv) Allowing a wider range of voices to be heard

Many churches include brief interviews of different members of the congregation within their services. Once again, however, we will default to hearing only the voices of those who are most active in our church programmes and projects. Why not ask a young person to pray for teachers? Why not interview a business person about how they seek to honour God in their work? Why not ask someone involved in politics to pray for issues in the news that week?[44]

(v) Finishing well

Graham Kendrick makes the valuable point that a final song can be chosen to be a transition point between congregational worship and the worship in the rest of life. The song can be introduced in a way which both draws together the various 'threads' of the service and which encourages the congregation to offer up the work of the coming week as worship to God. More liturgical traditions may have other ways of doing something similar, but it is important that we reflect on the leadership challenge of helping people maintain the perspective of worship as they move into the rest of their week.

(vi) Rediscovering the whole-life perspective of the Psalms

The Bible itself provides us with a wonderful resource for whole-life worship in the book of Psalms. The Psalms address such a vast range of life situations and give us tools and models to enable us to bring those situations to God in worship, whether in our personal devotions or in congregational settings. Graham Kendrick, who identifies learning to pray the Psalms as the single most important source of sustenance in his spiritual life for over a decade,[45] comments, 'What if young people started out being trained in how to pray the Psalms from the start? It would make a huge difference and would instil in them a whole-life Christian worldview and spirituality.'

---

[44] The London Institute for Contemporary Christianity encourages churches to include brief 'This time tomorrow' (TTT) slots in their services (Hudson, *Imagine Church*, p. 100).

[45] See also his creative use of the Psalms in the practice of *Psalm surfing* on <www.grahamkendrick.co.uk/about/psalmsurfing>.

Luke 22:7–30
12. Remember me

How are great people remembered? The pharaohs are remembered by their pyramids; Horatio Nelson is remembered by his statue in Trafalgar Square; Jane Austen is remembered by her literary achievements and country home in Hampshire; Prince Albert is remembered by his concert hall in London; Vladimir Lenin and Chairmen Mao by their mausoleums in Red Square and Tiananmen Square respectively.

How is Jesus remembered? By a broken loaf of bread, recalling his body disfigured on a cross, and by a cup of wine, representing his blood poured out as a sacrifice. What is more, this is specifically how he commanded his followers to remember him. As Christians we risk becoming so familiar with this symbolism that we take it for granted. So consider how strange it is that the Creator of the whole universe should be remembered with two everyday essentials of life; how unexpected that the one in whom the very glory of God was made manifest, should ask to be remembered in his moment of deepest shame; how extraordinary that the one who claimed that his coming had inaugurated the *eternal* kingdom of God should be remembered by an acted parable of his death.

Many Christians call the shared meal in which that parable is acted out, *Holy Communion* – what Allen Ross describes as 'the dramatic celebration of communion with God through the sacrifice of Christ'.[1]

Some families who have lost a loved one seek to keep the memory of them alive by regular visits to a grave – perhaps on a birthday or at Christmas. For some this can be very helpful. However, when the pattern continues indefinitely, it can sometimes seem to lock the

---

[1] A. P. Ross, *Recalling the Hope of Glory: Biblical Worship from the Garden to the New Creation* (Grand Rapids: Krugel Publications, 2006), p. 391.

family into decades of raw grief from which there is little recovery. Is Communion intended to have a similar impact on us? Was it to keep his followers in continuing sadness for his suffering that Jesus called us to remember him in bread and wine? I once heard someone comment on their church which ran a communion service every Saturday night. 'It's very helpful,' they said. 'It means we can get it over and done with before Sunday even begins!' So is Communion a dismal moment of commanded mourning which is the duty of every Christian regularly to undergo? Is it a moment of grief to endure or a moment of grace to savour at the heart of our worship?

It all began the day before Jesus died. It was the time of the Passover in Jerusalem,[2] the climax of the year for the Jewish people in which they celebrated their dramatic escape from Egypt many centuries previously. The feast was preceded by the ritual slaughter of the Passover lambs (7) in the temple, recalling the lambs slaughtered on that fateful night in Egypt. The lamb was then roasted and eaten in the Passover meal, in which the Exodus story was retold. This meal formed the setting for Jesus' last supper with his disciples, two of whom were sent into Jerusalem to *make preparations* (8).[3]

The full order for the celebration of the Passover (the Passover *seder*) only became established after the fall of the second temple in AD 70. However, much of the basic structure was in place before then (as the Gospel accounts of the last supper indicate) including the four cups of wine based around the four phrases of Exodus 6:6–7. The basic pattern seems to have been something like the following:[4]

- *The first cup of wine* ('I will bring you out . . .') is passed round, following a prayer of blessing. This introduces a preliminary course.
- A piece of *unleavened bread* (the *bread of affliction*) is broken and the story of the Exodus is introduced, after which the

---

[2] There can be little doubt of this, given the strength of emphasis in all three synoptic accounts. However, this raises tensions with the evidence in John that the crucifixion was prior to the Passover (18:28; 19:14; 19:31). The best solution appears to be that Nisan 14, the day of the Passover in AD 33, was reckoned by Galilean Jews, including Jesus, to last from Thursday sunrise to Friday sunrise (the Pharisaic Calendar) and by Judean Jews (and therefore residents of Jerusalem) to last from Thursday sunset to Friday sunset (the Sadducean Calendar). Therefore Galileans would slaughter the Pascal Lamb on the Thursday and Judeans on the Friday. See H. W. Hoehner, *Chronological Aspects of the Life of Christ* (Grand Rapids: Zondervan, 1977), pp. 85–90, cited in Ross, *Recalling the Hope of Glory*, p. 392.

[3] 'Citizens were expected to make rooms available to pilgrims because Jerusalem was a national possession' (Ross, *Recalling the Hope of Glory*, p. 392).

[4] See C. L. Blomberg, *Jesus and the Gospels* (Leicester: Apollos, 1997), p. 331; also Ross, *Recalling the Hope of Glory*, p. 394; and J. Nolland, *Luke 18:35–24:53*, WBC 35C (Waco: Word Books, 1993), p. 1048. There is no precise agreement on the details.

(traditionally) youngest son asks, with a series of four questions, why 'tonight is different from other nights'.

- In response an extended *liturgy* (the *haggadah*) tells and interprets the whole story.
- *Psalms* are sung, praising God for his deliverance (usually 113 – 114).
- *The second cup of wine* ('I will free you from being slaves to them') is passed around.
- The *unleavened bread* is blessed, broken and passed around to be eaten with the *Passover lamb*, along with bitter herbs.
- The *third cup of wine* ('I will redeem you') is shared.
- Further *psalms* are sung (usually 115 – 118).
- The *fourth cup of wine* ('I will take you as my own people . . .') is passed around.

Presumably the meal Jesus and his disciples ate followed a similar pattern. However, as they recline around the table, Jesus says to them, *I have eagerly desired to eat this Passover with you **before I suffer*** (15). The atmosphere changes instantly. From now on what Jesus says will have the intensity of 'last words' before death. He continues, *For I tell you, I will not eat it again **until it finds fulfilment** in the kingdom of God* (16).

The claim is quite simply staggering. The Passover meal, which had for generations anchored the identity of the people of God in the story of their exodus from Egypt, was yet to find its true fulfilment. It pointed beyond itself to the coming, triumphant reign of God, just as the exodus story it celebrated pointed to the great story of salvation that was about to be played out in the closing moments of Jesus' earthly life.

So it was that, as this unforgettable meal continued, Jesus transformed the Passover celebration into an acted parable of his coming suffering, becoming what Allen Ross calls 'the new centre of the worship of God'.[5]

In the rather formal solemnity of what Holy Communion has become in most of our churches, it is not unusual for congregations to spend most of the time with their heads bowed and their eyes closed. To the extent that the time is used for reflective prayer this is perhaps understandable. It is, however, a rather strange way to engage with an acted parable! I will never forget hearing a Christian psychiatrist speak about a Christian suffering from depression, who explained to him why she so valued Holy Communion as part of Christian worship. 'When I am depressed,' she said, 'I find it hard to know that God loves

[5] Ross, *Recalling the Hope of Glory*, p. 391.

me. However, in communion I don't only hear it; I can smell it, taste it, feel it and see that he loves me.' An emphasis on the physicality, tangibility and visual nature of Communion is something we would do well to recover. It is not merely a familiar ritual; it is an enacted parable, a great drama to be experienced and seen. It is from that perspective that we will explore this first communion.

1. *Look* at the bread: remembering his sacrifice (19)

Of the Gospel writers, only Luke mentions Jesus taking a cup before the meal (17–18). He could be referring to either of the first two of the Passover cups, though the strong connection with the previous verses may suggest that it was the first cup, shared at the start of the meal. As he takes the cup he gives thanks (*eucharistēsas*) – for this meal is to be a celebration of grace as well as a memorial of suffering.

Just a few short streets away, Passover lambs have been sacrificed in the temple; in just a few short hours Jesus will himself be sacrificed on the cross. Immediately before the lamb is eaten in the main course of the Passover meal, Jesus lifts the unleavened bread which will accompany it. *He took bread, gave thanks and broke it, and gave it to them, saying, 'This is my body given for you; do this in remembrance of me'* (19).

The symbolism of the meal is transformed and focused onto Jesus himself: the bread *is his body*.[6] Not only is he the 'bread of life',[7] he is also the 'bread of affliction' who carries the suffering of his people. He breaks the bread which *is his body*, for his body is to be tortured and torn on the cross as he, the true Passover Lamb (1 Cor. 5:7), dies for our liberation and salvation. Unlike the animal sacrifices that preceded it, this is a voluntary sacrifice: his body will be *given*[8] not taken. Fulfilling everything those sacrifices prefigured, his body is given *for us*[9] as he stands in our place, as our representative and

[6] This strong use of metaphor is common in Jesus' teaching. He *is* the gate, the door, the way . . . etc. There is absolutely no need to make the metaphor walk on all fours by saying it is his body in a literal, physical sense.

[7] John 6:35.

[8] I am assuming the longer reading of vv. 19 and 20 (reflected in most English translations) which has gained considerable scholarly support in recent decades. For a defence of this view see Nolland, *Luke*, p. 1041.

[9] Commenting on this phrase in the Pauline-Lukan tradition, Gordon Fee notes, 'The words "for you" are an adaptation of the language of Isa 53:12, where the Suffering Servant "bore sin for many" . . . Whenever [Paul] uses this preposition in reference to Christ, it expresses either atonement, his death on "our behalf" . . . or substitution, his death in "our place"' (G. D. Fee, *The First Epistle to the Corinthians*, NICNT (Grand Rapids: Eerdmans, 1987), p. 551.

substitute, before the bar of divine judgment. The death he will die is the death that we deserve.

This, surely, is the most solemn moment of Holy Communion. We look at the bread; we remember his body: the reality of his incarnation, his true and glorious humanity, the unity in him of the church (1 Cor. 10:17). We watch as the bread is broken; we remember his terrible suffering on the cross. We see the bread held out to us as a gift; we remember that he suffered willingly and that he suffered for us. Our pride is broken as we are faced with the reality of our sin. Our hearts are moved as we are faced with the strength of his love and the majestic strength of his obedience. We look, we take, we feel, we smell, we receive and, as we eat, we taste the life-giving goodness of costly grace. The bread enters our bodies as food to sustain our physical lives; we gratefully embrace the abundant grace of Christ that it represents, as food to sustain our souls.

2. *Look* at the wine: remembering his accomplishment (20)

In the same way after the supper . . . (20) confirms that it was time for the third Passover cup. This was the 'cup of blessing'[10] that was associated with the words 'I will redeem you with an outstretched arm and with mighty acts of judgment'.[11] In that redemption, the blood of the first Passover lamb was shed to save the people from their slavery in Egypt and draw them into covenant with God at Sinai. At the end of that supper Jesus takes the cup and claims its significance and its symbolism for himself and his followers. *This cup is the new covenant in my blood, which is poured out for you.* A new act of redemption is about to take place in which he, the true and final Passover Lamb, will offer his blood to save people from all the nations of the world and draw them into a new covenant relationship with God.

At least three streams of Old Testament thought flow into these words.[12] First, it recalls the covenant between God and Israel made at Sinai in Exodus 24, which was sealed with the blood of animal sacrifices sprinkled on the people to symbolize their being cleansed from sin and set apart for God. Second, it draws on the promise of a new covenant, glimpsed in Ezekiel 34 – 37,[13] and made explicit in Jeremiah 31:

[10] 1 Cor. 10:16, esv.
[11] Exod. 6:6.
[12] See the analysis in D. G. Reid (ed.), *The IVP Dictionary of the New Testament* (Leicester: Inter-Varsity Press, 2004), p. 672, and in Ross, *Recalling the Hope of Glory*, pp. 396–397.
[13] See esp. Ezek. 36:24–32; 37:26.

'The days are coming,' declares the LORD,
  'when I will make a new covenant
with the people of Israel
  and with the people of Judah.
It will not be like the covenant
  I made with their ancestors
when I took them by the hand
  to lead them out of Egypt,
because they broke my covenant,
  though I was a husband to them,'
                declares the LORD.
'This is the covenant that I will make with
    the people of Israel
  after that time,' declares the LORD.
'I will put my law in their minds
  and write it on their hearts.
I will be their God,
  and they will be my people.
No longer will they teach their neighbour,
  or say to one another, "Know the LORD,"
because they will all know me,
  from the least of them to the greatest,'
                declares the LORD.
'For I will forgive their wickedness
  and will remember their sins no more.'[14]

Third, the language of *pouring out* recalls the language of sacrifice in Leviticus,[15] together with Isaiah's shocking realization that the time would come when the Lord's own Servant would become such a sacrifice, who would 'pour out his life unto death', and be 'numbered with the transgressors. For he bore the sin of many, and made intercession for the transgressors'.[16]

In taking the cup, Jesus identifies himself as the true, suffering Servant of the Lord who will identify himself with sinners, bear their sin for them and give his life to bring about their forgiveness. In doing so he will establish the new covenant relationship with God which Jeremiah had promised, a transforming and personal relationship, made possible because he has dealt with our sin once and for all. It is unlikely that the disciples appreciated all this fully. Nonetheless, in time they came to understand what Jesus was doing

[14] Jer. 31:31–34.
[15] See Lev. 4:34; 17:11–14.
[16] Isa. 53:12.

and to see that drinking the wine[17] was for them a 'participation in the blood of Christ'[18] which, through faith, renewed their covenant relationship with God and gave deep assurance of their cleansing from sin.

For us too, the receiving of the wine of Communion in our worship is to be not only a solemn reminder of suffering, but also a living encounter with the grace of Christ, which we experience with trembling joy. We watch the wine being poured out; we remember his blood poured out on the cross in sacrifice. We see the cup offered to us; we hear the invitation of grace that this sacrifice was for us. We lift the wine to drink; our hearts bow in confession that we stand in need of this grace. We gratefully receive the wine into our bodies; we rejoice that Christ has 'loved us and freed us from our sins by his blood'.[19] In the silence of reflection the Holy Spirit assures that we are the children of God, set apart for Christ and held by him in glorious covenant security. Sometimes we do not feel that we are free, that we are set apart for Christ, that we are adopted into the family of God, but as we drink the wine, we smell, we feel, we taste the sweet savour of costly grace, and our hearts lift again to the music of divine love.

I believe Protestant Christians have been right to emphasize Holy Communion as a symbolic meal by which we remember Christ, rather than a sacrificial meal by which we re-enact his death. Nonetheless, I do find myself flinching when it is made to sound little more than a pictorial aide-memoire, like a picture in a diary to help us remember an appointment at the dentist! The symbolism of communion is not *mere metaphor* and the remembering of communion is not *mere recollection*! According to Calvin the symbolism is of the highest order.

> By the showing of the symbol the thing itself is also shown. For unless a man means to call God a deceiver, he would never dare assert that an empty symbol is set forth by him . . . And the godly ought by all means to keep this rule: whenever they see symbols appointed by the Lord, to think and be persuaded that the truth of the thing signified is surely present there. For why would the Lord put in your hand the symbol of his body, except to assure you of a true participation in it?[20]

[17] This is assumed in Luke's account but made explicit in Matt. 26:27–28 and 1 Cor. 11:25.

[18] 1 Cor. 10:16.

[19] Rev. 1:5.

[20] J. Calvin, *Institutes*, IV:17.10, p. 1371, quoted in W. Grudem, *Systematic Theology* (Leicester: Inter-Varsity Press, 1994), p. 995.

In other words, while the bread and the wine are a symbol (there is no physical change in them), they are not an 'empty symbol', but a means through which Christ truly presents himself to us, so that as we receive them we feed on him in our hearts by faith, with thanksgiving.[21] Similarly, the remembering is not mere recollection, but a rich, active encounter with the abundant grace of God in Christ, a 'participation' in his body and blood (1 Cor. 10:16), and a renewal of our covenant relationship with him. We *do this in remembrance of him.*

Often our thinking about communion stops there. However, Luke's account of the supper continues until at least verse 30. There is more to see.

3. *Look* at yourself: self-examination (21–23)

In all three synoptic Gospels, the story of Judas Iscariot is 'wrapped around' the account of the last supper and the prayers of Gethsemane. It is hard to imagine a more poignant way to portray the contrast between self-serving greed, on the one hand, and self-giving love, on the other.

Three factors come together to produce Judas' shameful betrayal. *First, the desire of the religious leadership to dispose of Jesus quietly* which was very difficult, given that tens of thousands of pilgrims were in Jerusalem for the Passover. What they needed was a way to arrest him away from the glare of publicity. *Second, the sinister strategy of Satan* who, we read in verse 3, *entered Judas.* What he needed was an insider who knew Jesus' movements and was prepared to reveal them. *Third, the callous greed of Judas himself* whose only requirement was a monetary reward. Something of his coldness of heart comes through in the brief mention of his story in the middle of the last supper. *The hand of him who is going to betray me is with mine on the table* (21).

We have all experienced the power of a shared meal to deepen our relationship with another person. In the world of first-century Judaism this was well understood so that to share 'table fellowship' with someone was to express trust and acceptance.[22] Judas, however, was quite prepared to sit with Jesus in this most intimate of gatherings and to participate in the feast, while at the same time awaiting his moment to betray the Master. His shameful duplicity is truly shocking. 'The role of the betrayer cannot, however, be comfortably

[21] Holy Communion Rite, *The Alternative Service Book 1980* (The Central Board of Finance of the Church of England, 1980).
[22] Which is why Jesus' own habit of eating with 'tax collectors and sinners' caused such consternation, see Luke 7:34.

left with Judas. The unresolved questioning of the Apostles in v23 leaves each of us to face the possibility of being one who betrays Jesus, though linked intimately to him through the communion fellowship of the church.'[23]

To take Communion is to share table-fellowship with Jesus – it is a participation (*koinōnia*, a sharing, a fellowshipping) in his body and blood (1 Cor. 10:16). The very fact that we participate in the meal should therefore lead us to ask whether we too are betrayers of Jesus in some area(s) of our lives. Communion involves us looking at ourselves. Perhaps the apostle Paul had Judas in the back of his mind when he wrote to the church in Corinth,

> Whoever eats the bread or drinks the cup of the Lord in an unworthy manner will be guilty of sinning against the body and blood of the Lord. Everyone ought to examine themselves before they eat of the bread and drink from the cup. For those who eat and drink without discerning the body of Christ eat and drink judgment on themselves.[24]

Holy Communion is, as we have seen, intended to be a living, faith-renewing encounter with the grace of Christ. Part of that encounter is to submit to the painful grace of self-examination, in order then to receive the healing grace of restoration.

4. *Look* at your Host: formation (24–27)

Who is greater, the one who is at the table or the one who serves? Is it not the one who is at the table? But I am among you as one who serves (27).

These words of Jesus overturn the usual convention, as he clearly acknowledges. Normally, the one who is at the table is greater than the one who serves, but the greatness of Jesus is an altogether different kind of greatness. He came among them *as one who serves* (27b). His service was about far more than serving at the table; its ultimate expression was in the cross itself. As he said, 'the Son of Man came not to be served but to serve and to give his life as a ransom for many'.[25] All this is prefigured and anticipated as he serves them at his table.

In terrible irony, it was a row among the disciples about *which of them was considered to be the greatest* (24) which occasioned Jesus' comments about the greatness of serving. We may wonder how they could descend to such a squabble, given all that they have just

[23] Nolland, *Luke*, p. 1060.
[24] 1 Cor. 11:27–29.
[25] Mark 10:45.

173

witnessed. We would do better, though, to reflect on how prone we ourselves are to using the structures and activities of church life to establish 'pecking orders' in our fellowships. Jesus responds by comparing their behaviour with the pagans whose relationships and thoughts of greatness are structured around status, authority, manipulation and deference (25). Among those whom he had chosen to be the founding leaders of his church, however, such attitudes had no place. In his kingdom the evidence of greatness is a willingness to serve in humility. *But you are not to be like that. Instead, the greatest among you should be like the youngest, and the one who rules like the one who serves* (26).

'Who is the greatest?' the disciples ask, and the only possible answer to that question is that Jesus is the greatest. Yet what is he doing at the table? He is serving. The disciples are to look and to learn. The communion table is still the Lord's Table (1 Cor. 10:21). He is the host at his table, not the person who presides. He is present at his table by the Holy Spirit, to serve us,[26] and we are to look to him, the divine host who serves his people.

We are not meant to leave the communion table unchanged. Our encounter with Christ, through participation in his body and blood, is to be one of formation. Thoughts of greatness are overturned by the God who kneels beside us to serve. Proud hearts are humbled and hard hearts melted by the tender ministry of the Servant King. Our power-shaped ambitions are subverted and our jealousy-distorted relationships healed as we encounter him, who is among us *as one who serves* (27). We look to our Host; we contemplate his self-giving glory; we are formed into his likeness.

5. *Look* at the banquet: anticipation and proclamation (28–30)

After the sharp rebuke of verse 27, Jesus speaks words of deep re-assurance: *You are those who have stood by me in my trials. And I confer on you a kingdom, just as my Father conferred one on me, so that you may eat and drink at my table in my kingdom and sit on thrones, judging the twelve tribes of Israel* (28–30).

Christian celebration of Holy Communion has a strong forward-looking aspect. The apostle Paul reminds us that we eat the bread and drink the cup, 'until he [Jesus] comes'.[27] This is the focus of these final

---

[26] 'In the Lord's Supper . . . the essential drama consists of the taking, blessing, breaking and giving of bread and the taking blessing, pouring and giving of wine. We do not (or should not) administer the elements to ourselves. They are given to us; we receive them' (J. R. W. Stott, *The Cross of Christ* [Leicester: Inter-Varsity Press, 1986], p. 260).

[27] 1 Cor. 11:26.

verses. Just a few days earlier, Jesus had said, 'The kingdom of heaven is like a king who prepared a wedding banquet for his son.'[28] The idea had its origins in the prophecy of Isaiah who had spoken of a coming day of restoration when 'the LORD Almighty will prepare a feast of rich food for all peoples, a banquet of aged wine – the best of meats and the finest of wines'.[29] This 'Messianic banquet' becomes one of Jesus' favourite images to convey the abundance and joy of the new creation and of the table-fellowship with God that we will enjoy within it. There is a striking glimpse of this banquet a few chapters earlier in Luke, where Jesus is a guest at a banquet, hosted by a 'prominent Pharisee' (Luke 14:1). He challenges his host that when he gives a banquet he should 'invite the poor, the crippled, the lame, the blind' and promises that he will then 'be blessed'. He goes on to tell a parable of a 'great banquet' (Luke 14:15–24), which reflects the 'feast in the kingdom of God' (that is, the Messianic banquet), and describes the generous host sending his servants 'into the streets and alleys of the town [to] bring in the poor, the crippled, the blind and the lame'. These were precisely the people who were excluded from Jewish worship, but now Jesus is claiming the right to overturn expectations and invite them to the Messianic banquet, for it is *his* banquet.

Now, at his last supper with his disciples, Jesus draws a striking connection between the Lord's Table, around which we sit in Holy Communion, and the Messianic banqueting table from which we will feast in the new creation. This eschatological table is his own – *my table* (30) – and to his faithful apostles he guarantees a place at that table. The role of those founding apostles in the kingdom is doubtless unique, but their invitation to sit around the banqueting table of Christ is *not*, for Isaiah's promised banquet was 'for all peoples' and Jesus had already made it clear that all people (even the most unlikely) were invited (Luke 14:15–24). The link between the Lord's Table and the Messianic banquet is therefore relevant for us too. All who share true communion with Christ at his table now, will also share in the consummated fellowship, abundance and joy of the new creation. We therefore rejoice with the apostle Paul that 'whenever we eat this bread and drink this cup, we proclaim the Lord's death *until he comes*'.[30] In Communion we not only look back to the cross in grateful recollection, we also look forward to the coming kingdom in joyful anticipation. Until that time, however, through the preaching of the gospel and through the great, visual drama of Holy Communion, the worshipping church proclaims Christ crucified, risen and ascended, even as we wait for his return.

[28] Matt. 22:2.
[29] Isa. 25:6.
[30] 1 Cor. 11:26.

Psalm 51
13. The voice of repentance:
A broken man

It is a deeply unnerving experience to realize that another person has seen right through us, exposing our darker motives and more selfish choices. A few years ago, a dear friend opened their heart to me on what they saw as a flaw in some of my attitudes, explaining how they had been feeling as a result of my actions. After some defensiveness, I had to face the fact that they were right. It was a painful episode which left me feeling unmasked and a little vulnerable. That is the kind of experience which lies (according to its heading) behind Psalm 51, which is surely the greatest of the seven *penitential psalms*.[1] In the words of M. D. Goulder, 'Among the outpourings of the human heart agonised by the consciousness of sin, this Psalm stands pre-eminent.'[2]

In John's Gospel Jesus is identified as the 'light of the world',[3] who both revealed the glory of God and exposed the depths of human sin.

This is the verdict: light has come into the world, but people loved darkness instead of light because their deeds were evil. Everyone who does evil hates the light, and will not come into the light for fear that their deeds will be exposed. But whoever lives by the truth comes into the light, so that it may be seen plainly that what they have done has been done in the sight of God.[4]

---

[1] These are Pss 6; 32; 38; 51; 102; 130 and 143.
[2] M. D. Goulder, *The Psalms of the Sons of Korah*, JSOTSup 20 (Sheffield: Sheffield Academic Press, 1982), quoted in M. Wilcock, *The Message of Psalms 1–72*, BST (Leicester: Inter-Varsity Press, 2001), p. 185.
[3] John 8:12.
[4] John 3:19–21.

It is hardly surprising, then, that Jesus' public ministry began with an uncompromising call to repentance and faith. 'After John was put in prison, Jesus went into Galilee, proclaiming the good news of God. "The time has come," he said. "The kingdom of God has come near. Repent and believe the good news!"'[5]

It follows that if our worship is truly to be shaped by the coming of Christ, we will need to learn to respond to God using the voice of repentance. For this, there is no better teacher than King David, whose own bitter realization of personal sin and failure led to the writing of this psalm.[6] The story is recorded in 2 Samuel 11 – 12.

King David was Israel's finest king, who had enjoyed unprecedented success in subduing the nation's many enemies. His military campaigns were generally conducted in the springtime before the heat of summer made journeys uncomfortable. However, on this occasion David had sent out his armies under the direction of Joab, his commander in chief (2 Sam. 8:16; 11:1), while he remained at home in Jerusalem – perhaps with a little too much time on his hands. In the cool of an evening, David walked on the roof of his palace and saw a woman – Bathsheba, the wife of Uriah, one of his loyal soldiers. She was washing, she was beautiful and, since he was the king, David decided she should be *his*. Throughout, the text is unambiguous in asserting *David's* responsibility for all that ensued – Bathsheba had no power to refuse the king.[7] After making a few enquiries, he brought her to his palace and slept with her. A few months later, Bathsheba 'sent word to David saying, "I am pregnant."'[8] David attempted to cover up his sin (see Ps. 32), pulling her husband off the battlefield and encouraging him to sleep with his wife, but Uriah was too honourable to comply. With increasing desperation, the king arranged for him to be killed by leaving him

---

[5] Mark 1:14–15.

[6] Scholarly opinion remains divided on the extent to which we should treat the superscriptions of the psalms as authentic and historical. Peter Craigie with Marvin E. Tate in *Psalms 1-50*, WBC 19 (rev. ed., Nashville: Thomas Nelson, Inc., 2004), p. 31 acknowledges that the titles form a part of the canonical text of the Hebrew Bible, but concludes (since he takes them as the work of post-exilic editors) that 'they are frequently of more importance for understanding the role of particular psalms in the context of the Psalter and in the historical context of Israel's worship than they are for understanding the original meaning and context of the individual Psalms'. However, there seems little compelling evidence against the possibility that they represent very early tradition, and if we are to follow the lead of the NT (Mark 12:36; Acts 2:29; 13:35–37), it seems we should treat them as canonical and therefore reliable. See D. Kidner, *Psalms 1-72*, TOTC (Leicester: Inter-Varsity Press, 1973), pp. 32–33.

[7] By noting that Bathsheba had 'purified herself from her uncleanness' the text both highlights her own purity and makes plain that she was not pregnant at the time.

[8] 2 Sam. 11:5.

unprotected in the front line of the battle. Bathsheba became *another* wife in David's royal collection . . .

This is a story of a bad decision that that led to lust, adultery, deception and murder – and all committed by Israel's finest king. There is no attempt to soften the shock we feel; Scripture does not try to 'airbrush' the sin and frailty out of its leading figures. Joab's battle report reaches David, with its stark postscript, 'Moreover, your servant Uriah the Hittite is dead.' David's uncharacteristically flippant response hints at the inner turmoil he is trying to suppress. 'David told the messenger, "Say this to Joab: 'Don't let this upset you; the sword devours one as well as another. Press the attack against the city and destroy it.' Say this to encourage Joab."'[9] Nonetheless, the narrator is clear that 'the thing David had done displeased the LORD'.[10]

Into this situation God sends the prophet Nathan, with a story to tug at David's heartstrings.

> He said, 'There were two men in a certain town, one rich and the other poor. The rich man had a very large number of sheep and cattle, but the poor man had nothing except one little ewe lamb that he had bought. He raised it, and it grew up with him and his children. It shared his food, drank from his cup and even slept in his arms. It was like a daughter to him.
>
> Now a traveller came to the rich man, but the rich man refrained from taking one of his own sheep or cattle to prepare a meal for the traveller who had come to him. Instead, he took the ewe lamb that belonged to the poor man and prepared it for the one who had come to him.'[11]

Blind to his own hypocrisy, David erupts with anger against the rich man and insists that he must die. Nathan, with perhaps the most devastating put-down in history, turns the full fury of David's anger back on him. 'Then Nathan said to David, "You are the man!"'[12] David is unmasked. He responds to Nathan, 'I have sinned against the LORD.'[13] This is the realization that calls forth the heartcry which is Psalm 51.

Bernard W. Anderson begins the preface of his book on the Psalms with these words: 'The book of Psalms has a unique place in the Christian Bible. One reason for its singular role, as noted by Athanasius,

[9] 2 Sam. 11:25.
[10] 2 Sam. 11:27.
[11] 2 Sam. 12:1–4.
[12] 2 Sam. 12:7a.
[13] 2 Sam. 12:13.

an outstanding Christian leader of the fourth century, is that most of scripture speaks *to* us while the Psalms speak *for us*.'[14] In other words, most of the psalms are not like sermons, or the teaching epistles of the New Testament, giving direct instruction to the people of God; rather they are prayers and songs addressed to God. Psalm 51 does not list some interesting 'bullet points' about the forgiveness of God; instead it gives us an invitation, a pathway, a means of approach that enables us to encounter for ourselves the God who forgives. In this psalm, then, are words which speak *for* us; words which we are invited to make our own; words that give us language for worship when we know *we* have done wrong. Nonetheless, these words are still God's words to us, his gift to us. Their inclusion within Holy Scripture assures us that such words have his approval and are met not with his rejection but with his embrace. So it is that this psalm gives us insight into the heart of the God who is there. He is the kind of God who does not despise *a broken and contrite heart* (17), but loves sinful people and invites them to approach him to find mercy.

There is little agreement among commentators on the structure of the psalm.[15] We will follow a simple three-part division, allowing the psalm to walk us along the contours of repentance.

1. The cry of repentance (1–6)

The voice of heart-wrenching repentance is heard clearly in the raw simplicity of these verses.

a. His appeal to God (1–2)

> Have mercy on me, O God,
>   according to your unfailing love;
>   according to your great compassion
>   blot out my transgressions (1).

---

[14] B. W. Anderson with S. Bishop, *Out of the Depths: The Psalms Speak for Us Today* (Louisville: Westminster John Knox Press, 2000), p. ix. He seems to be referring to a paraphrase from Athanasius' *Letter to Marcellinus*.

[15] An attractive alternative to the structure I am proposing is the chiastic structure put forward by T. Longman III and D. E. Garland in *Psalms*, Expositor's Bible Commentary, vol. 5 (Grand Rapids: Zondervan, 2008), p. 433. Their outline is:

  A Prayer for individual restoration (1–2)
      B Confession and contrition (3–6)
         C Prayer for restoration (7–12)
      B' Thanksgiving (13–17)
  A' Prayer for national restoration (18–19)

In repentance, David makes no attempt to bargain with God. He knows he has nothing with which to negotiate. His only hope lies in the heart of God, for he is the God of *unfailing love* and *great compassion*. So he makes his appeal for mercy, forgiveness and cleansing. However, this is no cheap desire for easy forgiveness; David has been forced to face reality and to come to terms with how profoundly flawed he is. This is the 'reality' that he now opens up to the cleansing grace of God, using three distinct terms to describe his failure.

Blot out my **transgressions** (1b), which Alec Motyer described as specific 'acts of wilful, open-eyed rebellion'.[16] The focus is on the nature of sin as rebellion against God. David longs for his acts of rebellion to be blotted out, their record fully erased.

Wash away all my **iniquity** (2a), that is, his inward perversity. The focus is on 'the interior aspect of sin, the warp in human nature'.[17] David bemoans not only his actions, but what those actions reveal about his inner, moral corruption. He longs for that corruption to be washed away and his heart made pure.

Cleanse me from my **sin** (2b), that is offences, 'missing the mark',[18] actions which fall short of what God has asked.[19] The focus here is on the specific instances of sin. David does not allow his concern about inner, moral corruption to become generalized and unfocused, but faces the particular offences he has committed and asks for cleansing.

Sin as rebellion; sin as moral perversity; sin as specific offences: David's recognition of his guilt leaves no stone unturned. He is facing the reality of his profound failure, for this is the reality he is appealing to God to deal with.

b. His acknowledgement of failure (3–6)

After the appeal for God's mercy comes a still deeper acknowledgement of his moral failure. David offers no excuses, pleads no mitigating circumstances and seeks no place to hide: *I know my transgressions, and my sin is always before me* (3). He also knows that his sin is, in the profoundest sense, against God (4). We might

---

[16] Alec Motyer in addresses to the UCCF staff conference at Scargill House, Kettlewell in 2000. Similar material is available in his article on Psalms in *NBC*. The Hebrew is *pešaʿ*, 'Covenant Treachery . . . The vast majority of the instances of *pešaʿ/pšʿ* in the OT signify rebellion directed against Yahweh' (*NIDOTTE*, vol. 3, pp. 707–708).

[17] Motyer, ibid.

[18] Motyer, ibid.

[19] 'It is possible to see in this term a basic, non-theological meaning of miss/fail existing, alongside its familiar meaning of sin' (*NIDOTTE*, vol. 2, p. 87).

protest that he should be more concerned about what he has done to Bathsheba and her late husband – and without doubt, he has wronged them deeply and injured them terribly. There is, however, a unique sense in which sin is, by its nature, an act of defiance against God. God's laws are not mere moral games he plays with us; they are *expressions of who he is*. There is no ultimate measure of goodness other than the nature and glory of God himself. Conversely, therefore, that which is sinful is that which is contrary to *his nature*. In this profound sense, then, all sin is *against God*; it is a rejection of his goodness and glory. It follows that God is the final judge of sin (4b). So, in David's case, he has chosen unfaithfulness and impurity over against the faithfulness and purity which are character-istic of God; he has chosen lies, deceit and cover-up over against the truth and light which come from God; God is the source of life, yet David has chosen to take the life of a man made in God's image. David has sinned against God.

His acknowledgement of guilt goes even deeper in verses 5–6. His recent failure with Bathsheba and Uriah may be uppermost in his mind, but it is not an isolated incident. On the contrary, the whole narrative of his life has been tainted by sin, from the moment of his conception (5).[20] There is some uncertainty in the trans-lation here, but in the Hebrew both verses 5 and 6 begin with the same word (*Behold*[21]) which may suggest that the two verses should be interpreted together. If so, the NIV[22] captures the sense well

> Surely I was sinful at birth,
>   sinful from the time my mother conceived me.
> Yet you desired faithfulness even in the womb;
>   you taught me wisdom in that secret place (5–6).

In other words David is reflecting on both the essence and the ambiguity of human nature in its fallenness. On the one hand, our problem with sin is indeed embedded deep within our nature (5); on the other hand, a sense of moral responsibility, an awareness of right and wrong, and even an understanding that 'faithfulness' is somehow

[20] The popular view in some older commentaries that v. 5 expresses a view that sexual intercourse is itself sinful is neither required by the text here nor consistent with Scripture as a whole, which acknowledges it to be a good gift of God in creation. 'Nowhere in the Old Testament is the legitimate act of coition referred to as sinful' (E. R. Dalglish, *Psalm Fifty-One in the Light of Ancient Near Eastern Patternism* [Leiden: Brill, 1962], p. 119, quoted by M. E. Tate, in *Psalms 51–100*, WBC 20 [Nashville: Thomas Nelson, Inc., 2000], p. 19).

[21] As in ESV and KJV.

[22] The 2011 edn; the 1984 edn takes a different approach.

desirable to God, were also hard-wired by him into our humanity (6), so that we are all without excuse.

Here is a model of repentance which goes far beyond a quick postscript to our prayers ('. . . and forgive us all our sins, in Jesus' name. Amen!'). For David, repentance is about embracing the cost of facing reality with painful honesty, as he acknowledges the depth of his failure and makes his appeal to the mercy of God. It is likely that many of our difficulties as Christians follow from our failure to follow his example. Sometimes we see repentance as prayer to pray to become a Christian, rather than a lifelong discipline of transformation. Often our 'repentance' is qualified with many excuses and fails to carry with it a serious desire to change. As a result sin is not squarely faced and its power over us is not seriously challenged. In this psalm, however, the voice of repentance rings with a deep authenticity, which confronts personal failure with honesty, accepts personal responsibility without qualification and seeks personal transformation with strong resolve. Such repentance, coupled with faith in God's grace and wisdom, is key for real change in the Christian life. If we are shallow repenters, we will be shallow Christians, trapped in sinful habits and not growing spiritually; if we want to be growing Christians we must learn to worship God with the costly voice of authentic repentance, which leads to continuing transformation.

2. The heart of repentance (7–12)

A week after we got married, Alison and I moved into our small new home in Nottingham. The house was in a reasonable condition but we quickly concluded that the entrance hall, stairs and landing needed to be decorated. With no prior experience to draw on, we rolled up our sleeves and got to work, stripping off the old wallpaper. It would, though, have been a very unsatisfactory job if we had stopped there, having done nothing more than to expose the bare rough walls. The whole point of taking off the old paper was so that we could replace it with the new paper we had chosen. Sometimes our ideas about repentance and holiness are so focused on the things we are called to 'take off' that we lose sight of the new things we are called to put in their place. Repentance is about profound change: a change of mind leading to a change of behaviour. It is about turning around: turning *from* sin, perversity and rebellion and turning *to* purity and faithfulness. Both elements are key in these verses, which take us to the heart of David's repentance.

a. A plea for cleansing (7–9)

When we need to repent from something, there are often voices in our hearts which show us that we really want to hold on to it: 'I repent of my pride (but please may my colleagues be careful to affirm me); I repent of my lust (but please can my eyes still wander); I repent of my greed (but please can responsible consumption begin tomorrow)'! By contrast, David's turning from sin is without equivocation. *Cleanse me* (7a); *wash me* (7b); *hide your face from my sins* (9a); *blot out my iniquity* (9b).

There is, however, an awkward question that lurks not far beneath the surface of this psalm: *how* can God forgive David? What kind of God would turn a blind eye to a man who has abused his power to seduce a vulnerable woman and kill off her husband? Would not such a God be complicit with David's sin and therefore unworthy of our worship? This psalm does not seek to provide a full answer to that question, but there is a small hint: *Cleanse me with hyssop, and I shall be clean; wash me, and I shall be whiter than snow* (7).

Why does David ask to be cleansed with hyssop? Hyssop was a plant (probably an aromatic herb),[23] which was associated, in the Old Testament, with the sprinkling of sacrificial blood. So in Exodus, as the angel of death hovers over Egypt, the Israelites take hyssop, dip it in the blood of a sacrificed lamb and use it to sprinkle the blood on their door posts (Exod. 12:22). The angel of death will pass over the household with blood on the doorposts, because the Passover lamb has already died as a sacrifice in their place. It was also used in cleansing rituals for various kinds of uncleanness (Lev. 14:6–8; Num. 19:6, 18). It seems, then, that David understood that blood must be shed and sprinkled on him for his sin to be forgiven; a price had to be paid, a penalty borne. His problem, though, was that in the Old Testament there *was* no sacrifice prescribed for murder or adultery.[24] In some sense, then, it seems that David is reaching for a better sacrifice than the law could provide, confident that the Lord had within himself the resources finally to deal with human sin. The fulfilment of his prayer was found at the cross, where Jesus the perfect human being and consummate king, stood in the place of a broken and rebellious humanity to die as a sacrifice for our sins, bearing their penalty for us, so as for God 'to be just and the one who justifies

---

[23] '"Hyssop" probably refers to a small bush known technically as *Origanum Maru L*, the Syrian Marjoram' (Tate, *Psalms 51–100*, p. 6).

[24] 'Sins such as adultery or murder are not provided for in sacrificial instructions, and the execution of the adulterer or the murderer is required' (Tate, *Psalms 51–100*, p. 28).

those who have faith in Jesus'.[25] So confident is David in the sufficiency of the grace of God, that he is able to affirm that he *will be clean* and *whiter than snow* (7) and to anticipate the restoration of *joy* (8) because his sin has been decisively *blotted out* (9).

b. A desire for renewal (10–12)

I have sometimes challenged a congregation immediately to expel all thought of chocolate from their minds! Most (especially the chocolate lovers!) find it impossible. The very suggestion that we should not think about chocolate stimulates us to think about it, rather as Paul found that the commandment against coveting caused sin to produce in him 'every kind of coveting'.[26] The only way to expel the thought of chocolate is to replace it with a thought of something still more compelling! Similarly, though the path to transformation begins with a decision to turn from sin, it must continue with a positive decision to put holiness and purity in its place. This desire for positive, inner renewal is clearly the focus of these verses:

> *Create in me a pure heart* ... (10a) *renew a steadfast spirit within me* ... (10b) *Do not ... take your Holy Spirit from me*[27] ... (11) *Restore to me the joy of your salvation and grant me a willing spirit, to sustain me* (12).

The renewal David seeks is not merely a quest to be restored to public respectability; it is a deep renewal of the heart and the will by the work of the *Holy* Spirit of God.[28] We should not read back into these verses a fully developed doctrine of the work of the Holy Spirit in sanctification.[29] Nonetheless (like the cry for cleansing of sin through sacrificial blood in v. 7), this *is* surely a far-sighted prayer, which throws a long trajectory right into the world of the New Testament, shaping the understanding of the apostolic authors, who experienced the fullness of what David longs for here, by the Spirit poured out at Pentecost.

[25] Rom. 3:26.

[26] Rom. 7:8.

[27] Probably reflecting David's fear that his experience would mirror that of King Saul, from whom the empowering Spirit of God departed (1 Sam. 16:14).

[28] It is possible that all three references to the spirit/Spirit in these verses refer to the Spirit of God (see Tate, *Psalms 51–100*, p. 25). It would be anachronistic to read back into these verses a fully developed NT doctrine of the Holy Spirit. Nonetheless, we should not hold back from the conclusion that David is talking about the Spirit of God and has understood both that the Spirit of God shares fully the holiness of God and that his inner work is key to our moral transformation.

[29] See, for example, Rom. 8 and Gal. 5.

Practically, this means that our repentance needs to be much deeper and much more intentional than we often make it. For example, following an inappropriate outburst in an argument we might pray a little superficially, 'Lord please help me to get rid of a bad temper.' That is, however, to leave the job less than half done! The key question for transformation is, 'what kind of character is the Holy Spirit working to develop in me, and how can I be more responsive to him, more in step with what he is doing?' For the Spirit does not want simply to 'take away' my 'bad temper', he wants to replace it with love, joy, peace and patience, which are the fruit of nurturing a close relationship with him (Gal. 5:22). Or to take another example, a young unmarried couple who have lost control of their sexual desires for each other. For them, a quick prayer – 'Lord, help us to stop sleeping together' – does not really constitute repentance. The key question for them is 'what kind of relationship does the Holy Spirit want us to build together?' This positive vision can then lead them to sustained prayer for God to enable them to grow into an unselfish love that will honour each other and will never take advantage, so that increasingly their relationship will be a beautiful picture of the love between Christ and his church.

3. The fruits of repentance (13–19)

As I write, our church family is in the process of establishing a centre to help people in the community who are in serious debt.[30] In our researching of this new initiative, we have frequently been very moved by the stories of those who, having been weighed down by crippling levels of debt, find their lives utterly transformed by becoming 'debt-free'. Profound gratitude, a positive effect both on the individual and on those connected with them and a desire to see others similarly helped seem to be typical responses. In the final verses of Psalm 51, David expresses a very similar reaction to his own experience of finding release from the 'debt' of his sin, in the forgiveness and grace of God.

a. Testimony (13)

Then I will teach transgressors your ways, so that sinners will turn back to you.

We might initially read this as David claiming some kind of moral superiority, but in the light of the rest of the psalm this is clearly impossible. The connecting *then* provides the key. It is precisely

---

[30] We are working in partnership with Christians Against Poverty, <www.capuk.org>.

because he has faced squarely the depth of his moral failure and found that it is met by still deeper divine grace, that he is motivated to speak to others. The deeper our experience of God's forgiveness, the more we will long to share that experience with others so that they may *turn back* to God themselves. Shallow repentance doesn't only lead to compromised living, it leads to missional indifference too. Conversely, it is when we grasp how good the gospel really is – how profound is the problem of our sin and how overwhelmingly rich is God's mercy to us in Christ – that we most desire to share it with other people.

b. Praise (14–17)

The connection between experiencing the grace of God and declaring the praise of God is made twice in these verses. First, in verse 14:

> **deliver me** from the guilt of bloodshed, O God,
>   you who are God my Saviour,
>   **and** my tongue **will sing** of your righteousness.

'God's righteousness manifests itself not only in judgement (v.4) but also in forgiveness and fidelity to his covenant (cf 1 Jn 1:9).'[31] Second, the prayer *open my lips . . . and my mouth will declare your praise* (15) is linked to the next two verses with a connecting 'for' in the original,[32] so that what follows is the reason for David's praise. David has understood that all he has *contributed* to this encounter was his sin and brokenness – there was, after all, no sacrifice (16) he knew of which could atone for the guilt of his bloodshed. However, what he has *received* is welcome, embrace and overwhelming grace from the God who does not despise his *broken spirit* and his *broken and contrite heart* (17). Shallow repentance leads to half-hearted praise, but deep repentance opens our lives to deep grace which, in turn, opens our mouths in heartfelt praise.

c. Restoration (18–19)

Many scholars see these last two verses as a later, editorial addition for Israelites who used this psalm as a model for their own repentance after the exile.[33] This may well be the case – after all, Jerusalem was

[31] Longman and Garland, *Psalms*, p. 439.
[32] See ESV and NRSV.
[33] 'It is far more likely that the generations between the captivity and the rebuilding made David's penitence their own, adding these verses to make their prayer specific' (Kidner, *Psalms 1–72*, p. 194). Some also suggest that it is intended to qualify the psalm's apparent lack of enthusiasm for animal sacrifice in v. 16.

in good shape at the time of David and scarcely needed building up (18)! However, it is also possible that David did write these words because he realized the adverse effect of his sin on the nation as a whole. Moral failure never happens in a hermetically sealed space. When we fail, there are always others who are affected in some way or another. If it is a significant leader who has failed, whole communities (including church communities) can be adversely affected and may take years to recover – especially if the leader fails to recognize their failure and repent. One of the responsibilities of leadership is to lead in repentance,[34] though in reality the fear of weakening their authority and damaging their reputation makes many leaders hard-hearted and slow to repent. In David's case, he sinned as the king of Israel and his actions had consequences which rippled far beyond himself – to Uriah, to Bathsheba, to his family and to the entire nation. That was not the whole story, though. It is a measure of the depth of David's spirituality that, once confronted with his failure, he was so quick to repent. He was quite literally the 'chief repenter' in Israel, whose example should be a challenge to all of us who lead today.

What David also understood was that, just as his sin had brought a cloud over the nation, so his repentance and renewal would bring blessing to the nations and a restoration of joy, worship and celebration – not least as other *sinners* followed David's example and *turned back* (13) to God. This, it seems to me, is the thrust of the final verses of the psalm.

> *May it please you to prosper Zion,*
> *to build up the walls of Jerusalem.*
> *Then you will delight in the sacrifices of the righteous,*
> *in burnt offerings offered whole;*
> *then bulls will be offered on your alta*r (18–19).

4. Conclusion

Repentance is a doorway to grace, a prelude to praise and a crucial step on the journey to renewal. It is an essential discipline for leaders and for all of God's people. A shallow practice of repentance produces a shallow appreciation of grace, which weakens our missional passion and dampens our desire to praise. It is therefore enormously important that we learn to let the voice of repentance sound often in our worship, both personal and corporate. In the

---

[34] I am grateful to my friend and former colleague Cassells Morrell for both teaching and modelling this principle to me.

words of Herman Veldkamp, 'The church is the only body on earth that confesses sin. Where the confession of sin dies out, the church is no longer the church.'[35]

Liturgical confessions help many to keep practising the discipline of repentance, though some find that there are dangers if words become too familiar. Clearly Psalm 51 has much to offer as a model for personal repentance in the prayer lives of individuals. Still, the title (*for the director of music*) does suggest that it was also intended for use in public worship, even though it is much longer than the public confessions we typically use and its language is self-disclosing and quite penetrating. Perhaps, then, we need to take the example of this psalm more seriously, giving more space in our public gatherings for the voice of repentance to be heard and developed. Why not weave together appropriate music, silent reflection and guided prayer to take people through the journey of this psalm (and others like it), so as to open their lives and open our churches to the deep reservoirs of grace?

[35] H. Veldkamp, *Dreams and Dictators* (St Catharines: Paideia, 1978), p. 202. Quoted in D. R. Davis, *The Message of Daniel*, BST (Nottingham: Inter-Varsity Press, 2013), p. 119.

Psalm 96
14. The voice of proclamation: A global call

In the autumn of 2011, the popular English choirmaster, Gareth Malone, began working with a new choir made up of the wives and girlfriends of military personnel who were on active service in Afghanistan. The BBC series 'The Choir' told the story of the journey they made, from their first hesitant attempts to sing together near their barracks in Devon, to their memorable appearance in the Royal Albert Hall at the Royal British Legion's Remembrance Parade. The composer Paul Mealor was commissioned to write a song for the choir, using a text compiled from letters the choir members had written to their husbands and boyfriends. The song he wrote ('Wherever you are') justly achieved widespread popular acclaim, as its poignant lyrics and evocative music moved the hearts of the listening public. There is nothing that can capture the mood of the moment quite so effectively as a *new song*. New songs have been used to send teams off on international sporting competitions, to encapsulate national grief in royal funerals[1] and national celebration wishes in royal weddings,[2] to bolster the sense of national identity in new states[3] and to unite the voices of dissident protesters.[4]

New songs are also powerful in the church. I well remember the excitement at a Spring Harvest event when the songwriter Stuart Townend first introduced his great song 'In Christ Alone' to the

[1] E.g. Elton John's rewriting of his 'Candle in the Wind' as a tribute to Diana, Princess of Wales (1997).

[2] E.g. Paul Mealor's setting of 'Ubi Caritas et Amor', commissioned and re-written for the wedding of HRH Prince William of Wales to Catherine Middleton (2011).

[3] E.g. *Ee Mungu Nguvu Yetu* was commissioned in 1963 to provide a national anthem for Kenya after independence from the United Kingdom.

[4] E.g. the *neuva cancion* ('new song') is a whole genre of protest music in the Spanish-speaking world (especially Latin America), which played a significant role in the upheavals of the 1970s and 1980s.

189

wider church. The writing of new songs has often been a feature of movements of spiritual renewal, as a rising generation finds new inspiration for worship in a new context. At their best, new songs foster creativity and vibrancy in our response to God and help to keep the church fresh and contemporary.

Psalm 96 begins with an invitation to sing a *new song* (1) to Yahweh, the God of Israel. Much of this song also appears in 1 Chronicles 16, following the bringing of the Ark of the Covenant into Jerusalem, perhaps suggesting that the song already had a place in the worship of Israel before its inclusion in the fourth book of Psalms.[5] The Greek translation of the Old Testament includes a heading for the psalm saying that it was for use 'when the house was being built after the captivity',[6] raising the possibility that it was after the exile that these old words were 're-mixed'[7] into a new song[8] to express the praise of the people of God in a new situation. The new song is a 'fresh outburst of praise to God. The occasion of praise is a new act of "salvation" . . . also known as "his marvellous deeds" and "his wonders"'.[9]

In his ground-breaking book *The Mission of God*, Chris Wright takes the idea of the new song a stage further, picking up the strongly missional perspective of this psalm. 'Among the many models for mission that we find in the Bible (in addition to the much over-used military one) is the concept of singing a *new song* among the nations.'[10] The song is a celebration of the saving acts of Yahweh and, whereas in many psalms it is the people of God who are called to sing to him,[11] the focus of Psalm 96 is to call *all the earth* to join in the song!

> The content of the new song is essentially a remix of the old songs of Israel – the name, the salvation, the glory and the mighty acts of Yahweh. What makes it new is *where* it is to be sung (in all the earth) and *who* is going to be doing the singing (all peoples).

[5] However, it is not certain that the Hebrew of 1 Chr. 16:7 does specify that this was exactly the song sung at the time (see NIV 2011, ESV, NRSV, *pace* NIV 1984); see D. Kidner, *Psalms 73–150*, TOTC (Leicester: Inter-Varsity Press, 1975), p. 347, fn. 1.

[6] See M. Wilcock, *The Message of Psalms 73–150*, BST (Leicester: Inter-Varsity Press, 2001), p. 98.

[7] This phrase comes from C. J. H. Wright, *The Mission of God* (Downers Grove: InterVarsity Press and Nottingham: Inter-Varsity Press, 2006), p. 134.

[8] The words 'Sing to the LORD a new song' do not appear in 1 Chr. 16 but only in Ps. 96.

[9] T. Longman III and D. E. Garland, *Psalms*, Expositor's Bible Commentary, vol. 5 (Grand Rapids: Zondervan, 2008), p. 723.

[10] Wright, *Mission of God*, p. 134.

[11] E.g. Ps. 33 begins, 'Sing joyfully to the LORD you *righteous*; it is fitting for the *upright* to praise him'.

What was an old song for Israel becomes a new song as it is taken up by new singers in ever expanding circles to the ends of the earth.[12]

In other words, this is a psalm which weaves together praise and mission, calling us to worship with the *voice of proclamation* as those who share God's heart for the whole world. As Christian worshippers who have received the good news of God's saving reign of grace in Jesus Christ, it is essential that we learn to value this voice for ourselves.

Anyone who is reasonably involved in church life will quickly realize that 'worship' (by which, sadly, people often only really mean singing) is one of the hot topics on which everyone seems to have an opinion. So much of our energy is expended on an in-house debate about style, preference and comfort which concerns only *how* we, as God's people, worship him. Psalm 96 cuts across our small concerns and invites us to embrace an altogether more thrilling global vision. It calls us to move our thinking beyond small, internal questions about *how* we worship to the great missiological question of *whom* the nations are worshipping and *how* they can hear the new song and be drawn into the worship of Yahweh.

A simple repeating pattern, based around a potent mix of worship, mission and theology, provides the structural architecture for the psalm.[13]

> All are called to worship . . . (1–2a) (WORSHIP)
> . . . so all must hear (2b–3) (MISSION)
> For the Lord is God overall (4–6) (THEOLOGY)
> All are called to worship . . . (7–9) (WORSHIP)
> . . . so all must hear (10) (MISSION)
> For the Lord is judge of all (11–13) (THEOLOGY)

1. All are called to worship (1–2a)

> *Sing to the LORD a new song;*
> *sing to the LORD, all the earth.*
> *Sing to the LORD, praise his name*

The call to *sing a new song* is made in the first place to Israel – perhaps celebrating the rebuilding of the temple in the aftermath of exile. Still, this vision of the psalm stretches far beyond the history of just

[12] Wright, *Mission of God*, p. 480. Note that Isa. 42:10 interprets the *new song* in this missional way.

[13] Based on Alec Motyer's article on Ps. 96 in *NBC*.

one nation. God's ancient promise to Abraham was that his offspring would be the means of blessing to all the nations (Gen. 12:1–3) and here the psalmist catches a rare glimpse of its fulfilment. The people of God are singing their *new song* in the hearing of a global audience. The song celebrates a radically alternative vision for human existence as it declares the unparalleled *glory* and unrivalled splendour of Yahweh and proclaims *his marvellous* [saving] *deeds* (3). As it is sung, proclaiming the story of salvation to the nations, one after another joins in the song, making it new again, as each one adds their own distinctive voice.

The vision of a global community called to the worship of Yahweh was, without doubt, an Old Testament one, as we have already seen. However, it was a vision that was all too rarely pursued in Old Testament history. It was only in the wake of Jesus' coming that the music of the *new song* burst onto the global stage in its fullness. He was the true Israelite who, fulfilling all that it meant to be the Servant of Yahweh, was made 'a light for the Gentiles, that [God's] salvation may reach to the ends of the earth'.[14] This same Jesus, having ascended to the Father's side, poured out his Holy Spirit – the Spirit of *mission* – on the church so that, filled with his power, they might sing the *new song* of salvation among the nations (Acts 1:8), calling *all the earth* to join in his praise.

This is a wonderful way to think about the mission of the people of God in every generation. We are a singing people, because the glory of the Lord and his acts of salvation have filled our hearts with joy. Our mission is to sing his song in the hearing of the nations, inviting them to share our joy and join in the song. As each new voice is added, the song is made new again, with each culture adding its own distinctive richness and style, blending with all the others into a glorious, global symphony to the praise of God.

In a fascinating study of the development of hymnody and worship music in the Turkish church, Jeremy Perigo comments:

> The church was born in culturally diverse worship. The outpouring of the Spirit at Pentecost sent the disciples out into the Jerusalem streets praising God in the particular languages of those gathered to celebrate from around the world (Acts 2:3–11) . . . Spirit-inspired praise uttered in indigenous language was a part of the church from the beginning.[15]

[14] Isa. 49:6.
[15] J. Perigo, 'Getting Past the Western vs. Indigenous Hymnody Debate: Viewing Turkish Hymnody through a Pneumatological Framework', presented at the 43rd Annual Meeting of the Society for Pentecostal Studies.

He goes on to quote Harold Best, who writes memorably,

> Pentecost tells us that one artistic tongue is only a start and a thousand will never suffice. There is not a single chosen language or artistic or musical style that, better than all others, can capture and repeat back the fullness of the glory of God. One culture has capabilities, nuances, and creative ways that others simply do not possess. This truism cannot be avoided. Cultures are not infinite. No single one can hold the wholeness of praise and worship or the fullness of the counsel of God.[16]

One Sunday morning many years ago my wife and I sat in a local church in a village in rural East Africa. Unable to understand any Swahili, I found I could make very little sense of most of the service, but to my surprise, there was a dreary heaviness to the gathering. After a while I noticed that, despite not understanding any of the words of the songs, I knew all the tunes. Some were English hymn tunes and others came from early American gospel songs. A rather solemn brass band accompanied the singing in a way that was reminiscent almost of a Western military parade. What was clear was that none of it was resonating with the people of the village. Towards the end of the service, however, the brass band put their instruments down. A group of local musicians began beating drums, playing their traditional instruments and singing their own, locally composed songs. The dreariness of the service lifted in an instant as everyone began to sing. The church was alive with the praise of God and we were hearing the new song – vibrant, clear and authentic.

Any discussion about worship must have as its overriding priority the glory of God, and in the light of that glory, narrow, parochial discussions about *how* we worship will always feel inadequate and shallow. A passion for the glory of God is the fuel of authentic worship, the motivation of biblical mission and the inspiration of true theology. It is this passion which sets our hearts beating in time to the rhythm of this psalm, as we realize that the magnificent splendour of the all-satisfying glory of God is such that he *must* be honoured, loved and worshipped by all the peoples of the earth. It is this passion which transforms us from being 'consumers' who look for worship 'just as we like it', into global ambassadors who long to see him praised by people completely unlike ourselves, as they receive his salvation and add their distinctive voices to the great song, to make it new again.

---

[16] H. Best, *Music Through the Eyes of Faith* (San Francisco: HarperCollins, 1993), p. 67.

2. . . . so all must hear (2b–3)

> *Proclaim his salvation day after day.*
> *Declare his glory among the nations,*
> *his marvellous deeds among all peoples.*

If Yahweh is to be loved and worshipped *in all the earth* (1), it is vital that *all the earth* should hear about him: the *new song* must be sung *among the nations* (3). So the psalm continues with strong encouragement to fill the earth with the sound of his truth.

Proclaim[17] *his salvation day after day* (2b) – that is, we are to tell the good news of his acts of salvation not as a 'hit and run' activity but in a continuing, day-after-day proclamation. We cannot be sure which particular 'acts of salvation' were in the mind of the author of the psalm nor the editors who included it in this book of the Psalms. Was it the original rescue from Egypt, the subduing of Israel's enemies under David, the return from exile and the rebuilding of the temple, or any one of numerous other deliverances God had granted? Perhaps it is best not to know for certain, so that the psalm is not limited by one historical context but available to resource the worship of God's people in many different situations. As Christian readers of this psalm, however, the frame of reference is clear. God's supreme acts of salvation (of which all the other deliverances had been an anticipation) have been accomplished through his Son, Jesus Christ, through his incarnation, death, resurrection and ascension to glory. Proclaiming 'Jesus Christ and him crucified'[18] remains at the heart of our mission.

Declaring his glory . . . his marvellous deeds (3). Our culture is marked by cutting satire and pervasive cynicism; the glory it so often celebrates is the thin and transient glory of mere celebrity. In such a culture (and in many other cultures too), the church is called to sing the new song: a song not of cynicism but of praise that celebrates the eternal glory of God and marvels at his saving acts.

Imagine for a moment that you have bought a new top-of-the-range car and you are describing it to a friend. Most of us would not just give a list of a few of the materials from which it was made, point out that it has four wheels and an exhaust pipe, quote a couple of statistics and then leave it at that. Rather we would say how sleek the design is, how powerful is the response when our right foot touches the floor, how comfortable the seats are, how efficient the engine is and how good it feels to drive, and then we would invite

---

[17] LXX *euangelizō*, the word from which we get our word 'evangelize'.
[18] 1 Cor. 2:2.

them to get inside while we take them for a spin! The analogy is imperfect but it gives us some feel for the model of mission in this psalm: a *new song* sung among the nations, that celebrates the saving goodness of God! In Western cultures today, many of us feel pressure to keep the new song rather toned down. If we speak of religious matters at all, we feel it expedient to do so in an understated way and with an air of sophisticated detachment. This psalm challenges us to think differently. We are not called merely to pass on some religious information, or to describe another option in the pluralistic world of religious possibilities; our mission is to declare the *glory* of Yahweh among the nations and to celebrate his *marvellous* deeds in the hearing of all people. Let the nations know of the Father who loves us, the Christ who died for our sins and rose in victory, and the Spirit whose transforming presence has entered our lives. Let them know that we love him and rejoice to know him. Let them know that his grace has won us, his glory satisfies us and his promises have become our eternal hope. Let them know that his glory is too magnificent for it to be only people like us who praise him; the new song can be theirs to sing as well. As the apostle Peter put it – we 'declare the *praises* of him who called us out of darkness into his wonderful light'.[19]

Tim Keller describes this vision as 'world-winning worship':

> God commanded Israel to invite the nations to join in declaring his glory. The vision of Zion was that it would be the centre of world-winning worship ... Throughout the Old Testament Scriptures believers are continually told to sing and to praise God before the unbelieving nations (Ps. 105, see also Pss 47:1; 100:1–5). As God's people praise him, the nations are summoned and called to join in song.[20]

We often assume that we are best to keep evangelism and worship as distinct as possible, with evangelistic 'events' stripped of the prayers and praise that make up our regular services. The Bible, however, calls us not to underestimate the missional potency of a worshipping church.

3. *For* the Lord is God overall (4–6)

Authentic praise and worship is by definition a response to God's initiative in revelation. As we have seen previously, true praise has

---

[19] 1 Pet. 2:9.
[20] T. Keller, *Center Church* (Grand Rapids: Zondervan, 2012), p. 300.

its reasons, and those reasons are discovered in biblical truth. This is why true worship and true theology must exist in a continuous two-way conversation if both are to flourish. The reasons for worship in Psalm 96 reflect the global, missional vision of the psalm as a whole – these are reasons for *all the earth* (1) to praise him.

a. His unrivalled greatness (4–5)

For great is the LORD, and greatly to be praised (4a, NRSV).

The greatness of God (his supreme power and sovereignty) should in some sense be reflected in the greatness of our responsive praise (its vehemence and energy): this is no mumbled hymn in a sleepy service! The focus, however, is on the unrivalled nature of that greatness. The psalmist challenges the politically correct consensus of our day with its superficial pluralism; he insists that *the LORD . . . is to be feared above all gods* (4b), that is, he is to be recognized, honoured, obeyed and revered above all other gods. The nations whom this psalm addresses have their 'gods' but Yahweh is by far supreme over them all. Indeed, 'Yahweh alone is God, and all the other deities are "fakes." They cannot be gods, because Yahweh alone has made . . . the heavens.'[21]

Many commentators have noted the numerous connections between Psalm 96 and Isaiah 40 – 66. One of those connection points is a powerful critique of idolatry. For example Isaiah 44:9–20[22] includes an extended parody of idol-making.

> All who make idols are nothing,
> and the things they treasure are worthless . . .
> He cut down cedars . . .
> Half of the wood he burns in the fire;
> over it he prepares his meal,
> he roasts his meat and eats his fill.
> He also warms himself and says,
> 'Ah! I am warm; I see the fire.'
> From the rest he makes a god, his idol;
> he bows down to it and worships.
> He prays to it and says,
> 'Save me! You are my god!'[23]

It is utter folly to worship what our own hands have made; rather, we are to worship the One *who made us with his hands*, the Lord

---

[21] Longman and Garland, *Psalms*, p. 723.
[22] See also Isa. 40:18–24 and 41:21–24.
[23] Isa. 44:9–17.

our great Creator! With this assertion of Yahweh's unrivalled greatness, the new song 'radically displaces the old gods whose former worshippers must now bring all their worship into the courts of the LORD'.[24] He alone is the Creator of all the earth; therefore all the earth is called to praise him.

b. His unfading splendour (6)

The psalmist pictures Yahweh enthroned in his heavenly sanctuary[25] with *splendour and majesty* before him, personified as if they were great angels in his royal entourage, together with *glory and strength*. The gods of the nations are lumps of wood, surrounded only by superstition and blindness; Yahweh is the eternal God surrounded with magnificent splendour in his heavenly sanctuary and since the sanctuary is heavenly and eternal, the splendour is unfading.

However, it is not enough simply to observe the splendour, majesty, strength and glory of God; these realities demand a response of worship. So in verse seven the cycle of the psalm begins again, calling the nations to *ascribe* these qualities to Yahweh.

4. All are called to worship . . . (7–9)

There is a sense of building intensity through these verses, like a spiral spring being wound up, turn by turn. The three calls to *sing* to Yahweh (1–2) are now matched by three calls to the nations[26] to *ascribe* glory to him (7–8). First they praise his *glory and strength* (7), perhaps because they see these things revealed in creation. Then they begin to recognize his uniqueness as their praise next acknowledges *the glory due to his name* (8a). Next the nations are pictured travelling from the ends of the earth to enter *his courts* (probably the outer courtyard of the tabernacle/temple), bringing their tribute offerings (8b) to Yahweh whom they now acknowledge as the only true God. Finally they fall before him in the overwhelming beauty of his holy presence (9a), and, with trembling (9b) joy, worship the God who *is to be feared above all gods* (4b).

[24] Wright, *Mission of God*, p. 134.

[25] Some commentators argue that this should be taken as the earthly sanctuary (the temple), but a reference to the heavenly sanctuary seems the more natural reading. It is nonetheless true that his splendour, majesty, strength and glory are evident in creation (Rom. 1:20).

[26] 'Families of nations' (7, NIV) is probably best understood as 'families/clans of the nations' (see ESV, NRSV), rather than as groups of nations.

The same vision, again, is found in Isaiah. Speaking to Israel of a time to come when 'nations will come to your light',[27] he reassures them:

> All from Sheba will come,
>   bearing gold and incense
>   and proclaiming the praise of the LORD.
> All Kedar's flocks will be gathered to you,
>   the rams of Nebaioth will serve you;
> they will be accepted as offerings on my altar,
>   and I will adorn my glorious temple.[28]

Today that vision is being fulfilled before our eyes. The people of Christ are singing the *new song* among the nations and as they do, the global church is growing throughout the world. Men and women from the nations are hearing the gospel and coming to join in the new song as they put their faith in Jesus. However, the vision of Psalm 96 reaches further even than this, right into the new creation. In his vision of the heavenly Jerusalem, the writer of Revelation records:

> I did not see a temple in the city, because the Lord God Almighty and the Lamb are its temple. The city does not need the sun or the moon to shine on it, for the glory of God gives it light, and the Lamb is its lamp. The nations will walk by its light, and the kings of the earth will bring their splendour into it. On no day will its gates ever be shut, for there will be no night there. The glory and honour of the nations will be brought into it.[29]

'Mission exists because worship doesn't', writes John Piper in the striking opening to his book *Let the Nations Be Glad.*[30] That is the heartbeat of this psalm. It should trouble us that though the Lord Jesus created every one of us, he is worshipped by so few of us; that though he is Lord of all, he is not obeyed by all; that though his splendour and glory are unrivalled in all the nations, still so many in the nations do not honour, love and treasure him. The connection between worship and mission does not stop there, though. 'Worship is the fuel and goal of missions,' Piper continues. 'It's the goal of missions because in missions we simply aim to bring the nations into the white-hot enjoyment of God's glory ... [it is the fuel of missions because] passion for God in worship precedes the offer

---

[27] Isa. 60:3.
[28] Isa. 60:6–7.
[29] Rev. 21:22–26.
[30] J. Piper, *Let the Nations Be Glad* (Leicester: Inter-Varsity Press, 2003), p. 17.

of God in preaching. You can't commend what you don't cherish.'[31] Psalm 96 invites us to go one step further still. Worship is not only the fuel and goal of mission, it is also one of the God-appointed *means* of mission as, singing the new song before the nations, we invite them to come and *worship the* Lord *in the splendour of his holiness* (9).

Mission is not a special-interest project for a few Christians; it is the calling of every worshipper.

5. . . . so all must hear (10)

While the niv implies that the message to the nations is simply that *the* Lord *reigns* (10a), most translations suggest that it is the whole of the verse that they must hear.

> *Say among the nations, 'The* Lord *reigns!*
> *Yes, the world is established; it shall never be moved;*
> *he will judge the peoples with equity'* (10, esv).

Over against the claims of the false gods, the people of God announce the unique reign of Yahweh. He is sovereign over all creation (*The* Lord *reigns*); he sustains all creation (*Yes, the world is established; it shall never be moved*); he will judge all creation (*he will judge the peoples with equity*).

6. *For* the Lord is judge of all (11–13)

We often take the idea of divine judgment to be rather bad news which we prefer not to mention if we can help it. In the world view of Psalm 96, we are mistaken, however, for in the final verses of the psalm judgment is seen as decidedly good news. God is coming to deal with evil and put things right, and at this news creation erupts with celebration!

> *Let the heavens rejoice, let the earth be glad;*
> *let the sea resound, and all that is in it.*
> *Let the fields be jubilant, and everything in them;*
> *let all the trees of the forest sing for joy.*
> *Let all creation rejoice before the* Lord, *for he comes,*
> *he comes to judge the earth.*
> *He will judge the world in righteousness*
> *and the peoples in his faithfulness.*

[31] Ibid.

The new song 'transforms the old world into the anticipated right-eousness and rejoicing of the reign of the Lord'.[32] God is going to come to our world: our world that is broken by human sin and rebellion; our world that is torn apart by injustice, violence and greed; our world in which innocent people are slaughtered by terrorists and the poor are kept poor and made poorer. When he comes he will put all things right and, from this marred and broken creation, he will 'create new heavens and a new earth' in which 'the sound of weeping and of crying will be heard ... no more'.[33] This is good news indeed; news which will bring liberty to the whole creation (Rom. 8:21). We must never forget, however, that in this judgment it is God who sets the terms. *He will judge the world in righteousness and the peoples in his faithfulness* (13b). This was the recognition that made the apostle Paul sing the *new song* so boldly to people in the ancient world, enslaved by idolatry and dead to the living God. He understood that God stepping in as judge to put things right would have to mean sinful humanity facing divine wrath and he did not hesitate to say so in his preaching (e.g., Acts 17:31). Describing how the Thessalonians' response to this message had been reported to him, he says, 'They tell how you turned to God from idols to serve the living and true God, and to wait for his Son from heaven, whom he raised from the dead – Jesus, who rescues us from the coming wrath.'[34]

Yahweh is the great ruler of all the nations and his glory is such that it demands the worship of all the nations. Since he demands the worship of all the nations, they must all hear his call to worship. Yahweh is also the judge of all the nations and he will come to put things right! Since he is the judge of all, *all* must hear how they should be ready to meet him at his coming.

7. Conclusion

This inspirational psalm is, on reflection, a rather challenging psalm to sing. Few of us, I suspect, are so passionate for the glory of God that we could say our hearts truly beat in time to its missional rhythm. Most of us, I suggest, have still to make the journey from the 'consumer worshipper' (one who looks to find worship done just the way they like it) to the 'missional worshipper' (one whose first priority is to enable others to sing the new song for themselves, even if they come from entirely different backgrounds and adopt culturally very different forms).

[32] Wright, *Mission of God*, p. 134.
[33] Isa. 65:17–19.
[34] 1 Thess. 1:9–10.

Of course we expect cultural sensitivity when we send mission partners to other countries, but what about such sensitivity in our own contexts, where the cultural gap between the generations and sub-cultures of our society can be as wide as that imposed by many oceans? I remember a staff meeting in our own church when we were reflecting on one of the previous day's services. A younger member of staff, who said that it had been a good service added, 'But what was that hymn? It was completely impossible to learn. The notes were all over the place!' In the same meeting another person who was a little older said, 'Of course, the trouble with the newer songs is that they're just not made for congregational worship – you can't sing them!' The cultural gap between the generations can be so large that the music of one is almost completely unintelligible to the other. The music of the newer songs typically has relatively static harmonies but is driven by complex rhythms, while the music of the older hymns has relatively simple rhythms but is driven by more complex movement of harmonies.[35] It is no wonder that many struggle to span the cultural divide! How then do we respond?

We need to accept that the missional task in our complex, multi-cultural society is likely to demand a great deal of flexibility on style. We should not expect all churches to be the same and we need to be slow to dismiss other churches as hopelessly traditional on the one hand or worryingly superficial on the other. Realistically, any style of worship is likely to feel alienating to at least some of the unchurched people who visit our churches. I suspect that, in the United Kingdom at least, the Christian community (particularly the evangelical community, of which I am a part) would be well served by an enthusiastic embracing of a wider range of cultural styles, rather than perpetuating our tendency to adopt a single, dominant, 'acceptable' style.

In his book *With One Voice*, Reggie M. Kidd develops the idea of Jesus as 'the singing Saviour'. He looks back to Psalm 22, the great abandonment lament quoted by Jesus on the cross, and points out that the psalm moves from the aloneness of abandonment to the fellowship of 'praise in the great assembly'.[36] 'The singer is surrounded in worship by Jew and Gentile (vv.23,27), poor and rich (vv.26,29) and generations past and generations to come (vv.29-31) . . . a vast and variegated assembly of

[35] If you doubt this, ask an organist to make an attempt on 'The Greatest Day in History' by Tim Hughes and Ben Cantelon and ask a guitarist to play Matthew Bridges' 'Crown him with many crowns' without skipping any of the chords. Both will be funny, but neither will work!

[36] Ps. 22:25.

worship'.[37] He goes on to suggest that, reflecting this diversity, the musical aspect of the church's worship should encompass a wide variety of cultural expressions from high art, through the everyday music of the people, to music on the cutting edge of contemporary artistic expression.[38] 'Let me suggest that every group brings its own voice, but no group brings the official voice.'[39]

Rather than give way to the attitudes of cultural supremacy that we would (rightly) never tolerate in our 'missionaries', we need to face the fact that in today's world *all of us are called to cross-cultural mission.* Whatever our preferences may be, singing the new song 'among the nations' will often mean singing it in a cultural form that is somewhat alien to us and when others join in the new song the cultural form may be different again. The worshippers whose worship has been shaped by Psalm 96 will be less inclined to complain that, faced with such an experience, their worship has been compromised and more inclined to rejoice that they have heard the song once again.

---

[37] R. M. Kidd, *With One Voice: Discovering Christ's Song in Our Worship* (Grand Rapids: Baker Books, 2005), p. 125.

[38] He refers to these three respectively as the 'Bach' voice, the 'Bubba' voice and the Blues Brothers, and makes clear that no one church is likely to encompass all these voices successfully, but that different churches can find their own distinct voice.

[39] Kidd, *With One Voice*, p. 126.

Part 3
Worship and the life of the Holy Spirit

2 Corinthians 3
15. The transformative Spirit

Lepe Beach lies on the south coast of England just a few miles from my home. With its nearby country park, beautiful views of the Isle of Wight and sheltered coastal waters, it is a favourite destination for many local families wanting a day out by the sea. Despite its current tranquillity, this unlikely, remote spot has a fascinating wartime history. In the early summer of 1944, the narrow country roads and secluded woodlands around Lepe started to fill with hundreds of troops, along with their associated vehicles and ammunition. It was from this quiet beach that they would leave for what is now recognized as one of the greatest feats in military history: the D-Day landings on the coast of Normandy. This was also one of the sites where the 'Mulberry Harbours' were constructed before being floated across the sea to enable necessary supplies to be landed for the use of the advancing allied armies. However, for the invasion to be sustained, a vast, secure, continuing supply of fuel was needed, and again Lepe was to play a strategic role. Four pipelines, each over seventy miles in length, were laid from here (via Shanklin on the Isle of Wight) to Cherbourg. The project was known as P.L.U.T.O. (Pipe Line Under The Ocean) and the pipes successfully supplied millions of tonnes of fuel to power the Allied invasion.

The life and mission of the Christian church similarly required access to a vast, secure and continuing supply of spiritual power as it was commissioned to advance across the globe with the gospel.[1] According to the risen Christ it was precisely in the ministry of the Holy Spirit that such power was to be found (Luke 24:49; Acts 1:8)

---

[1] I am grateful to my friend Rev. Gordon Tuck of Testwood Baptist Church for sharing this illustration with me. It is sometimes cautioned that analogies to the work of the Spirit which appeal to inanimate materials can deflect attention from his personhood. This is a proper concern of course, but it does not prevent the NT from using the analogies of wind (John 3:8) and fire (Luke 3:16)!

and the book of Acts tells the thrilling story of his world-changing work. We saw in the previous chapter of this book that the mission, theology and worship of the church are intimately connected and cannot be easily separated. We also began to explore the central significance of the Spirit's work to our worship in chapter 5. It is no surprise therefore that our focus should be upon him in the final section of this book. Our first passage focuses on the Spirit both as a glorious gift of the new covenant and as a transformational gift in the lives of Christian believers.

It is clear even from a casual reading of 2 Corinthians that Paul's ministry was under attack in Corinth. A closer reading reveals that his relationship with the Corinthian church had long been rather turbulent,[2] but as he writes it appears that the conflict has reached a crisis point.[3] Certain changes in his travel plans have led to the allegation that Paul is unreliable and ungodly (2 Cor. 1:15–17); support for Paul's collection for the suffering believers in Jerusalem has stalled (2 Cor. 8:7–11); some in the church continue to defy his earlier calls to withdraw from the idolatry and immorality of Corinth (2 Cor. 6:14 – 17:1);[4] some remain embarrassed by his unwillingness to accept patronage from the wealthier members of the congregation and are accusing him of obtaining support by manipulation (2 Cor. 11:7–11; 4:2; 7:2); most worryingly of all, people whom Paul regards as 'false apostles' are influencing the Corinthian church to the extent that he fears for the survival of his connection with the believers there (2 Cor. 10:12 – 12:13). Central to Paul's response is that the ministry of the *new covenant* (6) – and therefore his own ministry – is a *ministry of the Spirit* (8) and that its glory far transcends the ministry of the old covenant which was *of the letter* (6) (that is, it concerned obedience to the law of Moses). This bold contrast sets the tone for the whole passage, which Gordon Fee describes as 'one of the most significant Spirit passages in the Pauline corpus'.[5]

1. A heart-changing ministry (1–6)

The providing of written 'references' is a widely acknowledged aspect of good practice for businesses recruiting new staff and churches

---

[2] See, for example, the reference to 'another painful visit' (2 Cor. 2:1) and to his previous letter which 'hurt' them (2 Cor. 7:8).

[3] For a full discussion of the trouble see P. Barnett, *The Second Epistle to the Corinthians*, NICNT (Grand Rapids: Eerdmans, 1997), pp. 31–40 and D. E. Garland, *2 Corinthians*, NAC 29 (Nashville: B&H Publishing, 1999), pp. 26–33.

[4] And cf. 1 Cor. 5 and 8.

[5] G. D. Fee, *God's Empowering Presence* (Peabody: Hendrickson Publishers, Inc., 1994), p. 297.

receiving new people into membership (if their polity includes the idea of 'membership'). People are not always what they first seem to be, and the view of a third party can provide helpful reassurance and insight. In the first-century Roman world, travellers (especially itinerant speakers and philosophers) were similarly expected to carry letters of recommendation with them to help secure a good reception in a new town.[6] Paul is not against this practice in principle,[7] but he is clearly distressed by the suggestion that he would need such letters in Corinth, a church that he himself had planted (Acts 18). *Are we beginning to commend ourselves again? Or do we need, like some people, letters of recommendation to you or from you* (1)?

The previous chapter concluded with Paul contrasting his own 'sincerity' with the 'many' who 'peddle the word of God for profit'.[8] It is very likely that this is an early reference to the false apostles (2 Cor. 11:13) whose assault on Paul's authority becomes such a major theme later in the letter. One of their accusations (which appears to have taken root in the Corinthian church) is that Paul's failure to produce *letters of recommendation* (1) in effect means that 'his apostolic legitimacy exists because he says it does'[9] – he is *commending himself* (1). Paul responds with a somewhat fluid metaphor[10] which identifies the Corinthian believers themselves as his *letter* of recommendation. *You yourselves are our letter, written on our hearts, known and read by everyone* (2).

The approach is a masterstroke of pastoral tact, appealing directly to the hearts of the believers over the heads of the false apostles. They themselves are the only letter of recommendation he needs, for their transformed lives bear witness to the power and authenticity of his ministry (cf. 1 Cor. 9:2–3). Not only so, but his heartfelt affection for them is such that he speaks of them wherever he goes, so that this 'letter' is *known and read by everyone* (2). Nonetheless, this is not just a piece of great pastoral wisdom; Paul is making a deeper theological point. The 'peddlers' may have their letters of recommendation

---

[6] Linda Belville cites a letter from *Zenon Papyri* 2026 as typical. 'Philo, the bearer of this letter to you, has been known to me for a considerable time . . . Be so good, therefore, as to make his acquaintance and introduce him to other persons of standing, assisting him actively, both for my sake and for that of the young man himself. For he is worthy of your consideration . . .' (L. L. Belville, *2 Corinthians*, IVPNTC (Leicester: Inter-Varsity Press, 1996), p. 87.

[7] His letter to Philemon is a notable example of the practice, after all.

[8] 2 Cor. 2:17.

[9] Barnett, *Second Corinthians*, p. 162.

[10] For example, the letter is initially said to be written on Paul's own heart (v. 2) but then written on the fleshly hearts of the Corinthian believers (v. 3). The ties to the new covenant promises are such that the second of these is probably paramount in his thinking, but his affection for them is such that the letter is also carried on his own heart.

but in the end the only approval they contain is human approval. Paul's apostolic ministry, by contrast, rests on divine commissioning (2 Cor. 1:1; cf. 1 Cor. 4:3–4) and he is unwilling to make it subject to the whims of human approval. The commendation he seeks is neither from himself nor from other people but from God himself, and this is exactly the kind of commendation he is claiming here, for the Corinthians are *a letter from Christ, the result of our ministry, written not with ink but with the Spirit of the living God, not on tablets of stone but on tablets of human* [lit. 'fleshly'] *hearts* (3).

These words are rich in Old Testament allusions. The tablets of stone recall the giving of the Ten Commandments to Moses, inscribed on tablets of stone (Exod. 31:18) while the idea of the Spirit of God writing on human (*'fleshly'*) hearts recalls the new covenant promises of both Jeremiah (Jer. 31:31–34) and Ezekiel:

> I will give you a new heart and put a new spirit in you; I will remove from you your heart of stone and give you a heart of *flesh*. And I will put my Spirit in you and move you to follow my decrees and be careful to keep my laws.[11]

As Barnett points out, Ezekiel's promise assumes that the stone tablets of the law have been internalized as 'hearts of stone' in the Israelites who have been hardened and desensitized through their disobedience. However, the promise of the new covenant is that the law of God will be 'internalised in hearts made alive by the Spirit of the living God'[12] so that they are inwardly moved to obedience. It is precisely this work of the Spirit that the new believers in Corinth have experienced as a result of Paul's ministry there. The Holy Spirit has changed their hearts (just as Ezekiel had promised) and the reality of his powerful work is so tangible, that it can be *read by everyone* (2). The way is thus prepared for Paul's dramatic conclusion that God has made him (and his co-workers) *competent as ministers of a new covenant* (6), which brings life by the Spirit rather than death through the law (*the letter*, 6b).[13]

Precisely how much of Paul's argument here (and in the verses that follow) is a response to the specific theology of the 'peddlers' is debated by the scholars.[14] However, given the emphasis on their

---

[11] Ezek. 36:26–27.

[12] Barnett, *Second Corinthians*, p. 169.

[13] Paul's understanding of how the letter 'kills' is clearly set out in Romans 7:7–11.

[14] Barnett is very clear that 'Paul is connecting the newcomers' ministry with the Mosaic covenant' (*Second Corinthians*, p. 169). Others are generally more cautious. Fee accepts that 'it seems likely that the contrast between himself and Moses . . . is in some way in response to the opponents' but expresses misgivings as to whether

Jewish credentials in later chapters (e.g. 2 Cor. 11:22), it seems likely that the extended contrast here between Paul's own (new covenant) ministry and the (old covenant) ministry of Moses is calculated to place the ministry of his detractors in Corinth firmly on the side of Moses. 'Paul implies that the ministry of those who have newly arrived, who bear "ink-written" letters, and who promote "tablets of stone" is hopelessly anachronistic. Their day has ended; another has dawned. The work of the Spirit is the evidence of that.'[15]

Whatever Paul may or may not be implying about the theology of his opponents, his claim for his own ministry is clear. Through the preaching of his gospel, the promises of the new covenant are being fulfilled. The *Spirit of the living God* (3) is at work: not just issuing instructions but changing hearts; not only confirming the condemnation and death that arise from human failure, but imparting life (6), by his indwelling presence.[16] The same transformation is described in the opening chapter of the letter, using different metaphors which underline the assurance and confidence that the Holy Spirit gives. 'Now it is God who makes both us and you stand firm in Christ. He anointed us, set his seal of ownership on us, and put his Spirit in our hearts as a deposit, guaranteeing what is to come.'[17] He is the eschatological Spirit, his indwelling presence foreshadowing the final dwelling of God among his people in the new creation (Rev. 21:3) when we the servants of Christ will see his face (Rev. 22:4).

Throughout Scripture, true worship involves a response of obedient faith to the word of God and a reverent, joyful encounter with the presence of God.[18] Jesus defines what this means in the new covenant era when he explains that 'the true worshippers will worship the Father *in the Spirit* and in truth'.[19] There is therefore no truly Christian worship that does not take seriously the indwelling presence of the Holy Spirit, moving in our hearts and amongst God's people. It is his presence that imparts spiritual life to our hearts (6); his presence that stirs hunger for Christ in our hearts (John 16:14–15);[20] and his presence that moves our hearts towards holiness so that our worship becomes transformational and not self-indulgent.

The ministry of the Spirit is a heart-changing ministry.

'we can thereby recreate either the theology or the origins of the opponents on the basis of what is said here' (*God's Empowering Presence*, p. 299).

[15] Barnett, *Second Corinthians*, p. 170.

[16] Notice the promise of the indwelling Spirit in Ezek. 36:27: 'I will put my Spirit *in* you . . .'

[17] 2 Cor. 1:21–22.

[18] This is the conclusion of ch. 2 of this book.

[19] John 4:23 and see ch. 5 of this book.

[20] John 16:14–15.

2. A glorious ministry (7–18a)

We have spent most of our family holidays under canvas. For many years we had a large frame tent which we took to various parts of Britain and (latterly) France. We had some excellent times, but the need for artificial light in the evenings became something of a headache. We tried everything: gas lamps, battery torches, eco-friendly wind-up lanterns and candles. They all provided some light for us for a time, but it was rarely enough and it never lasted very long. However, as our children grew up we stumbled on a radical solution – a folding camping trailer, which was able to plug in to mains electricity. Suddenly holidays had evenings again, which we spent bathed in the bright, unfading light of an electric light bulb! We never looked back.

The remaining verses of our passage turn on a very similar contrast. The ministry of *the letter* (6b) (that is, the Law of Moses) was, without doubt, a glorious ministry. Through Paul's preaching of the gospel, though, the Corinthians have become the recipients of a ministry that is far more glorious: namely the ministry *of the Spirit* (6c, 8). However, it seems that the problem in Corinth is that, under the influence of the false apostles, they *are* looking back. Paul is arguing passionately that they should think again. His argument is based on a Christian reflection on the account of Moses' radiant face in the book of Exodus.[21]

When Moses came down from Mount Sinai with the two tablets of the covenant law in his hands, he was not aware that his face was radiant because he had spoken with the LORD. When Aaron and all the Israelites saw Moses, his face was radiant, and they were afraid to come near him. But Moses called to them; so Aaron and all the leaders of the community came back to him, and he spoke to them. Afterwards all the Israelites came near him, and he gave them all the commands the LORD had given him on Mount Sinai.

When Moses finished speaking to them, he put a veil over his face. But whenever he entered the LORD's presence to speak with him, he removed the veil until he came out. And when he came out and told the Israelites what he had been commanded, they saw that his face was radiant. Then Moses would put the veil back over his face until he went in to speak with the LORD.[22]

---

[21] Barnett, in line with most contemporary commentators, describes Paul's approach as a 'Christian Midrash' (*Second Corinthians*, p. 178).

[22] Exod. 34:29–35.

a. Greater glory (7–11)

The glory of the ministry of the old (Mosaic) covenant is unmistakable in the Exodus account. Moses descends from Mount Sinai carrying the two tablets of the Decalogue and his face is radiant with the glory of Yahweh, with whom he has spoken. Paul is quite ready to acknowledge this *glory* (7), but he insists that the new covenant *ministry of the Spirit* is *more glorious* still (8). The argument is built around three 'how much more . . .' contrasts.[23]

(i) Contrast one: The ministry of death and the ministry of the Spirit (7–8)

The groundwork for this contrast has all been done in verses 1–6. The old covenant wrote God's law *in letters on stone* (7);[24] the new covenant writes God's law on *tablets of human hearts* (3)[25] by the indwelling Holy Spirit. The old covenant therefore *brought death* (7) because it gave no power to perform what it commanded; the new covenant, however, *gives life* (6) because the indwelling Spirit motivates and energizes the obedience of the people of God so that they live the (true) life to which they are called.[26] Nonetheless, this old covenant ministry was truly glorious: it *came with glory* (7), evidenced in the radiant face of Moses. How much more glorious, then, is the life-giving new covenant *ministry of the Spirit* (of which Paul himself has been made a *minister*, 6), who opens our blind eyes to see the 'light of the knowledge of God's glory in the face of Christ'.[27]

(ii) Contrast two: The ministry that brings condemnation and the ministry that brings righteousness (9)

The bringing together of the two words *condemnation* and *righteousness* take us firmly into the setting of the law court.[28] The old

---

[23] This form of argument from the lesser to the greater (*ad minori ad maius*) is a particular form of the *a fortiori* argument which is commonly found in Paul's writing and in Jewish legal texts.

[24] A clear reference to Exod. 34:29.

[25] Cf. Jer. 31:33; Ezek. 36:26–27.

[26] This is not a claim to sinless perfection under the new covenant, but a recognition of the reality of the work of the Spirit in bringing inner renewal, such that we (increasingly) live the life of the people of God. 'The flesh renders the law impotent, the Spirit empower us to obey it. This is not perfectionism; it is simply to say that obedience is a necessary and possible aspect of Christian discipleship. Although the law cannot secure this obedience, the Spirit can' (J. R. W. Stott, *The Message of Romans*, BST [Leicester: Inter-Varsity Press, 1994], p. 221.

[27] 2 Cor. 4:4–6.

[28] 'In this verse, righteousness is defined by contrast with condemnation; it means acquittal, justification, the act by which God puts man in the right relation with himself' (C. K. Barrett, *The Second Epistle to the Corinthians* [London: A & C Black, 1973], p. 116.)

covenant law reveals the righteous requirements of God, but by itself it serves only to deepen our guilt and condemnation due to our inability to keep it.

> Now we know that whatever the law says, it says to those who are under the law, so that every mouth may be silenced and the whole world held accountable to God. Therefore *no one will be declared righteous in God's sight by the works of the law; rather, through the law we become conscious of our sin.*[29]

Of course Paul is not here denying the reality of salvation in the Old Testament: after all he is unequivocal that both Abraham and David were 'justified' in the sight of God (Rom. 4:1–8). His point is that it was by their faith in the promise of God that they were justified, not by their obedience to the law,[30] for the law by itself condemns us. However, the new covenant ministry of the Spirit so unites us with Christ that he is condemned for our sin on the cross, while we are acquitted (justified, counted righteous) on account of his righteousness. As Paul put it a little later in 2 Corinthians, 'God made him who had no sin to be sin for us, so that in him we might become the righteousness of God'.[31] It is little wonder that he concludes that this new covenant ministry *that brings righteousness* (lit.) *overflows with glory (9)!*[32]

(iii) Contrast three: The ministry that is transitory and the ministry that is lasting (10–11)

Three times in this passage, Paul describes the glory of the old covenant ministry as *transitory* or *passing away* (7, 11, 13). The same Greek verb is used on each occasion and it is translated by other versions as *brought to an end* (ESV) or having been *set aside* (NRSV).[33] The reference is still to Exodus 34 in which the face of Moses was radiant with the glory of God – so much so that the Israelites were unable to *look steadily* at it (7). Paul, however, looks back at the radiant glory of Moses' faith from the vantage point of new covenant faith. Having seen the true 'glory of God in the face of Jesus Christ',[34] he understands that the glory revealed in Moses was a wonderful step

---

[29] Rom. 3:19–20, emphasis added.

[30] Rom. 4:1–3 and see his critique of those who look to the law for righteousness before God in Rom. 10:1–4.

[31] 2 Cor. 5:21.

[32] See Barnett, *Second Corinthians*, p. 186.

[33] The verb is *katargeō*, 'abolish, nullify . . . Though *katargeō* is elusive in translation . . . its basic meaning of rendering something inoperative is clear and constant' (*NIDNTT*, vol. 1, p. 73).

[34] 2 Cor. 4:6, ESV.

along the journey of salvation history, not its destination point. Its true purpose was to point forward to the greater glory that would be revealed when the 'Word became flesh and made his dwelling among us',[35] at which point the former glory of the old covenant would be *brought to an end* or *set aside*.[36] So it is that *what was glorious has no glory now in comparison with the surpassing glory* (10) which has been revealed in Christ. The glory of Christ, perceived by us through the ministry of the Spirit, represents the climax of divine revelation. There is nothing that will supersede it; indeed there is nothing that *could* supersede it.[37] It is the *glory of that which lasts* (11)!

We saw in chapter 5 of this book that the worship which the Father desires and which Jesus makes possible is worship 'in the Spirit and in truth'[38] and we saw how this transforms and fulfils the pattern for worship in the book of Exodus. This passage is beginning to fill out our understanding of what that might mean. Under the old covenant, God was present among his people in the tabernacle and, in a partial way, his presence could be accessed through animal sacrifice. Under the new covenant, however, the indwelling Holy Spirit brings the presence of God into our hearts, the very core of our beings.[39] He bears his own internal witness to the holy will of God, writing his law on our hearts. He opens our eyes to see the glory of God in the face of Christ, assuring us that his work on the cross is sufficient for our full justification. His indwelling life is itself a foretaste and a down payment of the Christ-saturated life of the new creation, assuring us that the glory we now see in part *is* the glory that lasts – the same glory we will see in full, when we see our Saviour face to face. New covenant worshippers delight in his presence in their hearts, nurture their awareness of his glorious unseen ministry and respond to him with obedience to his prompting, joy in his Christ-exalting work and deep assurance of our eternal hope.

b. Unveiled glory (12–18a)

There is nothing more disappointing for tourists than to visit a great

---

[35] John 1:14.

[36] 'According to Paul, that glory [i.e. the glory of Moses' face] was only ever a sign pointing forward to the great and permanent glory to come; it was not an "end" in itself' (Barnett, *Second Corinthians*, p. 183).

[37] See Heb. 1:1–4.

[38] John 4:24.

[39] In Hebrew thinking the heart is not only the centre of the emotions and feelings but also of the intellect and will. 'You think in your heart, and your heart shapes your character, choices and decisions. It is also the centre of a human being as a moral agent' (C. J. H. Wright, *Deuteronomy*, New International Bible Commentary [Peabody: Hendrickson Publishers, Inc.], p. 99).

building and find that the outside is covered in the scaffolding and tarpaulins of construction workers, so that its true magnificence cannot be seen. This, according to Paul, is the experience of worshippers under the old covenant from whom even the lesser glory which adhered to Moses is veiled. In sharp contrast, the worship of the new covenant is *bold* and bare-faced (12)[40] because *whenever anyone turns to the Lord, the veil is taken away* (16) so that they enter his presence with *freedom* (17).

Paul is continuing his Christian reflection on the shining face of Moses in Exodus 34. Throughout the previous section he has consistently maintained that the glory of Moses' face was a transitory glory, a glory that pointed beyond itself to the glory of Christ, which would therefore be set aside when he appeared. What concerns him, however, is that so many among his own (Jewish) people refused to see the glory of Moses in this way. In their view Moses (and the law covenant which was established through him) was to be seen rather as 'the final embodiment of God's salvation'.[41] To make matters worse, some with this view appeared to be infiltrating the church in Corinth. It seems to Paul that there is something obscuring their vision, so that they are unable to see the true nature of Moses' glory. This, he concludes, has been the way from the beginning, because *Moses . . . would put a veil over his face to prevent the Israelites from seeing the end of what was passing away* (13). Moreover, Moses veiled his face *because their minds were hardened* (14, NRSV) – perhaps he understood that if they saw the glory on his face, their misunderstanding of its significance would only be intensified and therefore he kept his face veiled.[42] This 'veiledness' of Moses' true glory persists, for *to this day the same veil remains when the old covenant is read. It has not been removed, because only in Christ is it taken away* (14b). The temporary veil over Moses' face has now become a lasting veil over the hearts of the people (15).

However, there is hope, because *whenever anyone turns to the Lord, the veil is taken away* (16). This seems like a wonderful and straightforward resolution of the situation: when we turn to Christ, we begin the glorious experience of unveiled worship! This is true (see v. 14), but the argument is a little more complex, because whereas we might expect Paul to go on to clarify that the Lord to whom we turn is *Christ* (reflecting general New Testament usage) he instead continues *now the Lord is **the Spirit*** (17).[43] We are probably best to

---

[40] Gk, *parrēsia*.

[41] R. P. Martin, *2 Corinthians*, WBC 40 (Waco: Word Books, 1991), p. 68.

[42] Ibid.

[43] This phrase (together with its parallel in v. 18) has been (wrongly) taken by some virtually to equate Christ and the Spirit.

imagine that Paul had the text of Exodus 34:34 in front of him: 'But whenever [Moses] entered the LORD's presence to speak with him, he removed the veil until he came out.' So, Paul notes that when Moses turned to 'the LORD' (Yahweh), he removed the veil. In an analogous fashion then, he explains that *whenever anyone turns to the Lord the veil is taken away* (16). He then immediately explains how the analogy works by clarifying that *the Lord* (to whom we turn) *is the Spirit* (17).[44] The point, then, is not that Yahweh *is* the Spirit, nor that Christ *is* the Spirit,[45] but that, just as the veil was removed when Moses turned to Yahweh, so the veil is removed whenever a person turns to embrace the new covenant ministry of the Spirit, who opens their eyes to see the glory of God in the face of Christ.[46] That glory is an unveiled glory, for *where the Spirit of the Lord is there is freedom* (17b)[47] – freedom from the veil, freedom to behold, freedom to worship.

We are now more than ready for Paul's glorious declaration that, as new covenant believers who have embraced the Christ-exalting ministry of the Holy Spirit of God, we *with unveiled faces contemplate*[48] *the Lord's glory* (18a). In a moment we will see the conclusion of Paul's argument, but it is worth pausing to savour this moment. This is the worship which the Holy Spirit has made possible by uniting us with Christ. Shadow has given way to reality; a transitory glory has given way to lasting glory; the veiled glory of the old covenant has given way to the unveiled glory of the new! The way is thus open for worship which is *very bold* (12) as we claim our new covenant right to draw near to God (Heb. 10:22) in the Holy Spirit and to feast our souls on the holy magnificence of his glory unveiled to us by Christ. Here, surely, is a vision of worship that is wonderfully intimate yet profoundly reverent; deeply experiential yet nurtured in the soil of gospel truth; gloriously satisfying yet provoking ever deeper hunger for the consummate glory of the new creation.

---

[44] Fee expresses it as 'Now "the Lord" stands for the Spirit' (*Empowering Presence*, p. 311).

[45] Note that the Spirit is 'the Spirit *of the Lord*' in v. 17b, so Paul cannot be equating Christ and the Spirit.

[46] I think the clearest explanation is probably that of Linda Belville in *2 Corinthians*, pp. 109–110.

[47] 'The meaning of "freedom" here has been much debated and, at the popular level, much abused. In context it refers primarily to the freedom from "the veil" as that has been interpreted in v15, as lying yet over the hearts of those in the synagogue at the hearing of the old covenant' (Fee, *Empowering Presence*, p. 313).

[48] It is possible that this should be translated 'we . . . reflect the Lord's glory' (NIV 1984) but the balance of opinion is in favour of the NIV 2011. For the arguments, see Fee, *Empowering Presence*, pp. 316–317.

3. A transformative ministry (18)

I trace my own love of music – especially my aspiration to play the piano – back to a particular moment in my childhood. I had already begun to have piano lessons which I tolerated with moderate interest, but one day my parents took me to one of the evangelistic 'tent crusades' that were popular at the time. A smartly dressed choir was led by a flamboyant pianist-conductor whose extraordinary energy and dexterity left me completely mesmerized. From that day on I had a vision of what I wanted to be – which proved more motivational than any number of piano lessons! Similarly, our passage finishes with Paul concluding that our unveiled contemplation of the glory of Christ by the Spirit gives us a transformative vision of what we want to be as the people of God: *We all, who with unveiled faces contemplate the Lord's glory, are being transformed into his image with ever-increasing glory, which comes from the Lord, who is the Spirit* (18).

Paul's gospel was always (superficially at least) vulnerable to the attack that it gave insufficient motivation for moral transformation.[49] If the ministry *of the letter* (6) (that is, the Mosaic Law) has truly been *set aside* (7, 11, 13, NRSV) by the coming of the *ministry of the Spirit* (6, 8), what will guide and motivate the new covenant people of God to holiness? Paul's answer is that the ministry of the Spirit is a transformative ministry. He develops this idea in a number of ways in his letters[50] but here the focus is on the contemplation of the glory of Christ *with unveiled faces*, to which the Spirit leads us. This vision of what we want to be as the people of God proves to be more motivational and more transformative than any number of attempts at moral education, for as we contemplate his glory we are *transformed into his image with ever-increasing glory* (18).

An important test of authentic worship, therefore, is whether or not it motivates us to Christ-likeness. Or, to put the challenge a little differently, authentic worship must be *Christ-centred, contemplative and transformational*. It must be *Christ-centred*, for it is the unveiled vision of *his* glory which motivates our transformation. It must be *contemplative*, because it is not enough for us simply to know the truth about Jesus; we need space, encouragement and help to reflect on that truth, consider it, absorb it into our hearts and respond by loving Jesus for who he is. It must be *transformational*, because the Lord whose glory we contemplate is holy and the Spirit who

[49] He frequently had to offer a defence at this point, see e.g. the extended argument in Rom. 6 – 8.
[50] See especially Rom. 7 – 8 and Gal. 5.

energizes our contemplation is the *Holy* Spirit. We cannot claim truly to love and worship Christ if we do not desire to be transformed into his likeness.

1 Corinthians 12 – 13
16. The empowering Spirit I: The gifts of the Spirit for the church

Now to each one the manifestation of the Spirit is given for the common good (12:7).

With these positive and deeply encouraging words the apostle Paul introduces his first list of spiritual gifts in 1 Corinthians 12.[1] Three points are immediately clear:

- Spiritual gifts are for all of God's people, for they are given *to each one.*
- Spiritual gifts demonstrate the reality and power of the Holy Spirit's presence in the life of the church, for they are a *manifestation of the Spirit.*
- Spiritual gifts are given not for the glory of those who exercise them but for the benefit of the whole church, for they are given *for the common good.*[2]

A wonderfully compelling picture of the life of the church emerges. Here is a *collegial* community in which spiritual power is not concentrated in the hands of one or two outstanding leaders, but distributed to each one by the wisdom of God. Here is a *supernatural* community which is not simply a social club of people who share a common interest, but a living organism – a body, animated by the present and active Spirit of God. Here is an *inclusive* community which grows not by the parading of the small number of gifts given to celebrity performers but by giving space for the diverse contributions of every member to flourish. Those who gather for worship

---

[1] This verse also gives the heading to D. A. Carson's masterly exposition of these chapters, *Showing the Spirit: A Theological Exposition of 1 Corinthians 12–14* (Grand Rapids: Baker Book House Company, 1987).
[2] Gk, 'for (sc. general) profit', hence 'the common good'.

in this kind of church will not come as spectators but as participants, not only to receive but also give, not only to be blessed but also to be a blessing. Given such an attractive vision for the life of the church, and given the breadth of support for it in the New Testament,[3] we might expect that the widespread exercise of spiritual gifts within the churches would be welcomed enthusiastically. The reality has always been more complex, however, as we will see in this chapter and the next. Nonetheless, our understanding will be better served if we avoid approaching these chapters as a 'problem passage' and simply do our best to understand and apply what Paul says.

1. The gifts of the Holy Spirit and the body of Christ (1 Cor. 12)

Now about the gifts of the Spirit,[4] brothers and sisters, I do not want you to be uninformed (1). Paul seems to regard a proper understanding of spiritual gifts as a high priority for the Corinthian believers in their congregational life and worship. Their problem is not their interest in these things, but the superficiality of their interest. So he writes not to stamp out their enthusiasm but to fill out their understanding.

a. Understanding the gifts of the Spirit (1–11)

(i) Discerning their authenticity (1–3)
Ignorance surrounding the things of the Spirit is dangerous. The Corinthians of all people should have known this, because the profound ignorance of their pagan past had led them into allegiance *to dumb idols* (2). Paul therefore provides them with the essential criterion by which they are to assess whether or not a person truly has the Holy Spirit and whether or not their gifts are a *manifestation of the Spirit* (7).

Therefore I want you to know that no one who is speaking by the Spirit of God says, 'Jesus be cursed,' and no one can say, 'Jesus is Lord,' except by the Holy Spirit (3). There is much debate among scholars as to the precise point being made here. It seems unthinkable that Paul is seriously entertaining the possibility that the statement 'Jesus

---

[3] Other relevant passages include Acts 1 – 2; Rom. 12:3–8; Eph. 4:7–13; 1 Pet. 4:10–11.

[4] The Greek word here, *pneumatikōn*, can be taken as either masculine (in which case the reference could be to 'spiritual people', as in 1 Cor. 14:37) or neuter (in which case the reference is to the 'things of the Spirit' and therefore to spiritual gifts, as in 1 Cor. 14:1). Either is possible here and the reference could even be intentionally ambiguous (see Carson, *Showing the Spirit*, pp. 22–23). That spiritual gifts are at least in view here is clear from the subsequent argument.

be cursed' would be tolerated in a meeting of the Christian church. Some suggest he is referring back to experiences of 'ecstatic speech' in the pagan past he mentioned in verse 2. Others say he is talking about fearful Christians who are seeking to resist the moving of the Holy Spirit by making a blasphemous utterance.[5] It is likely that his point is far more straightforward. For Paul the essential criterion for the presence of the Holy Spirit is not the presence of spiritual manifestations but the confession of Christ as Lord,[6] and anything or anyone falling short of that confession cannot be *speaking by the Spirit of God*. 'The presence of the Spirit in power and gifts makes it easy for God's people to think of the power and gifts as the real evidence of the Spirit's presence. Not so for Paul. The ultimate criterion of the Spirit's activity is the exaltation of Jesus as Lord.'[7]

(ii) Celebrating their bountiful diversity[8] (4–11)

The New Testament includes six lists of spiritual gifts[9] and no two lists are the same. Willow Creek's *Network Course*[10] helpfully assembles these into a single list of twenty-three gifts, and even this should probably not be seen as exhaustive.[11] This breadth of gifting bears witness to the boundless creativity of the Holy Spirit who is able to manifest (7) himself in numerous ways within the church. By contrast, there often seems to be a drive within churches to replace that glorious and creative diversity with a narrow uniformity. In some contexts the place of musical gifts assumes such centrality in the worship of the church that other forms of ministry are pushed to the side; in other settings the teaching ministry of a lead pastor may be so dominant that few other gifts have room to flourish; some traditions give such emphasis to the gift of tongues that Christians who do not exercise this gift feel relegated to a lower tier of spirituality; others may place so much weight on their understanding of

---

[5] Thiselton discusses eleven different options in A. C. Thiselton, *The First Epistle to the Corinthians*, NIGTC (Grand Rapids: Eerdmans, 2000), pp. 918–927!

[6] The suggestion that the expression 'Jesus is Lord' could be uttered merely as empty words arises from the anomalous situation of churches in the West today in which serious persecution is rare. In the first century to confess Christ as Lord was to accept hostility, rejection, material loss and possible martyrdom. See G. D. Fee, *The First Epistle to the Corinthians*, NICNT (Grand Rapids: Eerdmans, 1987), pp. 581–582.

[7] Fee, *First Corinthians*, p. 582.

[8] The phrase belongs to Carson in *Showing the Spirit*, pp. 31ff.

[9] 1 Cor. 12:8–10; 1 Cor. 12:28; Eph. 4:11; Rom. 12:6–8; 1 Cor. 7:7; 1 Pet. 4:11.

[10] B. Bugbee and D. Cousins, *The Network Course Participants Guide* (Grand Rapids: Zondervan, 2005), p. 64.

[11] See the discussion in W. Grudem, *Systematic Theology* (Leicester: Inter-Varsity Press, 1994), pp. 1019–1022.

prophetic words that the systematic teaching of Scripture comes to be seen as rather mundane and lacking in contemporary relevance.

The problem in Corinth appears to be an over-emphasis on the gift of tongues as the authenticating sign of spiritual fullness.[12] However, Paul's argument is relevant to all attempts to squeeze the creative life and power of the Holy Spirit into the pre-formed mould of our personal preferences, theological preoccupations and ecclesiastical traditions. The Holy Spirit is the Spirit of bountiful diversity who wishes to show himself among his people in many different ways. This is hardly surprising, for biblical monotheism believes that diversity is inherent to the one God whom we worship as Father, Son and Holy Spirit. This is in fact the basis of Paul's argument: *There are different kinds of gifts, but the same **Spirit** distributes them. There are different kinds of service, but the same **Lord**. There are different kinds of working, but in all of them and in everyone it is the same **God** at work* (4–6).[13]

In keeping with his emphasis on the diversity of gifts given by the one God, Paul goes on to list nine such *manifestations of the Spirit* in verses 8–11. Attempting to define all these gifts in detail is beyond the scope of this exposition.[14] We will return to the nature of prophecy and tongues in the next chapter, but a few general observations can be made. First, attempts to break the list down into sub-categories have not been very successful. We are better to regard it (along with the other lists) as more *ad hoc*. Second, we should be cautious about arguing back from present experience to the text. Having experienced a powerful and authentic *manifestation of the Spirit*, a person may notice some possible affinity with one of the gifts in the New Testament lists and assume that what they have just experienced is the same thing as the original text describes.[15] It may or may not be, of course, but simply to assume it is to run the risk of making their particular experience normative for other Christians. Third, a preoccupation with such definitions may lead us to miss Paul's real point. His concern is to broaden the Corinthians'

---

[12] Granted that this is something of a 'mirror reading' of the text, but it seems likely in the light of 13:1 and the argument of 14:1–25. 'The problem is almost certainly an *abuse* of the gift of tongues' (Fee, *First Corinthians*, p. 571).

[13] 'Here we encounter the earliest "clear" Trinitarian language' (Thiselton, *First Corinthians*, p. 934).

[14] The main commentaries offer various suggestions. I have generally found Carson's material in *Showing the Spirit* (pp. 38–41; 77–100) most convincing. For a more cautious and extensive treatment see Thiselton, *First Corinthians*, pp. 936–965.

[15] For example, I wonder if popular definitions of the *word of knowledge* (a supernatural endowment of knowledge about a particular situation) may be vulnerable to this criticism. My point is not that the Holy Spirit would never give such words, but that there is very little certainty as to whether this is what Paul meant by the phrase.

understanding of the ways in which the Spirit manifests himself in the life of the church, not to replace their narrow thinking with another (necessarily) narrow set of definitions. The fact that just a few verses later (28) he gives another list in which he repeats three gifts from the earlier list and then adds four more rather confirms this conclusion.

b. Valuing the gifts of the Spirit (12–31)

The church will inevitably be damaged when too much attention or status is attached to one spiritual gift. The damage arises because those who do not exercise this one gift may be tempted to regard their gifts and contribution as worthless, while those who do exercise it may become spiritually proud. As we have already seen, in Corinth it seems that the favoured gift was the gift of tongues, but the same problems can easily arise when the status of any gift is inappropriately elevated. With his customary pastoral insight, Paul tackles the problem head on.

(i) Valuing our unity (12–14)
Paul introduces one of his favourite metaphors for the church: namely that it is the *body of Christ* (12, 27). Inherent to this image is both the unity of the church and the diversity within the church, for (12) the *one body* (the church) is made up of *many parts* (its individual members). The basis for the unity of these many members within the one body is their common experience of the Holy Spirit by whom they were *all baptised* and of whom they have all been given *to drink* (13).[16] The challenge, then, is to value our unity within the body of Christ, predicated on our common experience of the Spirit, rather than allowing our diversity to create divisions or petty jealousies.

(ii) Valuing our gifts (15–20)
Paul now extends the body metaphor with a touch of humour, to challenge those who feel that they lack those gifts which they regard as possessing higher status. First he imagines a *foot* (15) feeling that it does not really belong to the body on the basis that it is *not a hand*. Similarly he imagines an *ear* (16) feeling that it does not really belong to the body on the basis that it is not *an eye*. The image is clearly

---

[16] Some have suggested that reference to being *given the one Spirit to drink* implies a decisive experience of the Spirit subsequent to conversion, but the whole point of the argument here is that *all* members of the body share a common experience of the Spirit. It is best to regard the two metaphors of baptism and drinking as parallel, though the second does seem to imply an active responsibility to go on appropriating the benefits he brings.

absurd, for a body needs all of its parts in order to function properly (17). It is the same in the body of the church. God has deliberately built diversity into the church, uniting in one body people with a whole variety of backgrounds, gifts and functions (18). This is what makes the life and worship of the Christian church so wonderfully rich. Given that this is the work of God, we need properly to value our own gifts and contributions, rather than wishing that we had the gifts of others, for if we were all the same and all had the same gifts and functions we would not be a body at all (19).

(iii) Valuing the gifts of others (21–26)

Next Paul employs the body metaphor to challenge the elitists who regard their gifts as superior and the gifts of others as dispensable. He imagines an eye talking to a hand, explaining that the hand's services are no longer required, and a head talking similarly to a pair of feet (21). Again the image is absurd, for a body needs all its parts to function well, including the parts which appear weaker[17] or less presentable[18] (22–23). Indeed, those parts of the body which are not usually seen are in fact treated with special care and modesty (24a). Similarly in the church God gives special honour to those whose contributions are less visible and are easily overlooked (24b), so as to ensure that none regard themselves as superior and all are cared for equally (25–26). There is therefore no basis for any Christian – however gifted – to regard themselves as superior to another. We must all learn to value the gifts of others – a principle that is just as important to high profile pastors and worship leaders today as it was to the 'tongue-speakers' of ancient Corinth.

(iv) Valuing our place within the body of Christ (27–31)

Now you are the body of Christ, and each one of you is a part of it (27).

Both the spiritually insecure and the spiritually proud are addressed by these concluding words. For all its difficulties and divisions, the church in Corinth is nothing less than *the body of Christ* and all the believers need to understand that they have a place within it. None are so gifted as not to need the rest of the body; none are too lowly to be without a role within it. God has given to the body the diverse range of gifts needed to establish and build up the church (28)[19] and

[17] Probably the internal organs (Fee, *First Corinthians*, p. 613).

[18] Probably the sexual organs (ibid., pp. 613–614).

[19] The enumeration of this list has attracted much discussion but we should not read too much into it. The enumeration of the first three ministries probably acknowledges their particular role in establishing and building up the local congregation. 'The gift of tongues is not listed last because it is the least but because it is the problem [in Corinth]' (Fee, *First Corinthians*, p. 619).

our role is not to seek to flatten out this glorious diversity into a dull uniformity(29),[20] but to value the whole range of the gifts he has given – including those he has given to us to exercise.

The final imperative (31a)[21] *eagerly* to *desire the greater gifts* is best understood as anticipating the argument of chapter 14, which prioritizes all the intelligible gifts over the (unintelligible) gift of tongues in the particular context of public worship. Before he opens up this argument, however, Paul pauses to lift the discussion onto an entirely different plane, as he expounds the *most excellent way* of Christian life and service: the way of love.

2. The gifts of the Holy Spirit and the priority of love (1 Cor. 13)

Leon Morris memorably concluded his commentary on this chapter by saying, 'the commentator cannot finish writing on this chapter without a sense that soiled and clumsy hands have touched a thing of exquisite beauty and holiness . . . yet no commentator can excuse himself from the duty of trying to make plain what these matchless words have come to signify for him.'[22] The dramatic change of style from the surrounding material has led some to speculate as to whether this chapter may have been composed on a separate occasion and simply inserted by Paul at this point.[23] However, C. T. Craig's comment that 'almost every word in the chapter has been chosen with this particular situation at Corinth in mind'[24] is well-judged. More probably, Paul's change of style is adopted for rhetorical purposes, to signal his sense that in moving from talk of supernatural power for the church to talk about love in the church, he is not 'coming down' from mountainous heights but rising up to something that is truly sublime and Christ-like. Our worship may be enriched by the most impressive array of spiritual gifts, it may be expressed with the most striking creativity, it may be tuned to its particular cultural context with the utmost skill, yet it is all without spiritual value if the worshipping community is not a community of authentic, self-giving love.

---

[20] Clearly these questions all expect to be answered negatively because, as Paul has continuously asserted, the creative Spirit produces a diversity of gifts in the church. God does not intend uniformity but for us to have different gifts.

[21] See Fee, *First Corinthians*, pp. 623–625.

[22] L. Morris, *1 Corinthians*, TNTC (Leicester: Inter-Varsity Press, 1985), p. 186.

[23] This possibility is discussed in Fee, *First Corinthians*, p. 626.

[24] C. T. Craig, *The First Epistle to the Corinthians*, Interpreter's Bible, vol. 10 (New York: Doubleday, 1953), p. 165, quoted in Thiselton, *First Corinthians*, p. 1029.

a. The necessity of love (1–3)

If I speak in the tongues of men or of angels, but do not have love, I am only a resounding gong or a clanging cymbal (1).

The fact that Paul chose to begin with *speaking in tongues* re-inforces the opinion that he regarded the Corinthian view on this gift as particularly problematic. Paul is in fact very positive about the proper exercise of the gift of tongues, as we will see, but he insists that it is love and not tongues which is the *sine qua non* of true spiritual maturity. We might expect him to stop at this point but instead he pushes the point still further. In the next chapter Paul will urge the Corinthians to give priority to the gift of prophecy, but those who exercise this gift – or those with a gift of miracle-working faith – are *nothing* (2) if they minister without love. Still more striking, it is possible even to give of oneself sacrificially in service of the poor and of God, and to do so without love (and very possibly with an air of patronizing self-righteousness!). The end result will be to *gain nothing* (3). Without love, no action – however spiritually dramatic, insightfully truthful or personally costly – has value in the sight of the God who 'is love'.[25] What, then, is this love?

b. The nature of love (4–7)

Our thinking about love is typically rather self-centred: we want to 'find love' or to 'fall in love', but in either case we are looking to meet a need in ourselves. In the coming of Jesus, however, an altogether different kind of love was seen; a determined and self-giving love which did not arise from any need in himself, but which was simply the outflow of his nature. Paul does not offer here a definition of this love so much as a description of how it is actively expressed.[26]

(i) The long-suffering generosity of love (4a)

Love is patient – it does not wait, poised to pounce on another's failings but has a long fuse, 'a godlike quality that is eloquent of love's self-restraint'.[27] If patience is the self-restraint of love, then *kindness* is love in action. Love moves out to the 'other' in gentleness, under-standing and compassion.

---

[25] 1 John 4:8.

[26] Again Craig's comment is instructive, 'The nature of love is expressed by Paul in a series of verbs, the active character of which many not be fully indicated by . . . adjectives' (Craig, *First Corinthians*, 10:172, quoted in Thiselton, *First Corinthians*, p. 1046).

[27] Morris, *1 Corinthians*, p. 180.

(ii) The self-giving orientation of love (4b–5a)

Paul has already addressed the tendency of some in the Corinthian church to brag about their gifts, while others were inclined to be jealous of those whose gifts seemed more spectacular. He now insists that this division in the church is in fact a failure to love, for love *does not envy* and *it does not boast* (4b). Moreover love does not 'cherish inflated ideas of its own importance',[28] by self-congratulation (*it is not proud*, 5), self-promotion (*it is not . . . rude*, 5, ESV) or self-assertion (*it is not self-seeking*, 5). This takes us to the very heart of Christian love, which does not seek to dominate or possess for the sake of the one who loves, but to give itself for the benefit of the one who is loved. How many church splits could have been avoided if those involved had taken to heart the priority Paul attaches to this kind of self-giving love?

(iii) The forgiving heart of love (5b–6)

In *Mere Christianity* C. S. Lewis wrote, 'Everyone says forgiveness is a lovely idea, until they have something to forgive'.[29] Similarly the call to love seems attractive when relationships are good, but is much more demanding in times of conflict. Nonetheless, it is precisely in such times that the true quality of our love is revealed, for the love celebrated in this chapter *is not easily angered* and *it keeps no record of wrongs* (5b). I remember a moment in my own life when I was convicted to delete a series of files from my computer which concerned a period of conflict in my own ministry. To keep them would have been a failure to love, for love has a forgiving heart, which takes no pleasure in raking over the supposed failures of others but delights only in seeking *truth* fair-mindedly (6).

(iv) The enduring persistence of love (7)

Love never tires of support, never loses faith, never exhausts hope, never gives up (7).[30] When all else fails love finds a way. This is the love to which we are called – though in the final analysis we have to acknowledge that such love is only to be found in God himself.

c. The never-ending greatness of love (8–13)

The conclusion of Paul's evocative description of love has fully prepared us for his assertion that *love never fails* (8). His perspective, however, is now shifting from the interpersonal to the eschatological: love will continue forever! By contrast the gift of prophecy will not

---

[28] J. B. Phillips' translation.
[29] C. S. Lewis, *Mere Christianity* (Fontana Books: Collins, 1952), p. 101.
[30] This is Thiselton's rendering of v. 7 (*First Corinthians*, p. 1057).

continue forever but *will cease* (8b) for God's final act of judgment will be so utterly definitive and complete, that there will be nothing left for the prophets to say. As Thiselton puts it, 'To prophesy [then] would be like switching on a torch in the full light of the noonday'.[31] Similarly the gift of tongues will not continue forever, for *where there are tongues, they will be stilled* (8c), as the intimate relationship with God which this gift so often fosters gives way to the face-to-face communion of the new creation (Rev. 22:4). The gift of *knowledge*[32] also will not continue forever but will *pass away* (8d) as the mystery of God and his ways is finally and fully revealed.

This passage has sometimes been used to argue that certain of the gifts of the Holy Spirit (including the gifts of tongues, prophecy and knowledge mentioned here) ceased to function in the church at the end of the apostolic age.[33] A detailed analysis of the arguments is beyond the scope of this book[34] but it seems to me that D. A. Carson is right to insist[35] that this passage does specify *when* these gifts will cease: namely *when completeness* [ESV, *the perfect*] *comes* (10). If so, the key question is to what this *completeness/perfection* refers. Is it (a) personal spiritual maturity, (b) the completion of the New Testament canon or (c) the consummation of the new creation when Christ returns? The first of these options seems most unlikely and out of step with Paul's challenge in this letter to those making exaggerated claims of maturity for themselves; the second option introduces a category (the canon of Scripture) which is, frankly, alien to this particular text; but the third option fits very well with the references to seeing *face to face* and *knowing fully* in verse 12. So my preferred conclusion is that Paul believes that the gifts (including those of tongues, prophecy and 'knowledge') do not cease until the moment of Christ's return.[36]

---

[31] Thiselton, *First Corinthians*, p. 1061.

[32] '"Knowledge" in this passage does not mean ordinary human knowing or learning, but refers rather to that special manifestation of the Spirit, the "utterance of knowledge" (12:8) which understands revealed "mysteries"' (Fee, *First Corinthians*, p. 644).

[33] Understood to be the point at which the NT documents were completed. Alan F. Johnson identifies Augustine, Aquinas, Calvin, Edwards and McArthur (among others) as taking this position (A. F. Johnson, *1 Corinthians*, IVPNTC [Leicester: Inter-Varsity Press, 2004], p. 254).

[34] And it should be noted, with Thiselton, that 'few or none of the serious "cessationist" arguments depends on a specific exegesis of 1 Cor. 13:8-11' (*First Corinthians*, p. 1063).

[35] Carson, *Showing the Spirit*, p. 69, against Richard Gaffin who argues that 'the time of their cessation is not a point he is concerned with' here (see Wayne Grudem (ed.), *Are Miraculous Gifts for Today?* [Leicester: Inter-Varsity Press, 1996], p. 55).

[36] I should perhaps make clear at this point that these are my own conclusions and should not be taken as the official positions of the organizations with which I am most closely associated (Above Bar Church, Southampton and the Keswick Convention), which seek to make space for a breadth of conviction on this issue.

These gifts of tongues, prophecy and knowledge, which were so highly prized in Corinth, were indeed of great benefit to the church. Their presence, however, was not evidence that they had reached full spiritual maturity, but rather that they were only part way there! Their knowledge of God and his ways (and therefore their prophesying) was only fragmentary and partial (9), reminding them that they had yet to reach the true knowledge of the new creation. The gifts are valuable now but they must not be prized as supreme, for the time will come when they are no longer required, as what is *in part* is replaced by eschatological *completeness* (10). The loveless, undisciplined manner in which the Corinthian believers have practiced the gifts, as if certain gifts were definitive of spiritual superiority, is not evidence of a maturity in which they should take pride, but of a childishness which they should put behind them (11).

Corinth was famed for its mirrors, made from polished metals. The image they produced was good by ancient standards, but still it was only an image – inverted and distorted through the 'mediation' of the mirror. So it is in our present knowledge of God and his ways: it is 'mediated' to us in various ways, including through the gifts of which Paul has spoken (12a). Yet the day will come when the mirror is thrown away and we shall turn and look into the face of God himself (12b) and will know him even as he knows us (12c). In the light of this breath-taking, sublime prospect the Corinthian pretensions of spiritual superiority crumble to dust.

The church in its charismatic life now is wonderful indeed, but it is only the beginning; something far greater still awaits us, as we have seen. Until our partial (9) knowledge of God is replaced by the *face to face* (12) knowledge of the new creation, the church will need to exercise the gifts of the Holy Spirit, but their time will come to an end. By contrast, *faith, hope and love* will *remain* (13) forever – and *the greatest of these is love*, the glorious centrepiece of this passage and the very nature of God himself.

It is generally recognized that this section of 1 Corinthians is one of the most significant passages on congregational worship in the whole of the New Testament. How striking then, that it should be centred around this glorious chapter on love. It seems clear that this emphasis urgently needed to be recovered in Corinth, divided as it was with pride, insecurity and jealousy around the exercise of particular spiritual gifts. We urgently need to recover the same emphasis in our churches today, which often experience conflict, division and bad feeling in discussions, both on the gifts of the Holy Spirit specifically and on congregational worship more generally. For those of us who find ourselves in the middle of such discussions, this chapter presents us with a sobering challenge. If it is more important to us that our worship is pleasing to God than to us, then the primary question to ask is not, 'how can I promote my particular desires, convictions and preferences in the church?' but rather, 'how can I learn to love well those who think differently from me?' If we fail to give due weight to that question, then all our worship and all our exercise of spiritual gifts really is nothing more than hot air and noise – or to use Paul's words, *a resounding gong or a clanging cymbal* (1).

1 Corinthians 14
17. The empowering Spirit II:
The gifts of the Spirit in the church

Matrix warning signs are a regular feature of motorway driving in the United Kingdom. At their best they provide drivers with advance notice of a range of hazards (closed lanes, poor weather, traffic congestion and obstructions on the carriageway, to name just a few). All too often, though, they appear to be inadequately managed, slowing traffic down or even bringing it to a standstill on account of hazards which have long-since disappeared. Of course, these warning signs are actually very valuable when they are used well, but I suspect that I am not the only driver who is so weary of seeing them misused that I am sometimes tempted to wonder if we would be better off without them!

There is a risk that our thinking about spiritual gifts may take a similar turn. Perhaps we were made to feel spiritually inferior because we did not exercise a particular gift; perhaps we were put under pressure when someone claimed that 'God had told them . . .'; perhaps someone prayed for our healing and then appeared to blame our lack of faith when we remained ill. Faced with such painful experiences we might be tempted to feel that the church would be well advised to excise these chapters from their Bible, or to keep them safely locked away in a previous period of salvation history, or even to ignore them altogether. However, it is very striking that this is not Paul's response when faced with a similar range of problems in the church in Corinth. Poor discipline, an over-emphasis on one particular gift, spiritual pride on the one hand and spiritual insecurity on the other, an elevation of the spiritual power of *gifts* over the spiritual fruit of *love*: all of these problems appear to have been evident among the Corinthian believers. Nonetheless, Paul still insists that it is 'for the common **good**' (12:7) that the gifts are given; he still calls the believers *eagerly to desire* spiritual gifts (1); he still says that he would like *every one* of them to *speak in tongues* and *even more to prophesy* (5). It seems that in Paul's mind, when it comes to spiritual gifts 'the answer to *misuse* is not *disuse* but *right use*'[1] to quote the memorable words of the late David Watson. There is no better place than 1 Corinthians 14, to which we may turn if we wish to learn what this 'right use' of spiritual gifts entails.

Follow the way of love and eagerly desire gifts of the Spirit, especially prophecy (1).

After scaling the heights of chapter 13, Paul returns to the discussion of spiritual gifts that he began in chapter 12. The strength of his encouragement *eagerly to desire* the gifts of the Spirit while also following *the way of love*, makes it clear that he does not intend us to regard these as mutually exclusive (as if we should chose the way of love over the desire for spiritual gifts) but as complementary. It is the way of love that provides the context in which the exercise of spiritual gifts will flourish. This chapter is of particular interest in a book on Christian worship because of the insight it provides into what happened when the Christians gathered together.[2] In this chapter, Paul's focus narrows to the gift of tongues (and its interpretation) and the gift of prophecy. Before following the flow of his argument, we must pause to seek to clarify what Paul meant by these terms in this particular context.

The gift of tongues. According to Thiselton we should speak of various 'species of tongues'[3] rather than seeking to identify tongues as a singular entity. This is a helpful reminder that Paul may not share our desire for tight definitions in the things of the Spirit – after all, he is keen to remind the Corinthians of the bountiful diversity of the Spirit's manifestations, as we saw in the last chapter. However, there are a number of things which are made clear in the text here. The *gift of tongues* is a form of speech which is directed not to people but to God (2). It is, therefore, a particular expression of prayer. It seems that this 'speech' carries a meaning of some kind since it is

---

[1] D. Watson, *Discipleship* (London: Hodder & Stoughton, 1981), p. 107.

[2] We should note that, while there was one 'church' in Corinth (1:2), it is quite possible that the one church gathered in a series of home meetings, probably in the larger houses of wealthier members. The highly participative nature of the gatherings Paul describes may well reflect in part the informality of this domestic setting. See P. H. Towner's article 'Households and Household Codes', in G. F. Hawthorne, R. P. Martin and D. G Reid (eds.), *Dictionary of Paul and His Letters* (Leicester: Inter-Varsity Press, 1993), pp. 417–419. See also the second point in D. A. Carson, *Showing the Spirit: A Theological Exposition of 12 Corinthians 12-14* (Grand Rapids: Baker Book House Company, 1987), p. 123.

[3] Reflecting the Pauline phrase 'different kinds of tongues' in 1 Cor. 12:10. See A. C. Thiselton, *The First Epistle to the Corinthians*, NIGTC (Grand Rapids: Eerdmans, 2000), p. 970.

capable of being interpreted (5),[4] but it need not follow that authentic tongues must always be identifiable human languages, for Paul seems to allow the possibility that the speech may reflect either angelic or human forms of speech.[5] Nonetheless, the 'meaning' is unknown both to the speaker (14) and to any who hear them (9), unless an interpretation is given (13). Those who exercise this gift *edify themselves* (4) in using it – so undoubtedly it can be beneficial – but, because the meaning is unknown to the speaker, the gift leaves their mind *unfruitful* (14) and engages their *spirit* (15) in some more immediate way. There seems to be some variety in the precise form in which the gift is expressed, with both spoken and sung examples referenced here (15). So the gift of tongues (here at least) is primarily a gift given to enrich prayer and praise; a way to engage intimately with God, which enables us to continue to communicate with him when familiar words run out or seem inadequate. This much, at least, is clear, though scholarly debate continues to rage on many of the questions surrounding this gift.[6]

By contrast, *the gift of prophecy* is a form of speech addressed not to God but to people, with the purpose of *their strengthening, encouraging and comfort* (3).[7] Paul's particular emphases here are first, that (in contrast to tongues) prophecy is intelligible both to the one who speaks and to those who hear (9, 19) and second, that prophecy therefore *edifies the church* (4–5, 12). Beyond that, however, the exact nature of New Testament prophecy is much debated and there seems to be little scholarly consensus. On the one hand, Wayne Grudem emphasizes a link with specific, spontaneous revelation with his definition of prophecy as 'the reception and subsequent transmission of spontaneous, divinely originating revelation'.[8] On the other hand, Thiselton questions the emphasis on spontaneity and allows for the inclusion of *pastoral preaching* within his definition of prophesying as 'the performing of intelligible, articulate, communicative

---

[4] It is important, however, not to assume that 'interpretation' is the same thing as 'translation'. If the experience described in Rom. 8:26–28 falls within the broad category of 'species of tongues' (as Thiselton argues) it may be that one aspect of this gift is to enable a verbal release of the deepest feelings of the human heart by the operation of the Holy Spirit, such that the 'interpretation' is not so much translation as a bringing 'to articulate expression' (Thiselton, *First Corinthians*, p. 978).

[5] As implied by 1 Cor. 13:1.

[6] For example, whether speaking in tongues is an 'ecstatic' experience, whether it bears any relationship to forms of 'ecstatic speech' in the spirituality of other first-century religions and how the tongues of this chapter relate to tongues elsewhere in the NT such as Acts 2.

[7] Though it should be noted that the Paul's idea of *encouragement* was probably rather more challenging and rather less therapeutic than ours.

[8] W. A. Grudem, *The Gift of Prophecy in 1 Corinthians* (Washington DC: University Press of America, 1982), p. 115, quoted in Carson, *Showing the Spirit*, pp. 93–94.

speech-acts, the operative currency of which depends on the active agency of the Holy Spirit mediated through human minds and lives to build up, to encourage, to judge, to exhort, and to comfort others in the context of interpersonal relationships'.[9]

There can be little doubt that for Paul prophecy included the speaking out of a spontaneously-given revelation, for this seems clearly implied in verses 29–31: *Two or three prophets should speak, and the others should weigh carefully what is said. And if a revelation comes to someone who is sitting down, the first speaker should stop. For you can all prophesy in turn.* It is striking that Paul seems to expect such spontaneous interventions within the life and worship of the Christian church. This is unquestionably threatening, both for leaders who prefer to retain tight control and for churches which run their services within well-defined timetables. Nonetheless, I see no reason why we should not seek to make sufficient space to welcome such spontaneity within the life of our churches;[10] I have personally benefitted greatly from this kind of ministry. I am much less certain, though, that spontaneity should be seen as a defining characteristic of prophecy. Are we sure, for example, that the *first speaker* had not prepared their material in advance?[11] The term *prophecy* seems to be the dominant, encompassing term for intelligible ministry in this chapter but there nonetheless seems to be a fluidity of meaning between the terms *revelation, word of instruction* and *prophecy*,[12] suggesting that we cannot tie down the meanings too tightly. Furthermore, *prophecy* is the term Paul chooses to use for his iconic example of the kind of intelligible ministry that will *build up the church* (12). From all that we know of the emphasis of Paul's wider ministry, with its deep foundations in the Scriptures and strong emphasis on their thoughtful exposition and application, it seems inconceivable to me that he would choose a gift that (by definition) did not *include* the thoughtful preaching of Scripture, as his example of edifying, intelligible ministry. What made the church in Corinth different from any other that Paul was concerned with? Surely what this church most needed for its edification (like every other church) was the faithful, spiritually sensitive preaching of Holy Scripture! It therefore seems best to see the category of 'prophecy' here as a broad

---

[9] Thiselton, *First Corinthians*, p. 1094.

[10] If Paul is describing a house-church gathering (perhaps of less than fifty people) it could be argued that, in larger churches, these expectations would attach more to prayer gatherings and community groups than to larger more structured Sunday services.In our church this is more exceptional within our public services, but we particularly seek to make space for it within our special prayer gatherings.

[11] V. 26 could easily be taken to imply this possibility.

[12] See vv. 6, 19, 26.

term, encompassing the kind of very specific situational guidance given by Agabus in Acts 21:10–14, the speaking out of spontaneous revelation received when Christians meet together (usually, but not exclusively, based on an insight into Scripture itself) and the spiritually sensitive preaching and application of Scripture in the church, whether prepared in advance or not.[13]

With this understanding in place we can summarize Paul's argument in the rest of the chapter.

1. The priority of prophecy in corporate worship, since it builds up the church (1–5)

Paul is very positive about the value of the gift of *tongues* (5) but he places special emphasis on the value of the gift of *prophecy* in public worship (1, 5). He believes that the priority for corporate worship is the *building up* (*edification*; 4, 12, 26) of the church, rather than that of the individual. This idea of *building up* of the church is expanded at various points in the chapter. It is not to do with strengthening its corporate self-esteem but rather *strengthening, encouraging and comforting* the people in the church (3); it involves a vision of congregational worship that is not individualistic but genuinely corporate and communal (16–17); it involves words of *instruction* (6, 19). It seems that the building up of the church always involves the apprehension of divine truth, since in each case it depends on intelligible speech, enlivened by the Holy Spirit (6, 19).

This, then, is the basis for the priority of prophecy over tongues in congregational worship. Prophecy *builds up the church* both because it is addressed to the congregation rather than to God (2–3) and because it does not require interpretation (5) since its content is not mysterious (2). The only exception Paul allows is if *someone interprets* (5) the tongues so that others can understand its meaning.

2. The problem of tongues in corporate worship, since they are unintelligible (6–19)

While Paul is warm in his appreciation of the value of the gift of tongues in his own life (18) and positive in his encouragement of others to exercise this gift (5), he is bold in questioning its value in public worship. *Now, brothers and sisters, if I come to you and speak in tongues, what good will I be to you, unless I bring you some revelation or knowledge or prophecy or word of instruction?* (6).

---

[13] Many preachers see this 'prophetic' task as central to their role, whether or not they would describe themselves as 'charismatic'.

For Paul, congregational worship is not simply the simultaneous expression of the worship of individuals, as if it were little more than a synchronized quiet time! Rather congregational worship is a shared, participative, interactive activity in which the contribution of one worshipper needs to be *intelligible* (9, 19) to all the other worshippers. If this principle is broken, the individual worshipper *will just be speaking into the air* (9b), which Paul clearly regards as a bad thing. Furthermore, the body will be divided, with the speaker and the (uncomprehending) listeners becoming *foreigners* to each other (11).

This is not to say that Paul forbids the exercise of the gift of tongues in the Christian congregation – indeed, in verse 27 he envisages up to three people speaking in tongues in a single meeting.[14] Whether he is encouraging this practice, or offering a concession to Corinthian enthusiasm for the gift is harder to discern, but we should not forbid what Paul does not forbid (39). Nonetheless, he is very clear that in public worship there should be no simultaneous tongues-speaking (27)[15] and that an interpretation must always be given (13, 27–28).[16] His argument gives an intriguing insight into the nature of corporate worship.

Otherwise when you are praising God in the Spirit, how can someone else, who is now put in the position of an enquirer, say 'Amen' to your thanksgiving, since they do not know what you are saying? You are giving thanks well enough, but no one else is edified (16–17).

So public prayer is not a performance to which we merely listen in; it is an engagement with God in which we participate, making the prayer our own by adding our *Amen* (16). Through this participation we are ourselves then *edified* (17). This is a practice that we need to teach explicitly to young and new believers, to enrich their experience of corporate worship. Such participation is impossible, however, if the prayer is spoken in tongues which are not interpreted.

3. The presence of unbelievers in corporate worship (20–25)

These verses are well-known for their difficulty, but their purpose is to take the argument one stage further for the priority of prophecy

[14] Though *if anyone speaks in a tongue . . .* (27) does seem to contrast with the more positive *Two or three prophets should speak . . .* (29).
[15] On this basis I would quite strongly question the practice of corporate singing in tongues in public meetings where unbelievers may be present.
[16] Whether by the speaker themselves (v. 13) or by another *interpreter* (v. 28).

over tongues, by considering their respective impact on unbelievers who may come in to the public meeting of the church. The conclusion is that such visitors will be convinced that the believers are *out of their mind* (23) if they hear them speaking in tongues (presumably an undesirable outcome), but will be convicted of the sin of their own hearts and of the holy presence of God in the church (a desirable outcome), if they hear *everyone prophesying* (24–52). That much is clear. The difficulty is with the statement that *tongues, then, are a sign, not for believers but for unbelievers; prophecy, however, is not for unbelievers but for believers* (22), which seems to go against the conclusion of these later verses. The key lies in the preceding quotation from Isaiah. *In the Law it is written: 'With other tongues and through the lips of foreigners I will speak to this people, but even then they will not listen to me, says the Lord'* (21).

In the original context (Isa. 28:11–12) the *tongues* were the (foreign) voices of the invading Assyrian army, whose victory over Israel was a powerful word of judgment from Yahweh. The unintelligibility of their voices, however, was itself a profound sign of the judgment under which they languished. It served only to deepen their confusion and harden their hearts, for having resisted the voice of prophets, God's voice had now become incomprehensible to them. In Isaiah's time, then, the 'tongues' of the Assyrians were a *sign* of God's judgment to the *unbelieving* majority, while the *prophetic* word had been a sign to the *believing* remnant that the door to repentance remained open. On this basis, the Corinthians can expect unbelievers to be hardened against the gospel if the church persists in its emphasis on the public use of tongues (23), while it can expect wonderful gospel fruit if it emphasizes prophetic ministry instead (24–25).[17]

4. Participation and order in corporate worship (26–40)

The (non-canonical) headings in most modern Bible translations tend to emphasize Paul's teaching on order in worship here.[18] This is perfectly appropriate, but there is a danger that we give insufficient weight to the expectations of extensive congregational participation here that Paul also assumes, so that the 'order' he envisages becomes more that of the graveyard than of the living body. The Corinthian believers do not come to watch a service but to be participants in dynamic, congregational worship. *When you come together **each of***

---

[17] For this view see Fee, *First Corinthians*, pp. 679–688, and (with more detail) Carson, *Showing the Spirit*, pp. 108–117.

[18] 'Good order in worship' (NIV); 'Orderly Worship' (NRSV, ESV); 'A Call to Orderly Worship' (NLT).

you has a hymn, or a word of instruction, a revelation, a tongue or an interpretation (26). Up to three people may *speak in a tongue* (27) and *two or three prophets should speak* (29). At the same time, those who listen do not do so passively but *should weigh carefully what is said* (29). Furthermore, there is an expectation that the Holy Spirit may, in his sovereign overruling, interrupt the flow with an immediate revelation (30) of some kind. I recently attended a church where something like this happened, and one speaker was asked to give way for another person to speak. It felt a little strange, but Paul seems to accept it as quite normal (30–31). Whatever our views on the charismatic gifts may be, we must surely acknowledge that our gatherings could be deeply enriched if they were guided by a similar expectation of active participation, rather than by the passivity of consumer Christianity.

Nonetheless, there is also an important focus here on orderly worship. The two key principles are set out in verses 26 and 40, framing the passage as a whole:

Everything must be done so that the church may be built up (26).

Everything should be done in a fitting and orderly way (40).

The first principle was unpacked fully in the earlier verses of the chapter. The second is applied initially to the use of the gift of tongues, ensuring that its use is limited in the public assembly and that it is never used publicly without interpretation (27–28). Next, it is applied to the use of the gift of prophecy, ensuring that the content of prophecy is actively weighed by those who hear it (29), that no one speaker is allowed to dominate to the exclusion of other voices (30–31), and that the gift is exercised in a disciplined rather than a frenzied manner (32).[19] This call for order is then rooted in the character of God who is *not a God of disorder but of peace* (33). A specific application of this principle of order must surely be that we should encourage prophetic gifts (using the term broadly) to be used in a humble way which invites testing and honours the wisdom of the wider church and its leadership. Preachers should not be threatened by the Berean spirit (which 'examines the Scriptures . . . to see if what [is] said is true'[20]), but should rather encourage it! Those claiming specific guidance for the church or the individual believer should avoid declaring 'God has told me . . .' and should express

---

[19] The point seems to be that the prophetic Spirit (*the spirits of the prophets*, 32a) is not quenched by such self-restraint (*the control of the prophets*, 32b), but rather honoured, since the fruit of the Spirit is self-control.

[20] See Acts 17:11.

what they believe God to be saying in a way that encourages those who listen to test whether it is consistent with Scripture.[21]

Finally the principle of order in the church is applied to the participation of women in the church (34–35). Assuming that we wish to avoid making Paul guilty of completely contradicting himself, we cannot take as absolute his encouragement for women to remain silent, for elsewhere in the letter (1 Cor. 11:5) he envisages them praying and prophesying. Fee argues against the authenticity of these verses.[22] Carson rejects Fee's arguments strongly and suggests Paul is speaking about the public judging of prophecy (which he takes to be the final responsibility of elders in the church).[23] An alternative scenario is that certain women in the church (perhaps the same ones who were abandoning the head-covering codes needed in that culture to prevent the shaming of their husbands[24]) were disrupting the order of the worship with questions and challenges to those who were speaking. Paul's response is that such questions should be dealt with privately at home.[25]

5. Conclusion

It is true that the passage of Scripture on which we have focused in the last two chapters represents Paul's response to a particular set of issues in a particular church at a particular time. On this basis, we should perhaps exercise some caution before we assume that every instruction he gives is intended to be normative for all churches at all times[26] – there may be an element of description rather than prescription here. To my mind, however, such arguments seem just a bit too convenient, especially when made by Western Christians who have lived and breathed the air of rationalism with its bias

[21] Cf. 1 Thess. 5:19–21. It is sometimes suggested that it is impossible to test a prophecy by Scripture, if its content is not taken straight from Scripture (i.e. if there is a claim to fresh revelation of some sort). This would clearly be true if it were a claim to fresh doctrinal insight (a claim which should, in my view, be rejected as incompatible with the sufficiency of Scripture). However, I do not see why it is so difficult to test a specific word of situational guidance, such as that in the prophecy of Agabus (Acts 21:10–14) against the wisdom of Scripture. Similarly words given in the public assembly can be tested to see whether they *strengthen, encourage and comfort* the believers (v. 3).

[22] Fee, *First Corinthians*, pp. 699–708.

[23] Carson, *Showing the Spirit*, pp. 129–131. Carson is of the view that Paul regarded eldership as restricted to men.

[24] See 1 Cor. 11:2–16.

[25] For this position see A. F. Johnson, *1 Corinthians*, IVPNTC (Leicester: Inter-Varsity Press, 2004), pp. 269–277.

[26] However, we should also be cautious about this caution (!), for it would be very easy to use it to filter out anything in Paul's writings that causes us discomfort!

towards anti-supernaturalism. These chapters remain the fullest and most extensive description we have of what the meetings of the early Christian churches were really like and we dare not disregard the importance of what they teach. On the contrary, the church will be well-served by a rediscovery of the 'bountiful diversity' of the Holy Spirit's manifestations in our gatherings, provided that it teaches and practises the disciplines of these chapters at the same time as making appropriate space to nurture the many gifts that they describe.

Ephesians 5:18–21;
Colossians 3:15–17
18. The dynamic Spirit

Last winter I decided that we had had enough of shivering our way through chilly December evenings in the poorly-insulated lounge of our bungalow. A trip to our local home improvement store and a couple of days of unpleasant, dusty work were sufficient to install the required insulation. Since the installation, however, I have rarely even thought about the thick blanket of glass mineral wool above our heads; it's just there – and we hope it is doing its job of keeping us a little warmer! I fear that, as Christians, many of us think in a similar way when it comes to the ministry of the Holy Spirit. We affirm (rightly) that we received the Holy Spirit when we came to faith in Christ, but in our day-to-day lives we rarely even think about him; he's just there (we trust) – and we hope he is doing his work of keeping us spiritually a little 'warmer'. The contrast with New Testament Christianity could hardly be more stark.

Do not get drunk on wine, which leads to debauchery. Instead, **be filled with the Spirit** (Eph. 5:18).

In the book of Acts the Holy Spirit baptizes (Acts 1:5; 11:16), comes upon (Acts 1:8; 8:16; 10:44; 11:15; 19:6), is received (Acts 8:15, 17, 19; 10:47), is poured out (Acts 2:17, 18, 33; 10:45), fills (Acts 2:4; 4:8, 31; 9:17; 13:9, 52), enables (Acts 2:4), speaks/tells/says/warns (Acts 4:8; 8:29; 10:19; 11:12; 13:2; 20:23; 21:11), sends (Acts 13:4), encourages (Acts 9:31) and so transforms the lives of individuals that they are said to be 'full' of his presence (Acts 6:5; 7:55; 11:24). In Paul's letters, the Spirit empowers the preaching of the gospel (1 Thess. 1:5; 1 Cor. 2:4; Rom. 15:19), brings joy to those who receive it (1 Thess. 1:6; Rom. 14:17), transforms hearts and lives (2 Cor. 3:17–18; Rom. 8:1–9; Gal. 5:17–25), manifests his presence in the church through spiritual gifts (1 Cor. 12:7), testifies to our adoption and final salvation (2 Cor. 1:22; Eph. 1:13–14; Rom. 8:15; Gal. 4:4–7), enlivens prayer (Eph. 2:18; Rom. 8:26–27; Eph. 6:18), gives power to God's people (Eph. 4:3; Phil. 1:27; 2:1), unites them (Eph. 4:3; Phil. 1:27; 2:1), gives them wisdom and understanding (Col. 1:9) and inspires their worship (Col. 3:16; Eph. 5:19). On three occasions (Gal. 3:5; Eph. 1:17; 1 Thess. 4:8), Paul speaks to believers explaining that God 'gives' (in the present tense) them his Holy Spirit. Particularly striking is Ephesians 1 where, having just blessed God for giving to his readers 'the promised Holy Spirit',[1] Paul immediately goes on to pray that 'the glorious Father may *give* you the Spirit of wisdom and revelation, so that you may know him better'.[2] The New Testament evidence is clear: we should not think of the Holy Spirit only as a one-off endowment whose presence, once received, can be safely ignored and taken for granted. He is rather the *dynamic* Spirit with whom the people of God are to cultivate a continuing relationship of expectancy, dependence, openness and joy.

Anyone who has installed new pieces of software onto their computer will be familiar with the license agreements that pop up before the programme can be used. Not usually possessing the patience to plough through the endless paragraphs of legalese that follow, I generally read the first couple of lines before ticking the box and getting on with using the programme. I fear that, as Christians, many of us have a similar approach to the Bible. We stick with a few familiar headline themes, gloss over the sections we perceive to be difficult or dull, hope we know roughly what it says and then get on with doing what we want to do; once again, a complete contrast with New Testament Christianity.

Let the message of Christ[3] *dwell among you richly as you teach and admonish one another with all wisdom* (Col. 3:16). The dynamic Spirit brings the powerful word of God into the life of the people of God in a rich, ongoing way. The word defines our mission (Matt. 24:14; 28:19–20; Acts 8:4; Rom. 1:1; 1 Cor. 9:16; Col. 1:25), brings us to spiritual life (1 Pet. 1:23; Jas 1:18), anchors our assurance (Rom. 1:16–17), is the basis of our hope (John 6:68; 1 Cor. 15:2; 2 Thess. 2:14; 2 Tim 1:10; Rev. 21:5; 22:6) and our unity (Phil. 1:5), brings us to maturity (Acts 20:32; Col. 1:28), sustains our spiritual lives (Matt. 4:4; John 6:63), shapes our obedience (Matt. 7:26; Jas 1:22–24), equips us for service (2 Tim. 3:16–17) and governs the church (1 Tim. 4:11–16). Christian leaders are responsible to preach that word in its

---

[1] Eph. 1:13.

[2] Eph. 1:17.

[3] Strictly speaking *the message/word of Christ* is the gospel, rather than the Bible as such. Nonetheless, it is clear that Paul saw the OT scripture as testifying to the gospel (Rom 1:2; 3:21) and the apostolic message as bearing witness to it (Rom 1:1), so the distinction need not be pressed.

fullness (Acts 20:27; Col 1:25) and to live lives of model obedience to it (1 Tim. 4:16; Jas 3:1). Christian people are called not to neglect the word or take it for granted but to have it *dwell richly* among them.

It is widely recognized that the books of Ephesians and Colossians are closely related,[4] so the close overlap of the two passages we are considering comes as no surprise. The following table shows how closely they mirror each other.

Ephesians 5:18–21	Colossians 3:15–17
Command: *Be filled with (by) the* **Spirit** (18)	**Command:** *Let the* **message of Christ** *dwell among you richly . . .* (16a)
Consequences: *Speaking to one another* (19a) *Sing . . . to the Lord* (19b) *Giving thanks to God* (20) *Submitting to one another* (21)	**Consequences:** *Teach and admonish one another* (16b) *Singing to God* (16c) *Do it all in the name of the Lord Jesus* (17a) *Giving thanks to God* (17b)

Both passages begin with an image of surplus and abundance (filling, dwelling richly); both envisage Christians gathering together to speak truth into each other's lives, sing praise to God and give thanks to him; both expect that the blessing of their gathering will overflow into transformed living in every sphere of their existence. The striking difference is that, while in Ephesians Paul begins with God's people *being filled by the Spirit*, in Colossians he begins with the word of the gospel dwelling *richly among them.* Of course we must not conclude that the Spirit *is* (to all intents and purposes) the word, nor that the word is the Spirit. Still it is surely clear that the word and the Spirit work together in the closest possible relationship, making authentic Christian worship a dynamic, supernatural event and not a mere social gathering or ministerial performance.

---

[4] 'So similar are the letters in theology, general content and even (at a number of places) in exact wording that scholars are united in thinking that these two letters have a very close relationship' (D. J. Moo, *The Letters to the Colossians and to Philemon*, PNTC [Nottingham: Apollos, 2008], p. 36). Although the consensus in biblical scholarship is against Pauline authorship of both letters, a good case can be made for their authenticity in both cases and I will assume it in this chapter. See Moo, *Colossians and Philemon*, pp. 28–40 and H. W. Hoehner, *Ephesians: An Exegetical Commentary* (Grand Rapids: Baker Academic, 2003), pp. 2–61.

This should not come as any surprise to us at this stage in our exploration of the biblical material on worship, for we have seen that the word of God and the presence of God have stood at the heart of the worship of the people of God throughout the story of salvation.[5] The people of Israel whom Yahweh called out of Egypt so that they could 'worship him in the desert'[6] were given his word (the law) to believe and obey, and his presence (in the tabernacle) to honour and celebrate. In many ways they fell short of this calling until the coming of Jesus, the true Israelite who showed himself to be the true worshipper, trusting God's word fully and honouring God's presence as holy. In the wake of Jesus' perfect obedience, a new worshipping community was born, united to him through faith; a community which receives God's word by the truth he reveals and encounters God's presence by the Spirit he gives. In a sense that was never fully realized in the Old Testament, we can now be the 'worshippers the Father seeks'[7] because Jesus has come to reveal to us the word of the gospel and to give to us the intimate presence of God through the ministry of the out-poured Holy Spirit. As Jesus explained to the Samaritan woman by Sycar's well,

A time is coming and has now come when the true worshippers will *worship* the Father *in the Spirit and in truth*, for they are the kind of worshippers the Father seeks. God is spirit, and his worshippers must *worship in the Spirit and in truth*.[8]

God's word speaks into the whole of life and his Spirit is given to empower our obedience and encourage our hearts in all of life, so that we become 'whole-life worshippers'.[9] Nonetheless, the passages we are exploring in this chapter primarily address the context of the gathered church,[10] ascribing a continuing significance and centrality to corporate worship. Together they give us some of the clearest calls in the New Testament to engage dynamically with the two great realities of the word of God and the Spirit/presence of God, which (as we have seen) are the essential ingredients of authentic worship:

*Let the **word** of Christ dwell richly among you* (Col. 3:16).

[5] This biblical trajectory is worked out fully in chs. 2–6 of this book.
[6] Exod. 7:16.
[7] John 4:23.
[8] John 4:23–24, emphasis added.
[9] See ch. 11 of this book.
[10] 'This verse [Col. 3:16] is one of the very few that provide us with any window at all into the worship of the earliest Christians' (Moo, *Colossians and Philemon*, p. 290). 'This passage [Eph. 5:19ff] goes on to deal with worship in the assembly' (A. T. Lincoln, *Ephesians*, WBC 42 [Waco: Word Books, 1990], p. 343).

*Be filled by the Holy **Spirit*** (Eph. 5:18).

The *commands* are both plural in their form, and the *consequences of responding to those commands* are experienced not primarily by the individual Christian in isolation, but by the church gathered together (speaking to *one another*, submitting to *one another*, teaching and admonishing *one another* and giving thanks). In other words we are right to nurture the expectation of a particular encounter with the dynamic presence of the Spirit and the indwelling richness of the word when we gather together, and so to see a unique significance, still, in the corporate worship of the church.

We can identity five implications for our understanding and practice of Christian worship.

1. We give a rich welcome to the word of Christ (Col. 3:16)

Let the message of Christ dwell among you richly as you teach and admonish one another with all wisdom through psalms, hymns, and songs from the Spirit, singing to God with gratitude in your hearts.

Eugene Peterson captures this thought memorably in the Message when he paraphrases this verse, 'Let the Word of Christ – the Message – have the run of the house. Give it plenty of room in your lives' (16a). The image is of the word of Christ (that is Holy Scripture, as centred on and interpreted through Christ) taking up 'permanent residence'[11] such that the whole community is transformed by its presence. We are called to let this word dwell *richly* among us. Our welcoming of the word 'should not be superficial or passing but . . . it should be a deep and penetrating contemplation that enables the message to have transforming power in the life of the community'.[12] Traditionally, this verse has been read primarily at the individual level (the word of God dwelling richly in our lives) and the original could be read in this way. However, 'the rest of the verse, with its focus on the worship of the collective body, suggests that Paul is urging the community as a whole to put the message about Christ at the centre of its corporate experience'.[13]

There is a fairly obvious (but much needed) application in terms of the teaching and preaching of Scripture within the life of the church. The word is not given a *rich* welcome when we place endless downward pressure on the time given to the exploration of Scripture within our services; or when it is only used as series of 'pegs' on which

[11] Moo, *Colossians and Philemon*, p. 286.
[12] Ibid.
[13] Ibid., p. 286; hence the translation of TNIV and NIV 2011, *let the message of Christ dwell **among you** richly . . .*

to 'hang' the favoured themes of the preacher or strategies for church growth that happen to be fashionable at the time; or when expectations are focused on witnessing another sparkling performance from our favourite celebrity preacher; or when we insist that the word must be primarily about us and our lives, rather than about God and his purposes; or when, obsessed with novelty, our only interest is in hearing something we have never heard before, rather than having our hearts wooed, won and fashioned again by the great and familiar themes of Scripture. On the contrary, churches which give the word a *rich* welcome will be glad to give it sufficient time within their services. Their hunger will be less for novelty or entertainment and more for the nourishing, bracing, humbling, heart-winning, worship-evoking delight of hearing the powerful voice of the speaking God through his unfailing and trustworthy word. They will embrace the truth that, while Scripture often calls for a practical response, sometimes it asks us simply to stand in trembling joy before the majesty, holiness and saving grace of God. They will commit themselves to hearing the whole of Scripture, whether familiar or new, comforting or challenging, warmly encouraging or shockingly difficult, reassuringly practical or stretchingly doctrinal. Their deepest desire will be simply to let Scripture say what it says and to receive that truth with humility and joy.

It is striking, however, that Paul's vision for what it means for the word of Christ to *dwell richly among* God's people extends beyond the sermon to our singing together.[14] Singing provides a wonderful vehicle for expressing response to God, but worship music must never become mere self-expression. For worship to be authentic it must be a response to the God who is there and who reveals himself through his word. It should therefore be the truth of Scripture that summons us to worship, that directs the theme and flow of our worship (including our singing) and that echoes clearly in the words of the songs we sing.

2. We nurture an expectant openness to the Holy Spirit (Eph. 5:18)

Do not get drunk on wine, which leads to debauchery. Instead, be filled with the Spirit.

---

[14] Comparison of NIV and ESV reveals that there is some uncertainty as to whether the *teaching and admonishing* (v. 16) stands in parallel (ESV) to the singing of *psalms, hymns and spiritual songs* (v. 16) or is the means by which the *teaching and admonishing* is delivered (NIV). Either way there is a focus on the biblical content of what we sing together. In support of the NIV see P. T. O'Brien, *Colossians, Philemon*, WBC 44 (Waco: Word Books, 1982), pp. 208–209, and Moo, *Colossians and Philemon*, pp. 286–288.

The same expectation of a continuing, dynamic experience of the Holy Spirit that we noted in the prayer of Ephesians 1 is reflected here in the call to *be filled with/by the Spirit*. The fact that Paul *commands* us to be filled, makes clear our responsibility to nurture a relationship of expectant openness to the Holy Spirit; the fact that the command is *passive* (*be filled . . .*) makes clear that we cannot fill ourselves; the fact that the command is in the *present tense* makes clear that this filling is not only a single experience[15] but a continuing expectation of his powerful presence being manifested among his people.[16] The contrast with being *drunk on wine* has been the subject of considerable debate,[17] and may well have a background in the orgiastic worship of the readers' pagan past. If so, the point may be less that they should 'come under the influence' of the Spirit in ecstatic worship (rather than being intoxicated by wine) and more that truly spiritual worship will evidence the fruit of self-control.

Gordon Fee warns us that 'one misses too much if this text is completely individualised'. He adds that there is great need 'for God's people individually to take this imperative with all seriousness. But in its immediate context the imperative has to do with community life'.[18] In other words we should think not only of individuals being filled by the Holy Spirit of God, but whole church communities so alive with his powerful presence that the vitality of their corporate worship and the quality of their daily lives, together demonstrate that God is truly among them.[19]

Probably the best way to understand what Paul really means by this command is to see the way it is reflected in his prayers throughout Ephesians. The fact that such prayers need to be prayed underlines our responsibility to seek the filling of the Spirit, while the nature of prayer reminds us that we are dependent on God and unable to fill ourselves. In chapter 1 Paul's prayer for 'the Spirit of wisdom and revelation' is explicitly directed towards the deepening of their knowledge of God and his purposes in Christ (Eph. 1:17–23). This knowledge is not only intellectual but also personal and relational as the Spirit opens their hearts and minds both to understand God's truth and to experience its reality in their lives. In chapter 3, he goes on to pray that, 'out of his glorious riches [God] may strengthen

---

[15] Though it is clear in the book of Acts that the Holy Spirit does sometimes give a special 'for the moment' filling of his power and presence (e.g. Acts 4:8).

[16] These points are all made in Hoehner, *Ephesians*, p. 704.

[17] See, e.g., O'Brien, *Ephesians*, pp. 388–391.

[18] G. D. Fee, *God's Empowering Presence* (Peabody: Hendrickson Publishers, Inc., 1995), p. 722.

[19] See 1 Cor. 14:25.

you with power through his Spirit in your inner being, so that Christ may dwell in your hearts through faith'.[20]

For Paul, then, the filling by the Spirit is a powerful work, an inner, spiritual work and a work which fosters deep fellowship with Christ. It is, furthermore, a work that brings us into a profound encounter with the vastness of the love of God, an encounter which expands the generosity of our missional imagination[21] and feeds our souls with rich, personal experience as we come to 'know this love that surpasses knowledge'.[22]

The conclusion of the prayer in chapter 3 is that Paul's readers 'may be filled to the measure of all the fullness of God'[23] and it is likely that this provides the framework for our understanding of what Paul means by our being *filled by/with the Spirit.* In other words, the end goal is not so much that the Holy Spirit fills us with his (singular) presence, but that by his presence he fills us with the fullness of the whole of the Holy Trinity.[24] It is hard to imagine a more thrilling expectation to bring to our experience of corporate worship. Gone is the pride that comes merely to evaluate or (worse) to find fault; gone is the consumerism that hopes merely to have things the way we like them; gone is the attitude of the spectator whose only interest is to watch others perform. In their place is an expectant, humble faith in the God who 'fills the hungry with good things'[25] and who comes to his people still by the dynamic Spirit, so that they encounter the Father's everlasting love and majestic holiness, the radiant glory and all-sufficient grace of Christ and the powerful, transforming presence of the Holy Spirit.

The encouragement for us is that Paul is confident that such a wealth of spiritual experience for God's people is entirely possible. 'Now to him who is able to do immeasurably more than all we ask or imagine, according to his power that is at work within us, to him

[20] Eph. 3:16–17.

[21] See Eph. 3:18. In the context of Ephesians, with its emphasis on the uniting of Jew and Gentile within the Spirit-filled community, these dimensions of the love of God probably have their primary application in moving us to embrace the diversity of people whom Christ welcomes into his church.

[22] Eph. 3:19a: the rich, paradoxical language employed here must surely suggest a depth of personal experience which is more than just cognitive.

[23] Eph. 3:19b.

[24] The technical debate here is whether the Gk of Eph. 5:18 *(en pneumati)* is to be understood in an instrumental sense (the Spirit is the *means* by which we are filled with the fullness of God) or as indicating the *content* with which we are filled (we are filled *with the Spirit* himself). The first view seems much closer to Paul's approach in his prayers in chs. 1 and 3 and is the one I am adopting. See O'Brien, *Ephesians,* pp. 391–392 for this position.

[25] Luke 1:53.

be glory in the church and in Christ Jesus throughout all generations, for ever and ever! Amen.'[26]

The challenge for us is both that Paul feels it necessary to pray for such experience of the Holy Spirit, as we have seen, and that he commands the believers to seek such experience in our passage. In other words, his work among us is not automatic: he comes to the hungry not to the self-satisfied; he comes in response to the prayers of God's people.

Practically, then, this is a call for passionate, committed prayer for the corporate worship of the church. Careful preparation, good organization and high quality training all have their place and should not be denigrated, but if our experience of corporate worship has become stale, the key question to ask is whether the church is truly praying. Nonetheless, alongside this, we need to ask whether our structures and leadership of corporate worship nurture the expectation of a powerful encounter with God, by the work of his Spirit. Do we acknowledge and welcome God's presence by the attitude of our hearts and the words we use to call people to worship? Do we provide accessible opportunities for prayer and counsel because we expect God to be at work? Do we leave any room for the unexpected?

As we have seen, Paul anticipates certain consequences in the life of the church when we take to heart these commands to *let the message of Christ dwell among* us *richly* and to *be filled with the Spirit.*[27] We will now consider each of these briefly.

3. We minister to one another as we sing (Eph. 5:19a; Col. 3:16)

. . . speaking to one another with psalms, hymns, and songs from the Spirit (Eph. 5:19a).

It seems surprising to us that Paul begins here. Our default is to assume that our singing is solely directed towards God, but Paul clearly believes that much of it is directed towards each other.[28] Many of the psalms in fact follow this pattern, telling the story of salvation in such a way that the community is taught, reminded and moulded,[29] or teaching the way of wisdom such that its lessons are

---

[26] Eph. 3:20–21.

[27] This is especially clear in the syntax of Eph. 5:18–21 where the initial command is followed by four dependent participial clauses in vv. 19–21: i.e. . . . *be filled with the Spirit: speaking to one another . . .; singing and making music . . .; always giving thanks . . .; submitting to one another . . .*

[28] This is clear in Eph. 5:18. It is also clear in the NIV translation of Col. 3:16, but less clear in the ESV and NRSV.

[29] See for example the salvation history psalms such as Pss 78, 105, 106, 136.

absorbed deep into the heart and life.[30] This *teaching function* of music is made explicit in the NIV translation of Colossians 3:16: *Let the message of Christ dwell among you richly as you* **teach and admonish** *one another with all wisdom* **through** *psalms, hymns, and songs from the Spirit.*

However, we should also consider more widely the effect on others of our participation in congregational worship. I may come to a gathering of the church full of struggle and doubt, finding it very difficult to lift my heart in praise to the Lord, but as I stand alongside you in the solidarity of congregational worship, my faith is encouraged by your faith, my praise stirred up by your praise even as my struggle and lament[31] may lead you to prayer and to a deeper authenticity of relationship with God: we *speak to one another* as we sing.

The songs we sing in corporate worship are described in both of our passages as *psalms, hymns and songs from the Spirit.* The terms are all used in the titles of the psalms (in the Septuagint) and attempts to distinguish sharply between them are generally felt to have been unsuccessful. It is possible, though, that we should understand *psalms* as referring to Christian use of the Old Testament Psalms, *hymns* as new compositions celebrating the person and work of Christ and *songs from the Spirit* as more spontaneous songs of response prompted by the Holy Spirit.[32] Whatever the precise distinctions may or may not be, the fact that Paul uses all three terms is at least a reminder that it is helpful for our musical repertoire to include both songs which are rich in biblical content and some simpler songs which give a vehicle for appropriate response.

4. We lift our hearts to God in song (Eph. 5:19b; Col. 3:16b)

Sing and make music from your heart to the Lord (Eph. 5:19b).

Paul now turns from the horizontal dimension of corporate worship to the vertical, as he encourages us to sing *to the Lord* [i.e. to Christ] (Eph. 5:19) or *to God* (Col. 3:16). The reference to the *heart* does not imply a silent, inward praise, nor only an emotional ('heartfelt') praise. 'Rather, *heart* here signifies the whole of one's being. The entire person should be filled with songs of praise; thereby expressing the reality of life in the Spirit.'[33] We are not called only to sing words; we are called to give the whole of ourselves to the

---

[30] See for example Pss 1, 37, 73 and 133.

[31] See the next chapter of this book for the much neglected theme of lament in corporate worship.

[32] See Moo, *Colossians and Philemon*, p. 290.

[33] P. T. O'Brien, *The Letter to the Ephesians*, PNTC (Leicester: Apollos, 1999), p. 396.

worship of God, choosing to lift our hearts to him as we sing his praise.

It has often been pointed out that we have relatively little biblical material on which to base our understanding of what characterized the gatherings of the earliest churches. It is clear from these passages, though, that singing played a significant part in their meetings. Indeed, the logic of Paul's argument is that one of the signs that the Holy Spirit is filling the church and that the word of Christ is welcomed in the church, is that God's people desire to sing, both as a declaration of their faith and as an act of praise and celebration.[34]

In order to bring this material together it may be helpful to pause and draw out some of the dynamics of corporate worship in a diagrammatic way, highlighting the interactions between the worshippers, their engagement together with God and the overflow of corporate worship into the everyday worship of whole life discipleship.

5. We go out to live the whole of life as worship (Eph. 5:21; Col. 3:17)

And whatever you do, whether in word or deed, do it all in the name of the Lord Jesus, giving thanks to God the Father through him (Col. 3:17).

We do not need to develop a theology of whole-life worship *in place of* a theology of gathered worship because according to Paul, the two belong together. Authentic corporate worship, which is

---

[34] Daniel Block argues from these passages that '(1) Music provides an outlet for demonstrating that one is filled with the Spirit. (2) Music is a means of promoting community in the body of Christ: we sing to one another. (3) Music is an expression of thanksgiving to God; believers need to be thankful in all circumstances. (4) Whether sung or played, music arising from a thankful heart brings glory to God' (D. I. Block, *For the Glory of God: Recovering a Biblical Theology of Worship* [Kindle edn., Grand Rapids: Baker Academic, 2014], loc. 4482.

Spirit-filled and rich with the truth of the gospel, is characterized by its effect on the worship of our whole lives. When we come together we meet to worship God by magnifying the glory of Christ and expressing the thanks and praise of our hearts; when we leave, we go to worship him by living for the glory of Christ (*do it all in the name of the Lord Jesus*) and seasoning every aspect of our lives with gratitude and praise (*giving thanks to God the Father through him*). The Ephesians passage makes essentially the same point as it calls us to *submit to one another out of reverence for Christ* (Eph. 5:21), and then works out that call in detail in marriage, family life and the workplace (Eph. 5:22 – 6:9). The same Spirit whose presence fills us as we gather for worship, empowers us as we go to worship in the whole of life; the same gospel message which we welcome in our corporate worship, is sufficient to direct and give meaning to all we do as we go to worship in our homes, families and workplaces.

The Christian life works on the 'overflow principle':[35] we can only authentically minister the grace of God to others from the overflow of the grace he has first ministered to us. Anything else would, of course, be a denial of the gospel. In the same way, God's plan is so to bless us in our gatherings for corporate worship that the blessing will overflow into the joyful obedience that transforms the whole of life into ceaseless praise.

[35] I am grateful to Rev. S. Silvester of St Nicholas' Church, Nottingham for helping me to see this.

Psalms 42 – 43
19. The voice of lament: A troubled soul

My wife, Alison, and I decided to go to church on the evening of 18 April, 1993. Our hearts were too broken to face the busyness and energy of the morning service but we knew the evening would be quieter and more intimate. In the early hours of the previous morning the carefree happiness of our early years of marriage had been shattered by our first encounter with devastating personal loss: our new son, Daniel, who had been born prematurely, had passed from the arms of his human parents into the arms of his heavenly Father, having lost his fight for earthly life. Raw with grief and wearied by many tears, we knew we needed to be with our church family. Poignantly enough, much of the service focused on the hope of glory, though the sadness of our situation was sensitively acknowledged. At the end the piano continued to play a chorus, which spoke simply of the Lord giving strength in weakness and riches in poverty.[1] Quietly, members of the congregation began spontaneously to join in the song and soon we were surrounded by the tender sound of our dearest friends and Christian family – still reeling from the shock of our unexpected loss and clearly sharing in our pain, yet sharing also in our faith that God had not abandoned us though we did not understand his ways. As the song faded, one and then another began to pray for us before a final song brought the evening to its close. It was a moment of deeply shared grief and intense encounter with God, which we will never forget,[2] providing us with an experience rather akin to that of King David who, after

---

[1] The song was 'Give Thanks with a Grateful Heart' by Henry Smith (Integrity's Hosanna! Music, 1978).
[2] We were members of Cornerstone Evangelical Church, Nottingham, and this provides a welcome opportunity for us to record our profound gratitude to the church for being to us everything that a church should be in such circumstances.

learning of the death of his son, 'went into the house of the Lord and worshipped'.[3]

I cannot write about the experience of that evening without overwhelming emotion. Still, more than two decades later what really strikes me is just how rare such experiences of shared sadness and communal grief are in our churches today. It was not always so. The hymnody of previous generations made space for the lament;[4] the church of today rarely does.[5] If we take the book of Psalms as our guide, it seems that the worship of ancient Israel was rather different. Using the 'genre analysis' to which we referred in chapter 7, the following table attempts to summarize the prevalence of different kinds of psalm.[6]

Psalms of lament	66
Psalms of celebration and affirmation	29
Hymns of praise	16
Thanksgiving psalms	16
Psalms of trust	10
Wisdom psalms	8
Salvation history psalms	5

What is immediately striking is just how prominent the psalms of lament are within the Psalter. Even if we take together all the psalms of celebration, affirmation, praise and thanks, still they are outnumbered by the laments. Reggie Kidd has pointed out that across the five books of the Psalms there is a sense of movement:

The Psalter helps to tell the story of a journey from suffering to glory and from lament to praise . . . In Books One through Three (Psalms 1–89), so called 'laments' outnumber 'hymns of praise' by a little more than two to one, while in Books Four and Five (Psalms 90–150), the proportion is reversed, and actually amplified – here 'Hymns' of praise outnumber 'laments' seven-to-three.[7]

[3] 2 Sam. 12:20.

[4] The hymns of William Cowper are notable in this regard, most famously 'God moves in a mysterious way, his wonders to perform'. A lesser known Cowper hymn, which begins 'My soul is sad and much dismayed . . .' is not a firm favourite in any church that I know of!

[5] Two wonderful exceptions are Matt and Beth Redman's 'Blessed be your name' and Stuart Townend's 'We have sung our songs of victory'.

[6] The analysis is based on material from G. D. Fee and D. Stuart, *How to Read the Bible for All Its Worth* (Grand Rapids: Zondervan, 1982), pp. 175–177. It should be noted, however, that these categories are not all precisely defined and that some may overlap, so the figures are at best only a rough guide.

[7] R. M. Kidd, *With One Voice: Discovering Christ's Song in Our Worship* (Grand Rapids: Baker Books, 2005), p. 29.

It is nonetheless telling that even at the end of that 'journey', lament remains a part of the worship of the people of God.[8]

Many of the psalms of lament give voice to the troubles of individuals (e.g. Pss 3; 22; 31; 39; 42; 139; 142), while others enable a community to grieve together (e.g. Pss 12; 44; 80; 94; 137). This is hardly surprising in the light of the 'saw-toothed history'[9] of Israel recounted in the Old Testament, with its many stories of personal struggle (not least those of David prior to and during his reign), its cycles of rebellion, judgment and restoration and its long descent towards exile, loss and destruction. It is perfectly possible that even the songs of individual lament sometimes found their way into the corporate worship of Israel. Some of the psalms of lament[10] take us through a process of grief or grievance, towards some kind of resolution. Others do not resolve.[11] God, it seems, wants us to keep talking to him, even when we can see no light at all and when all that we have to bring him is the outpouring of our heart's bewilderment in the face of the contradictions of life. Of course, believers in every age experience such bewilderment and many of them find themselves voicing their feelings to God. The problem is that when they complain to God or question him, they often imagine that they are moving towards the edge of faith with God looking on in deep disapproval. The psalms of lament give us over sixty reasons to conclude that it need not be so. These psalms are God's *gift* to us, his provision of words that we can use and make our own when our hearts are broken and our faith is troubled by personal loss or communal disaster. These psalms are God's *permission* to us to share honestly with him the untidy realities of our confused hearts, when we are passing through painful experiences. These psalms are God's *evidence* for us, that to speak to him in the voice of lament is not so much a sign of weakening faith as of robust and honest faith – precisely because we're talking *to God*. Perhaps most profoundly of all, because these psalms are, paradoxically, *God's word to us*, we may use them with confidence as *our words to him*, knowing that we will not be pushed away.

I was moved to read of a young theological student who had been called to hospital where his sick mother was in a critical condition. As he drove to the hospital, fearing the worst, he said, 'I wanted to sing Christian songs, but nothing I had really fitted. Everything was

---

[8] See, for example, Ps. 142 which, though confident in God's ultimate goodness, is raw in its expression of complaint to God.

[9] E. H. Peterson, *A Long Obedience in the Same Direction: Discipleship in an Instant Society* (Downers Grove: InterVarsity Press, 2000), pp. 86–87.

[10] Such as Pss 42 – 43, to which we shall turn shortly.

[11] Most notably Ps. 88, though Ps. 89 also ends on a dark note.

too triumphant and – if I can use this word – easy.' In the end he found refuge in the psalms of lament. 'In the Psalms I discovered the emotions I was feeling were shared by the Psalmist, and that the Psalms resonated with my experiences and how I was feeling.'[12] His experience has been paralleled by all too many believers over the years: some battling with depression, some whose introverted temperament is ill at ease with the exuberance of many hymns and songs, some who, like Job, experience successive losses in their lives and some who are troubled by the injustices, griefs and agonies of a suffering world. For their sakes – and to rescue us all from the shallowness of triumphalism – we dare not neglect the psalms of lament. If we are in any doubt, we should let the 'singing Saviour'[13] himself be our guide, for as he suffered on the cross for our salvation, the Lord Jesus sang with the voice of lament, making the words of the psalmist his own, 'My God, my God, why have you forsaken me?'[14]

1. Approaching Psalms 42 and 43

Psalms 42 and 43 very likely form a single poem, bound together by the common refrain of 42:5, 11 and 43:5,[15] so I will refer to it as a single psalm henceforth. It is a psalm which gives voice to the grief of an individual, but many of its themes are sufficiently familiar for many believers to find that it speaks for them also. One of the most striking features of the psalm is that it is full of questions – thirteen of them, in fact. Some of the questions are taunts from the lips of the sceptical, but most are the questions of perplexed faith, asked by a believer who feels far from God but who longs for him nonetheless (42:1). Exactly why he feels this way we cannot be entirely sure. The *Sons of Korah* mentioned in the heading of the psalm, were part of the Kohathite clan of Levites, whom 'David put in charge of the music in the house of the LORD after the ark came to rest there'.[16] The fact that they are mentioned in the headings of eleven of the psalms[17] suggests that they had become a recognized guild of musicians serving in the Jerusalem temple.[18] For the writer of our

---

[12] See M. Searles, 'Shaped by the Psalms' in the Oak Hill College magazine *Commentary*, summer 2014, p. 24, <http://www.oakhill.ac.uk/commentary/14_summer/index.html>.

[13] To use Reggie Kidd's suggestive phrase (*With One Voice*, pp. 84–86).

[14] Mark 15:34; cf. Ps. 22:1.

[15] As indicated in the NIV footnote.

[16] 1 Chr. 6:31–38.

[17] Pss 42; 44 – 49; 84; 85; 87; 88.

[18] M. Wilcock, *The Message of Psalms 1-72*, BST (Leicester: Inter-Varsity Press, 2001), p. 152.

psalm, however, the temple worship of Jerusalem is now a painful memory – he *used to go to the house of God* (42:4) and yearns to still (42:1–2) but he no longer can. He finds himself in *the heights of Hermon* (42:6), a snow-capped peak in the far north of Israel rising to about 3,000 m, in whose foothills the River Jordan rises. He is surrounded by unbelievers from *an unfaithful nation* (43:1) who taunt him with questions about his God who now seems completely absent (42:3, 10). Perhaps, then, an army from the north (possibly from Samaria) has carried out a raid on Jerusalem and taken away as hostages some of those who served in the temple – including the writer of our psalm.[19] We need not press for certainty, however, because this is a psalm not just for one situation, but for every situation in which the people of God feel far from and confused by his ways and yet long to come near to him again.

The psalm is broken into three obvious stanzas, each of which is concluded by a refrain. Within each stanza there appears to be a pattern which John Goldingay has identified helpfully. 'In each [stanza] the psalmist begins by *letting himself go*: he gives expression to his feelings. In each he goes on to *make himself think*: he turns his mind away from the present situation. In each, finally, in similar words he *pulls himself together*.'[20] We could summarize this cycle as:

- *Release* (letting oneself go: 42:1–3, 6–7; 43:1–2).
- *Reflection* (making oneself think: 42:4, 8–10; 43:3–4).
- *Reorientation* (pulling oneself together: 42:5, 11; 43:5).

As we will see, the psalm as a whole also displays something of the same pattern, moving from a stronger element of *release* in the first stanza to a more definitive *reorientation* in the third, via the *reflection* of the second. Traditionally the British culture in which I have grown up has been said to have little place for the rawness of emotion we find in psalms like this one, but this is changing. Many of us today place a high value on how we *feel* about things, to the extent that we run the risk of making ourselves the victims of our emotions. The pattern of this psalm offers us a third way, inviting us neither to suppress our emotions, nor to make them into an idol, but rather to face them and *speak truth* into them. Derek Kidner calls this process

---

[19] 2 Kgs 14:11–14 describes exactly such a raid.
[20] J. Goldingay, *Songs From a Strange Land: Psalms 42-51* (Leicester: Inter-Varsity Press, 1978), p. 27, italics mine. In his later commentary on the Psalms he replaces these three with 'Lament, plea and a looking to the future' (J. Goldingay, *Psalms: Psalms 42–89* [Michigan: Baker Academic, 2007], p. 21).

'self-communing'[21] and it is a deeply helpful model for all who wish to process the setbacks of life within the framework of biblical faith.

2. Feeling far from God (42:1–5)

The first question of the psalm encapsulates the writer's experience. *When can I go and meet with God* (2)? Perhaps he had been driven by his captors through a barren landscape (if this is indeed the setting of the psalm) on the way to Israel's northern mountains and had been struck by the sight and sound of a deer running by, audibly panting for water. As the deer had disappeared into the undergrowth and the visceral sound of its gasping faded, he had become aware of a continuing echo of its pantings deep in his own heart, and it is this echo which becomes the point of departure for his psalm. He is thirsty for God, with a thirst every bit as deeply felt as that of the parched creature.

> *As the deer pants for streams of water,*
> *so my soul pants for you, my God.*
> *My soul thirsts for God, for the living God* (1–2).

Yet in every sense, it seems that he is far away from God. *Geographically*[22] he is far from the Jerusalem temple and its worship which he so loved. *Emotionally* it feels that God has lost all interest in him, so that his *tears have been* [his] *food day and night* (3a). *Circumstantially* he can find no answer to the persistent taunts of his enemies who ask *'Where is your God?'*(3b).

With no resort to easy platitudes and feeling no need to disguise the raw feelings he is experiencing, the writer *pours out his soul* (4) to God. The sense of emotional release is intense, but he does not stop at that point. How he feels is important but it is not the only thing that is important; what he thinks matters too, so he must allow himself space to reflect. He knows about God that he is living and desirable (2). He knows about himself that he needs God and longs for him (1–2). So he takes himself through a journey of the mind, *remembering* his past experience of God.

> *These things I remember*
> *as I pour out my soul:*
> *how I used to go to the house of God*
> *under the protection of the Mighty One*

[21] D. Kidner, *Psalms 1–72*, TOTC (Leicester: Inter-Varsity Press, 1973), p. 166.
[22] Although Michael Wilcock suggests that the reference could be metaphorical: in his heart he is far from Jerusalem (*Psalms 1–72*, p. 154).

> *with shouts of joy and praise*
> *among the festive throng* (4).

This is not mere wistful nostalgia; it is reflection by means of the discipline of remembering (that was so deeply engrained in Hebrew spirituality).[23] The God he longs for is no stranger to him, for he has met him often; he has been to his house; he has experienced the joy of his people as he joined them in praise.

The final step in the first stanza may come as a surprise: he has *let himself go* and *made himself think*; now he *talks to himself* in a moment of profound personal reorientation, in which he directly applies the fruit of his reflection to the turmoil of his inner life.

> *Why, my soul, are you downcast?*
> *Why so disturbed within me?*
> *Put your hope in God,*
> *for I will yet praise him,*
> *my Saviour and my God* (5).

Superficially, talking to oneself is often associated with mental derangement in the popular imagination. More significantly, this direct challenging of personal feelings sits uneasily in a therapeutic culture that has grown up in the soil of existentialism. However, the willingness to confront our feelings with the truth of what God has revealed is a vital part of biblical spirituality – even of biblical worship. The confrontation (for confrontation it truly is) begins by daring to question our feelings, 'Look, you singing son of Korah, why are you feeling like this? Why are you so disoriented by your experience? Has God changed? Is he not still worthy of your hope and trust?' In the Western world today, our default position is to question our faith and trust our doubts. The Bible turns this upside down: we must learn to question our doubts and to trust our faith.[24] That is exactly what the psalmist is doing in this verse, which concludes with a positive encouragement to invest hope in the God who will not finally disappoint us (5b).

3. Feeling confused by God (42:6–11)

Though books on bereavement often describe a 'typical' process of grief, people who experience bereavement often find that their grief is rather untidy and fits no clear pattern. Similarly, while the elements

---

[23] See, for example, Deut. 4:10; 5:15; 7:18; 8:2, 18; 15:15; 16:3, 12.

[24] I am grateful to my friend and long-term pastor Peter Lewis for teaching me this principle.

of *release, reflection and reorientation* are all discernible here, they are woven together in the turbulent stream of consciousness that makes up this middle stanza. Once again a question stands at the heart of the writer's concerns: *I say to God my Rock, 'Why have you forgotten me?'* (9a). Sometimes God's ways are so confusing to us.

We quickly see that there is no denial or superficiality about the *reorientation* of verse 5; he is not instantaneously 'fixed'! His soul still *downcast* (6) and he has the integrity to face his emotions again, but again he takes an unexpected turn: *My soul is downcast within me; **therefore** I will remember you* (6a, emphasis mine).

Typically when we are downcast we want to forget God, but this poet knows better. The moments when we are downcast are the very moments when we most need to *remember* him, though we may have to fight hard to enable ourselves to do so. The reality of that struggle is clear in the rather harrowing verses that follow. He will indeed remember God, though not from his treasured earthly dwelling place (the Jerusalem temple) but from far away in the unfamiliar foothills of Mount Hermon, where the Jordan River rises:[25] that is precisely what pains him so. 'The streams that come together to form the Jordan pass through several waterfalls and cascades of crashing waters where deep calls to deep, and breakers and waves pass over rocks and bathers.'[26] Standing beside one of these foaming, watery cauldrons, he sees an image of the churning chaos of his heart and hears echoes of his confused inner conversation (7a). Mention of the *deep* shifts the metaphor to the roaring oceans themselves, whose mighty waves seem to be closing over him (7b).

Notwithstanding all the confusion, the desire to remember God remains. The waters whose cries seem to give voice to his confusion and whose waves threaten to engulf him, belong to God; they are *his* (7). The thought is 'both a further distress and a comfort'.[27] Superficially it would seem easier on his faith if the writer could avoid that conclusion – after all, how could he ever trust a God whose mysterious wisdom had in some sense permitted this disaster to happen? Probably every believer is tempted at some point in their life to suppose that God is less than he really is: less powerful, less sovereign, less knowing. This troubled poet understands, however, that to take that path is to saw off the final branch on which faith sits and so to court disaster. If *God* has lost control, *we* have lost the only hope that remains to us. So rather than diminish God and destroy hope, he will live with the paradox of a God whose love is

[25] No firm identification of Mount Mizar has been made, but it probably refers to a small hill in the vicinity of Mount Hermon.
[26] Goldingay, *Psalms 42-89*, p. 27.
[27] Ibid., p. 28.

always unfailing (8a) but not always apparent to him (9–10), who is always worthy of praise (8b) but also open to questioning (9–10). It is difficult to live with such paradox, but rather than stew over it he prays over it, bringing his questions to *the God of his life* (8b), his *Rock* (9b).

> *I say to God my Rock,*
>   *'Why have you forgotten me?*
> *Why must I go about mourning,*
>   *oppressed by the enemy?'*
> *My bones suffer mortal agony*
>   *as my foes taunt me,*
> *saying to me all day long,*
>   *'Where is your God?'* (9–10)

The questions hang, unanswered. The air remains thick with the painful taunts of his enemies. Yet the very fact that he finds himself still talking to God strengthens his conviction that God is not, after all, either forgetful or absent. For, though God is remote enough for the writer to feel deserted, he is still near enough for him to speak to. So after this sustained period of honest reflection, he is ready to address himself again with the reorienting words of the repeated refrain (11).

4. Finding hope in God (43:1–5)

Pastoral experience has taught me that people are often surprised at how long the pain of loss can linger. Particularly distressing is the sense of plunging again into despair, just as one was beginning to feel a measure of recovery, provoking a fear that the journey of grief may never end. The cyclical nature of this psalm reflects exactly this experience and so offers us the reassurance that, however painful this repeating pattern of recovery and setback may be, it is actually one of the stages on the road to healing. Still, the psalm is much more than just a grief process; it is testimony of troubled faith in which the grace of God penetrates new levels of the writer's pain with each 'cycle' of release, reflection and reorientation.

This final stanza is unquestionably the most positive of the three, indicating that real steps forward have been taken. Nonetheless, the question at the heart of this stanza is surely the most deeply felt of them all. *Why have you rejected me?* (2) God's inaccessibility (42:2) arises from the writer's trying circumstances; if God has forgotten him (42:9) it could (he might imagine) be because of some kind of divine oversight; but there is no way to soften the suggestion that

God has rejected him. Probably this is the most honest point of the psalm, expressing what he really has been feeling all along. Yet this deeper exposure of his heart to God becomes the means through which he discovers a deeper consolation from God.

Once again, strong emotion characterizes the opening of the stanza but for the first time he has the confidence to make a plea to God.

> *Vindicate me, my God,*
> *and plead my cause*
> *against an unfaithful nation.*
> *Rescue me from those who are*
> *deceitful and wicked* (1).

He is no longer simply absorbing the taunts of his enemies; he is determined that they should see that he was right to keep his trust in God. We have already commented on the raw honesty of verse 2, but it seems likely that the questions are asked with the faith that believes God will act, rather than the resignation that assumes he has forgotten. Confidence grows as he reflects on the *light* and covenant faithfulness[28] of God (3) which had guided Israel through the desert to the Promised Land. He pleads with God to send them to him again, for they will surely lead him back to the blessing for which he so longs.

> *Send me your light and your faithful care,*
> *let them lead me;*
> *let them bring me to your holy mountain,*
> *to the place where you dwell.*
> *Then I will go to the altar of God,*
> *to God, my joy and my delight.*
> *I will praise you with the lyre,*
> *O God, my God* (3–4).

So the psalm, which began with the psalmist longing to be in the place of worship (the Jerusalem temple) finishes with confident anticipation of his return. Whether that was a literal return or a true experience of God's presence in exile is not, perhaps, certain.[29] What we do know is that, having opened the depths of his heart to God in painful lament and reflected on his knowledge of God in thoughtful recollection, this exiled musician who had felt so far from God

[28] Translated 'faithful care' in NIV and 'truth' (in the sense of truthfulness and fidelity) in ESV/NRSV.

[29] Kidner suggests that a physical return may not be in mind, though the language does seem quite concrete (*Psalms 1–72*, pp. 167–168).

is starting to find his hope in God rekindled and his mind reoriented. His soul may still be *downcast* and *disturbed*, but now he can say with firm confidence, *Put your hope in God, for I will yet praise him, my Saviour and my God* (5).

'The situation creating sorrow still exists, but as the question is asked again, "why are you downcast?" the response can now be given with the conviction that God has heard and answered his prayer.'[30]

5. Conclusion

This psalm of lament speaks for believers in all generations whose circumstances lead them to wonder if God is absent or has forgotten or rejected them. What it offers is not a series of trite answers, nor even the expectation of rapid resolution, but rather an invitation to open the deepest reaches of our hearts to God and a vocabulary to enable us to do so. The fact it is found within Holy Scripture means that the psalm gives us *permission from God to speak to God*, expressing to him our most raw emotions and most awkward questions. It also provides *encouragement from God to think about God*, reminding us that honest confusion and faithful reflection need not be mutually exclusive and urging us to cling to what we know of God, even when there is so much that we do not know. Finally the psalm offers *a challenge from God to nurture faith in God* as we make the words of its refrain our own and use them to question our doubts, challenge our feelings and buttress our faith in the God who is our *Saviour.*

Is there a place for such expressions of lament within our worship services today? The answer must surely be yes, though it may be difficult to work it out practically in large gatherings of people coming from such a wide range of life situations. It would be a formidable challenge for songwriters to produce more songs of lament for cheerful churches today and a courageous worship leader who decided to use them extensively. We may, however, be surprised at the appeal such songs would have.[31] In most church gatherings we should remember that there will be those who are hurting and whose faith is under pressure, for whom even a few moments of quiet or a thoughtful prayer can be so helpful. We need to learn how to worship in sadness.

[30] P. C. Craigie, *Psalms 1–50*, WBC 19 (rev. ed., Nashville: Thomas Nelson, Inc., 2004), p. 329.

[31] One only needs to think of the popularity of the songs in the Claude-Michel Shonberg musical *Les Miserables* (many of which are powerful laments) to see that this genre is far from dead.

So the psalms of individual lament (such as the one upon which we have focused in this chapter) have their place in the corporate worship of God's people. However, the psalms of communal lament give us another, equally important model. Perhaps the best known of these is Psalm 137 in which the agonies and taunts of exile are poignantly recalled (1–4), the commitment to continuing faith expressed through gritted teeth (5–6) and the cry for vindication expressed with shocking honesty (7–9).[32] When there is breaking news of a transnational tsunami, an era-defining act of terrorism or an outbreak of war, these psalms give us a model of what real faith looks like in the face of disaster and give us the resources to keep worshipping God together when others have concluded that the time for worship has ended. They can also bring a new dimension to special prayer events which focus on particular needs and struggles in the locality or the wider world, as we allow our prayers of intercession to be seasoned and strengthened by the authenticity of lament. Sometimes a particular tragedy will shake the whole of a local community, leaving church leaders with a tough choice: is their role to 'be strong' and continue with 'business as usual' or should they take the risk of allowing people to express their emotions to God and, through sensitive leadership and prayer, bring the grief of the community to the God who is 'close to the broken-hearted'?[33] The psalms of lament give us permission sometimes to take the second option so that, along with a practical response to local need, the people of God are able to voice lament at a moment when others may find that they have no words.

We should not leave the psalms of lament without recalling again that they were heard on the lips of Jesus. In the psalm we have explored, our struggling poet asked when he could go and meet with God, why God had forgotten him and why God had rejected him. From the cross Jesus, the 'Singing Saviour', responds that he was forsaken so that we might be brought home, that he was rejected so that we might be accepted, and that he died, the righteous for the unrighteous, so that we might be brought to God. He sang in the voice of lament that we might join the new song of salvation. The suffering of his death and the victory of his resurrection are the guarantee that the time for lamenting will not last forever, for he will bring us to the new creation in which every tear is wiped from our eyes and there is no more death, or mourning or crying or pain (Rev 21:4).

[32] Pss 44 and 80 are among the other more striking examples of communal lament.
[33] Ps. 34:18.

Psalms 63 and 85
20. The voice of desire: A raging thirst

> The great hindrance to worship is not that we are pleasure-seeking people, but that we are willing to settle for such pitiful pleasures ... The great barrier to worship among God's people is not that we are always seeking our own satisfaction, but that our seeking is so weak and half-hearted that we settle for little sips at broken cisterns when the fountain of life is just over the next hill.[1]

Ask any pastor or organizer of a large Christian conference and they will tell you that people have very strong feelings about what they want when it comes to 'worship' (by which they normally mean congregational praise). Some want more freedom while others want more structure; some want more liturgy while others want more spontaneity; some want more space and quiet while others want energy and exuberance; some want jazz while others want 'soft rock'; some want an organ while others want a band; some want more hymns while others want more contemporary songs; some want more variety of creative expression while others want more simplicity and familiarity. Doubtless a good case can be made for many of these things, but having personally struggled all too often with the impossibility of satisfying such a wide range of competing desires, I cannot help wondering whether we run the risk of missing the most important desire.

It seems that we are sometimes willing to settle for the 'pitiful pleasure'[2] of having a 'worship experience' that merely conforms as closely as possible to our cultural identity and preferences. The

---

[1] J. Piper, *The Dangerous Duty of Delight* (Colorado: Multnomah Books, 2001), pp. 55–56.
[2] Ibid.

result is painful division, unhelpful distraction and life-sapping complacency. The aim of this final chapter is to cast a vision for worship that is motivated by an altogether different kind of desire: a desire for God himself which transcends the small matters of style and preference, and drives away complacency. We hear the voice of such desire, first in the song of a thirsty individual whose *whole being longs* for God (Ps. 63:1) and then in the song of a disciplined but expectant people who call for God to *revive us again* (Ps. 85:6) so that they might rejoice in him.

1. A raging thirst (Ps. 63)

> *You, God, are my God,*
> *earnestly I seek you;*
> *I thirst for you,*
> *my whole being longs for you,*
> *in a dry and parched land*
> *where there is no water* (1).

It is immediately clear that a person in covenant relationship with God (they can say that he is *my God*) may feel distant from him, so that they *long* and *thirst* for him, for a sense of his nearness. Sometimes the reason is obvious and the solution is clear: they are clinging to a sin of which they must repent; they are cherishing an idol which they must renounce; they have neglected the disciplines of Bible reading, prayer and corporate worship and need to reorder their priorities. Sometimes, though, there seems to be neither an obvious reason nor a clear solution, yet still they feel distant from God.

a. Thirsting for God (1)

The heading of the psalm indicates that the writer is David and that he is in the *Desert of Judah*.[3] This suggests either a time before his coming to the throne when he was fleeing from King Saul[4] or a time towards the end of his reign when his son Absalom had rebelled against him.[5] The reference to *the king* (11) probably suggests the second of these possibilities, but in either case David is under great

---

[3] Of course much scholarship is inclined to dismiss the headings of the psalms as unreliable later additions. Nonetheless, they are treated as the first verse of the psalm in Hebrew manuscripts, suggesting they should be taken seriously. For the view that they are in fact canonical see D. Kidner, *Psalms 1–72*, TOTC (Leicester: Inter-Varsity Press, 1973), pp. 32–33.

[4] See 1 Sam. 23 (note that the Desert of Judah was also known as the Desert of Ziph).

[5] See 2 Sam. 15:13–30.

pressure and his life is in serious danger. Deserts, of course, are dry places and those who travel in them experience raging thirst. For David the experience of a *dry and parched land* becomes a powerful metaphor, making him aware of a deeper thirst; a thirst for God, a deep longing that consumes his *whole being*.

Often on a Monday night I am tired. I have worked up to three full days since my day off and Sundays are usually full and emotionally intense. When I stop, my mind tends to wander towards the New Forest where my wife (Alison) and I usually spend our day off. I begin to long for the sensation of fresh air on my face, the invigoration of a brisk walk, the relief of my mind unwinding in relaxed conversation, the luxury of a cream tea in one of our favourite forest cafes. Of course this is not a desire of which I am immediately conscious all of the time, but the moment I take time to stop and reflect it is unquestionably there. Desire for God is rather similar. We can rush through life at a relentless pace and experience very little of it, but when we stop and have time to reflect (either by choice or because of an event over which we have no control) our thirst for God starts awakening within us. For David, it is the experience of intense *physical* thirst which rekindles his *spiritual* thirst; his longing for water reawakens and reinforces his longing for God: *my flesh faints for you **as in** a dry and weary land . . .* (1, ESV). That desire becomes the focus of his song.

To learn to sing with the voice of desire for God is to open up the possibility of worshipping him when we might feel least inclined to do so; when we feel distant from him and have little sense of his presence. In the course of my work I have had to spend considerable amounts of time away from home. This has not been without difficulty as I have felt far from those I love most. However, being away from Alison does not mean that I stop loving her. Indeed, my *desire* to be with her is as much an expression of my love for her as the joy I feel when we are together, and when I stop what I am doing in order to think of her, the longing for our reunion intensifies. So it is that the expression of desire for God is as much an expression of worship as the expression of joyful celebration when we sense his nearness, and when we learn to worship with the voice of desire, that longing for God deepens and intensifies.

In verse 2 the journey of the song moves into a different key.

b. Satisfied in God (2–5)

Verse two begins with the word 'so'[6] which links it strongly to the first verse. The point is that he is recalling past experience where he

---

[6] Untranslated by the NIV but see ESV and NRSV.

has sought God *in the sanctuary* (the tabernacle) with the same intensity of longing that he has just expressed, and been rewarded with a vision of God's *power and glory*.[7] It is this past experience of God that then propels him forwards to encounter the living God in all of his life – even in the desert place. He is determined so to fill his mind with the praises of God (3–4) that he will find his joy and satisfaction in God renewed (5). In his prayer, therefore, he both expresses his committed devotion to God and reasons with himself to contemplate the superlative goodness and love of God that call forth praise.

Because your love [ḥesed, i.e. steadfast, covenant love] *is better than life, my lips will glorify you* (3). His life is fragile, threatened both by treachery and by physical thirst, yet God's love is steadfast and unchanging. More than that, it is more important for him to know God's love than to satisfy his raging thirst or to defeat his enemies or to have his reign and peace restored. David is not here seeking to impress God (or us or himself) with an extraordinary statement of sacrificial devotion, as if God could be persuaded to reveal himself on account of the extravagance of David's praise. This is a statement about God's love for David not David's love for God. His words reveal his deep conviction that God, in his covenant love, is so desirable that it would be *better* to know his love even if he has nothing else at all, than to have everything else he desires and not know it.

Such an appreciation of the supreme worth of the love of God must call forth glorious praise from his heart: that is the argument David is making to himself. So his *lips will glorify*[8] God (3b); he will *praise*[9] (speak well of) God *as long as he lives* (4a) and will *lift up his hands* in God's name (4b), so that his body as well as his lips are taken up in worship.[10] The praise to which David is calling his heart is no half-hearted effort, offered with polite reserve or cool detachment; it is strong, articulate, passionate and even physical.

John Piper speaks of three stages of worship: in the lowest stage the heart feels little love for God, and yet 'is granted the grace of repentant sorrow for loving so little'; in the next stage 'we do not feel fullness, but rather longing and desire'; but 'there is the final

---

[7] 'With the same intense desire David had worshipped God in happier days at Zion, and God had revealed himself' (Kidner, *Psalms 1–72*, p. 225).

[8] Heb. *šbḥ*: 'commend, praise, glorify, honour' (*NIDOTTE*, vol. 4, p. 26).

[9] Heb. *brk*: 'God blesses human beings by speaking well of them, thereby imparting a "blessing" (good things) to them, and so they are "blessed" (*barûk*); human beings bless God by speaking well of him, attributing "blessing" (good qualities) to him, and so he is "blessed" (*barûk*)' (*NIDOTTE*, vol. 1, p. 764).

[10] 'To lift up . . . hands or eyes (John 17:1) to heaven was to give the body its share in expressing worship (Ps. 134:2) or supplication (Ps. 28:2)' (Kidner, *Psalms 1–72*, p. 226).

stage in which we feel an unencumbered joy in the manifold per-fections of God . . . in this stage we are satisfied with the excellency of God, and we overflow with the joy of his fellowship'.[11] This is precisely what David envisages as the conclusion of his journey of remembering (2), reasoning with himself (3a) and calling his heart to praise (3b–4). He anticipates this abundance of joy in verse 5: *I will be satisfied as with the richest of foods; with singing lips my mouth will praise you* (5). *With the richest of foods* is literally 'with marrow and fat'[12] – not perhaps the most appetising prospect to the twenty-first-century palette, but to David it represented the most lavish of banquets, providing a striking metaphor of intimate and satisfying communion with God.[13]

It might be argued that this represents the very worst kind of self-absorbed religion, as David uses the extravagant metaphor of the banquet to describe the intimacy with God for which he longs. Does this not sound rather too much like a consumerist quest for mere personal pleasure dressed up in the garb of religious language? Certainly we should guard against worship becoming a mere quest for a spiritual feeling or experience, detached from its moorings in biblical revelation. However, if we are going to take the language of this psalm seriously, we have to conclude that the pursuit of joyful satisfaction in God is a thoroughly *good and God-honouring thing.* Such profound satisfaction in the supreme worth of the God of covenant love is precisely the conclusion to which the whole of the section has been moving; it is the highest goal of worship. In the famous opening words of the Westminster Shorter Catechism:

Quest. 1 What is the chief end of man?
Ans. Man's chief end is to glorify God and *to enjoy him* forever.[14]

Or in John Piper's memorable words, 'God is most glorified in us when we are most satisfied in him'.[15]

However, while the goal of David's quest is to find renewed satisfaction in God, it does not follow that he can be sure of finding that satisfaction immediately.

---

[11] J. Piper, *Desiring God* (Leicester: Inter-Varsity Press, 1986), pp. 75–76.

[12] See M. E. Tate, *Psalms 51–100*, WBC 20 (Nashville: Thomas Nelson, 2000), p. 124.

[13] I am assuming (with the NIV, NASB, NLT, NIV and the new KJV) that v. 5 is the conclusion of vv. 2–5, rather than the introduction to vv. 6–8 (as ESV and NRSV). See also T. Longman III and D. E. Garland, *The Psalms*, Expositor's Bible Commentary, vol. 5 (Grand Rapids: Zondervan, 2008), p. 490.

[14] *The Westminster Confession of Faith* (The Publication Committee of the Free Presbyterian Church of Scotland, 1958 edn), p. 287.

[15] J. Piper, *The Purifying Power of Living by Faith in Future Grace* (Colorado: Multnomah Books, 1995), p. 9.

c. Clinging to God (6–8)

> *On my bed I remember you;*
> *I think of you through the watches of the night.*
> *Because you are my help,*
> *I sing in the shadow of your wings (6–7).*

We can almost feel David tossing and turning on his uncomfortable desert bed as dark sleepless hours drift by. He is still far from Jerusalem, far from the tabernacle, and his enemies are still threatening, but his anxious heart is stilled by bringing to mind thoughts of his God. He imagines God's care for him, like that of a mother bird encompassing her chicks in the warmth, shelter and protection of her wings. So the God whose saving presence is made manifest beneath the outstretched wings of the cherubim in the Most Holy Place,[16] protects and helps David – and he finds himself singing for joy at the thought of such security.

These reassuring thoughts of God are not automatic for him, however, and at times they seem to be slipping away from his grasp, like water draining through his fingers. He therefore has to hold fast to God with every fibre of his being. *My soul clings to you; your right hand upholds me* (8, ESV). This *clinging* to God 'carries the meaning of "follow hard after" him',[17] with a deep sense of resolve and determination: God may seem far away, but he will not let him go, nor give up his pursuit of him. Yet David also knows that he continues to cling only because God's *right hand upholds* him (8b).

The voice of desiring God has more than one register. The early verses of this song were brimming with deep emotion as David journeyed in his imagination from the raging thirst of the desert to the abundant satisfaction of a sumptuous banquet, stirring up passionate desire for God within his soul. Now we are with him in the restless watches of the night, as he soothes his heart with thoughts of God and clings to him with deep resolve. 'He [David] has learned to sing . . . while *awaiting* the Lord's help and a new demonstration of the strength of his "right hand."'[18] Perhaps it is the sound of the second of these registers that reveals most decisively the true strength of desire for God. For some of us it is not difficult in the intensity and delight of public worship to feel drawn to God and to persuade ourselves that we truly desire him above all else. Too easily, though, the desires are quickly forgotten over a coffee at the end of a service. However, when we cling to God and 'follow hard after him' even

---

[16] Cf. 2 Sam. 6:2, and see Tate, *Psalms 51–100*, pp. 77–78.
[17] Tate, *Psalms 51–100*, p. 128.
[18] Longman and Garland, *Psalms*, p. 491.

though he may seem far away; when we trust him though we cannot see him; when we keep pursuing him though we are in a dry and weary land: then we have learned truly to enter into the worship of this evocative psalm.

d. Confident in God (9–11)

The long sleepless desert night is over and, as the dawn breaks, we find David not just clinging to God but now having found confidence in him. His enemies will be destroyed and *become food for the jackals* (10), while David – now feeling himself to be less like a fugitive and more like a *king* (11) – will be restored to joyful fellowship with God (presumably anticipating his return to Jerusalem and its cherished tabernacle).

> *But the king will rejoice in God;*
> *all who swear by God will glory in him,*
> *while the mouths of liars will be silenced* (11).

The king will rejoice in God, for his ultimate victory is certain. The minds of Christian readers of the psalm are surely drawn down through the centuries to a moment when another king stood in a thirsty desert (Matt. 4:1), assaulted by an enemy that wanted to defeat and dethrone him. He was tempted to satisfy his hunger with that which was not from God but he refused, resolving to be satisfied only by God and his word (Matt. 4:4). He was tempted to doubt God's presence and put him to the test, as if God were merely useful, but he refused and honoured God as the Holy One who is to be desired simply for who he is (Matt. 4:7). He was tempted to seek glory for himself apart from God, but he resisted and determined to seek God's glory alone (Matt. 4:10). This king was, of course, Jesus and he was in every sense the model worshipper. Never did any king demonstrate a more all-consuming desire for God than King Jesus demonstrated in choosing obedience to his Father over the enticements of sin. He too was betrayed by those who were his own (John 1:11), standing in the place not just of the fugitive but of the condemned criminal on the cross, but he triumphed over all his enemies through his resurrection. In his obedience is our justification; in his victory is our confidence in God; in his revelation of the Father is the true rest of our souls (Matt. 11:28–29). He is the 'bread of life' who satisfies our deepest hunger and quenches our truest thirst (John 6:35) and it is *to him* and *through him* that we are called to worship with the voice of holy desire.

If we wish to become increasingly the kind of worshippers that the Father is seeking (John 4:23), we need to move our focus away from battling for a particular style of music, a more or less liturgical approach, a more conducive atmosphere in our buildings. These remain much-contested issues but they are not the real issue. More than anything else the renewal of our worship requires the deepening of our desire for God, the joyful anticipating of sharing in the banquet he has prepared for us and the strengthening of our resolve to cling to him even through the watches of the night.

We should not imagine, however, that desiring God is simply a solitary pursuit, for God has called us to be a worshipping community. We therefore conclude by listening to the voice of a people who, though disciplined by God, nonetheless expect great things of him, as they seek his face again; a people whose song is a cry for revival.

2. An expectant people (Ps. 85)

Will you not revive us again, that your people may rejoice in you (6)?

It was November 1949 and two godly women in their eighties on the Hebridean Island of Lewis were troubled by the spiritual state of their parish: not a single young person came to church services.[19] They began to pray regularly and passionately, their intercessions often lasting late into the night. They were gripped by Isaiah's prophecy that God would 'pour water on the thirsty land and streams on the dry ground'[20] and night after night they begged God to do just that in their community. At night one of the women received a vision of their church full of young people being addressed by a visiting speaker. The vision was shared with the local minister; he called his leaders together to pray with the women and they met twice each week for a month and a half. As they prayed, the Holy Spirit made his presence powerfully felt among them, bringing profound conviction of sin and stirring great longing for God, for holiness and for the work of the gospel in their parish. Soon hordes of people – young and old alike – were turning to Christ. The move of God spread rapidly through the surrounding parishes and islands; hundreds were converted and many communities transformed. *Revival* – the renewed outpouring of the Holy Spirit on the church, or in the words of George Whitfield, 'God, the Lord, came down amongst us'.[21]

---

[19] For a full account of the revival see Colin and Mary Peckham, *Sounds from Heaven: The Revival on the Isle of Lewis, 1949-1952* (Fearn, Ross-shire: Christian Focus Publications, 2009).

[20] Isa. 44:3.

[21] Quoted in R. C. Ortlund Jr, *Revival Sent from God: What the Bible Teaches for the Church Today* (Leicester: Inter-Varsity Press, 2000), p. 27.

In Psalm 85 we hear the voice of a corporate desire for God, as his people cry to him to revive them again. The psalm, which gives us a wonderful model for expressing such a desire, falls into four sections.[22]

a. Remember God's (past) blessings (1–3)

> *You, LORD, showed favour to your land;*
> *you restored the fortunes of Jacob.*
> *You forgave the iniquity of your people*
> *and covered all their sins (1–2).*

It is likely (but not certain) that this psalm is looking back to Israel's restoration to the land after the exile.[23] Whatever the precise context, the writer is looking back to a moment when, after a period of judgment on his people (3), Yahweh had moved to them again in the grace of forgiveness and *restored the fortunes of Jacob* (1). The language of recollection is stark and without sentimentality as the writer speaks frankly of the *iniquity* and *sins* of his people (2) and of God's response in *wrath* and *fierce anger* (3). The implicit theology of his recollection is similarly robust: *restoration* had come neither from negotiation nor self-improvement on Israel's part but solely through the *favour* (grace) of Yahweh, who forgives their sin freely (2) and sets aside his own wrath (3). For all their directness, however, these verses are full of faith-strengthening thankfulness for the restoring grace of God, made manifest in Israel's history.

Such remembering is a familiar part of biblical spirituality, as we have seen many times already in this book. Still, what is particularly clear in this context is that Israel's remembering of God's past blessing was not mere nostalgia; rather it became the soil in which faith was nurtured to seek the renewal of that blessing for the future. This is a particularly important check on our tendency to romanticize the memory of past revivals. Those who know me best tell me that I have a tendency to nostalgic romanticism: a sound, a smell, a sight from my past and I am easily transported into a world I once knew, but which my imagination has sanitized from anything that was negative or questionable. Such fantasies provide a poor guide by which to navigate my present life. In a similar way there is a

---

[22] See D. Kidner, *Psalms 73–150*, TOTC (Leicester: Inter-Varsity Press, 1975) and Ortlund, *Revival*, pp. 38–39. Longman and Garland (see also John Goldingay, *Psalms: Psalms 42–89* [Michigan: Baker Academic, 2007], pp. 611–616) treat v. 8 as transitional and link v. 9 with vv. 10–12, but this does not affect the interpretation greatly.

[23] 'It is most likely, though not certain, that the Psalm is a postexilic composition' (Longman and Garland, *Psalms*, p. 638).

certain kind of nostalgic remembering of the great revivals of history that can prove enormously stifling for the present renewal of the church – as if what God did in one community at one particular point in history is likely to look and feel exactly the same as what he does when he *revives us again* (6). Biblical remembering is not a wistful desire to live in the past, building churches that resemble museum pieces; rather it is a spur to look to the God of boundless power and dynamic creativity to step into a new situation in new ways to bring the same restoring, renewing, gospel grace that he has brought to his people in the past. It is worth adding that, in the 'global village' we now inhabit with its sophisticated networks of rapid communication, such encouragement to faith can come not only from reflecting on the revivals of the past, but also from the dynamic life of the global church in the present, where powerful gospel growth can be witnessed in many contexts.

b. Longing for God's restoration (4–7)

Restore us again, God our Saviour, and put away your displeasure towards us (4).

This is not a passing thought issuing in a brief 'arrow prayer'; it articulates a passionate longing for God on the part of his people. The intensity builds through the three questions of verses five and six. The God who has brought renewal in the past is repeatedly implored to step in to the life of his people once again and put away his *displeasure* towards them.

It is intriguing that there is no expression of repentance in this psalm – indeed 'sin is not even mentioned, except as forgiven in the past (v2) and warned against in the future (8b)'.[24] The word for *displeasure* here could equally be translated 'annoyance' or 'irritation', and is most likely a reference not to God's judgment but to his discipline.[25] It seems that Israel's problem was not so much one of outrageous and obvious sin (such as that which led to the exile) but of a lack of spiritual fervour, a sense of distance from God and the loss of his immediate favour. Theirs was not so much an open spiritual rebellion, but a quiet spiritual indifference which had probably grown over decades. Doubtless all the apparatus of religion continued to function as normal, but the passion, the hunger for God had been lost. Nonetheless, spiritually sensitive people were unsettled. They discerned that they were under God's discipline and they longed for a new season in their relationship with him, in which

---

[24] Ortlund, *Revival*, p. 39; see also Longman and Garland, *Psalms*, p. 640.
[25] See Ortlund, *Revival*, p. 39.

his stance towards them changed from discipline and anger towards restoration and renewal.

> *Will you be angry with us for ever?*
>   *Will you prolong your anger through all generations?*
> *Will you not revive us again,*
>   *that your people may rejoice in you?* (5–6)

The emphasis in verse 6 is on the personal pronoun: *will **you** not revive us again . . . ?* We cannot organize our way to revival with strategies, papers and conferences; it is a sovereign work of God for which we must humbly pray, believing that he 'fills the hungry with good things'.[26]

One of the great dangers in the Western church is that we are satisfied with far too little. Our material prosperity has deadened our spiritual ambition and we seem content enough if our church is just about holding its own (while others may be closing) and putting on services we enjoy. Meanwhile, an emerging generation has been largely lost and the rising tide of secularism threatens to engulf the ever-shrinking turf on which the faithful huddle together. We desperately need spiritually sensitive people who are not so readily satisfied; people who discern the discipline of God on the church and who (rather than moaning about it) join with those who first sang this psalm, to humbly, urgently and persistently cry for him to revive and restore us again. I was deeply encouraged at a recent conference to hear the response of a pastor who was asked what it was that had given his church such remarkable growth. I expected him to describe an impressive growth strategy and make a series of inspirational book recommendations! Instead he simply said, 'Well, we started a prayer meeting every Friday night and we think of it as the engine of the church.'[27] Such a response is all too rare, but it is thoroughly in tune with the approach of this psalm.

What happens when God's people join together to worship with the voice of fervent desire for him and he comes to revive his people? First, they *rejoice in him* (6b). God's reviving grace lifts their hearts above the preoccupation of success, wealth, popularity and the pursuit of a designer lifestyle and they overflow in joy for all he is to them and for the abundance of his grace. Second, they know God's *unfailing*

---

[26] Luke 1:53.

[27] The pastor was Tope Koleoso from Jubilee Church, Enfield, which is part of the Newfrontiers family of churches. What excited me was not the specifics of where, when and how frequently people met to pray, but that this was a strategy which put God's power rather than human ingenuity and method at the heart of the church's growth.

love in unmistakable experience. As Raymond Ortlund writes on this verse, 'they cannot endure the prospect of his love remaining a theoretical abstraction only',[28] but when God revives them, they know his love in glorious experience. Third, God grants them his *salvation* (7b) – not in this case the saving of individuals from eternal judgment, but the saving of a people from disgrace, discipline and decline, because God has stepped in and restored them again. It is a wonderful prospect, to stir up the prayers of God's people in every generation.

c. Trusting God's promises (8–9)

After the yearning prayer of the first seven verses, a 'solo voice'[29] enters with a brief prophetic oracle. God's people have opened their hearts to him and are now called to listen to his response, but what will it be? The suspense is only momentary.

> *I will listen to what God the* LORD *says;*
> *he promises peace to his people, his faithful servants –*
> *but let them not turn to folly.*
> *Surely his salvation is near those who fear him,*
> *that his glory may dwell in our land* (8–9).

Peace (*shalom*) is a heavily-freighted word in Scripture.[30] It speaks of Yahweh's gift of wholeness, welfare, peace and prosperity. This is what he promises to his *faithful servants.* John Goldingay comments that 'it is dangerous to be a prophet of well-being',[31] for in Scripture such prophets are frequently false prophets (e.g. Jer. 6:14). It is not surprising, then, that this *promise* goes with a warning to God's people not to *turn back to folly* (8b, ESV). So I do not believe we should take these words as a universal and unconditional promise that revival is guaranteed if only we ask for it; there remain seasons of exile, discipline, struggle and decline. Nonetheless, God's fundamental stance towards his people is one of *peace, shalom* and restoration. His salvation is *near those who fear him* so that he is more ready to bless than we are seriously to seek his blessing. The psalm does therefore invite us to pray for his restoration with expectancy and confidence. Where there are people hungry for God they will be fed; where there are people thirsty for the outpouring of the Spirit they will be satisfied;

---

[28] Ortlund, *Revival*, p. 50.

[29] Kidner, *Psalms 37–150*, p. 309.

[30] John Goldingay translates it 'well-being' (Goldingay, *Psalms: Psalms 42–89* [Michigan: Baker Academic, 2007], p. 610).

[31] Ibid., p. 611.

where there are people who are passionate for the glory of God, the God whose glory has been enfleshed in Jesus Christ will by his Spirit cause that glory to be seen and known in the hearts of many. 'When the saving knowledge of his glory extends powerfully to many people at once, it is called revival.'[32]

d. Imagining God's coming (10–13)

While not so common in evangelical spirituality, it is not unusual for the great prayers of Scripture to conclude with a mouth-watering vision of what it will be like when God answers the prayer,[33] and that is how this psalm concludes. Such use of godly imagination, firmly rooted in God's promises and covenant faithfulness, can enrich our prayer, build expectancy in our faith and stir up our longings for God. These words, however, are not mere wishful thinking, they are a glorious bringing together of so many things the writer knows to be true of God. First, all of God's covenant blessings are given to his people in full measure and all at once: *love and faithfulness meet together; righteousness and peace kiss each other* (10). Second, there is a vision of cosmic reconciliation and harmony as God's saving reign causes his 'will to be done on earth as it is in heaven'.[34] The faithful obedience of a holy people in a restored creation is pictured rising to greet the watching righteousness of heaven (11). Third, freed from its bondage to decay, the creation is liberated under the noble rule of the transformed people of God, and so *gives what is good* and *yields its harvest* (12).[35] All this, because God has stepped in with saving righteousness to make all things new (13).

The picture is so glorious that its true fulfilment reaches far beyond any revival experience to the consummation of the new creation itself (cf. Isa. 65:17–25; Rev. 21:1–4). However, every revival is an anticipation in the middle of history of what God will do at the climax of history, for in revival the knowledge of the glory of the Lord fills the church now as, ultimately, it will fill the whole earth. So it is that we nurture the longing for revival now, by filling our imaginations with a biblical vision of the ultimate glory to which the revival points.

3. Conclusion

Discussions about worship in the contemporary church have become both so polarized and so distracted that it is all too easy to

---

[32] Ortlund, *Revival*, p. 53.
[33] See e.g. Ps. 96:12–13 and Eph. 3:19–20.
[34] Matt. 6:10.
[35] Cf. Rom. 8:20–21.

read through a book on worship expecting little more than to find reinforcement for existing convictions, justification for personal preferences and ammunition for taking the fight to anyone who thinks differently! The call to learn to worship God with the voice of desire for him, is a call for all of us to resist such self-satisfied complacency. My prayer for all who read this book (and for myself) is rather that we grow so to long for God and his glory – revealed in us, among us and through us by his Spirit – that we become ever-increasingly 'the kind of worshippers the Father seeks':[36] worshippers whose appetite never diminishes for the glories of his word of truth and for the manifestation of his all-satisfying presence by the Holy Spirit.

> *You, God, are my God,*
>   *earnestly I seek you;*
> *I thirst for you,*
>   *my whole being longs for you,*
> *in a dry and parched land*
>   *where there is no wate*r (Ps. 63:1).

> *Will you not revive us again,*
>   *that your people may rejoice in you?*
> *Show us your unfailing love, LORD,*
>   *and grant us your salvatio*n (Ps. 85:6–7).

---

[36] John 4:23.

Study Guide

HOW TO USE THIS STUDY GUIDE

The aim of this study guide is to help you get to the heart of what John has written and challenge you to apply what you learn to your own life. The questions have been designed for use by individuals or by small groups of Christians meeting, perhaps for an hour or two each week, to study, discuss and pray together. When used by a group with limited time, the leader should decide beforehand which questions are most appropriate for the group to discuss during the meeting and which should perhaps be left for group members to work through by themselves or in smaller groups during the week.

PREVIEW. Use the guide and the contents pages as a map to become familiar with what you are about to read, your 'journey' through the book.

READ. Look up the Bible passages as well as the text.

ANSWER. As you read, look for the answers to the questions in the guide.

DISCUSS. Even if you are studying on your own, try to find another person to share your thoughts with.

REVIEW. Use the guide as a tool to remind you what you have learned. The conclusion sections where they occur will be useful. The best way of retaining what you learn is to write it down in a notebook or journal.

APPLY. Translate what you have learned into your attitudes and actions, considering your relationship with God, your personal life, your family life, your working life, your church life, your role as a citizen and your worldview.

Author's preface

1 What aspects of the author's experience shape his approach to the subject of worship (pp. 8–10)?

'. . . my intention is not to court controversy, but simply to do my best to allow Scripture to speak, in the hope that the question "What kind of worship do we like?" is gradually replaced by the better question: "What kind of worship is it that God seeks?"' (p. 9).

PART 1. WORSHIP AND THE GLORY OF GOD

Psalm 8; Hebrews 2:5–18
1. Worship and the music of creation (pp. 21–33)

1 Why is worship about much more than church music or even church services (pp. 21–22)?
2 What is the central theme of Psalm 8? How is it expanded in Psalm 148 and reflected in Romans 1 (pp. 22–24)?
3 In what ways can creation be compared to music (pp. 24–25)?
4 Why does verse 2 present such an unexpected contrast with verse 1 (pp. 25–26)?
5 How did Jesus reinforce the lessons of verses 2–4 in Matthew 21 (pp. 26–27)?
6 What is (and is not) the correct understanding of the question in verse 4 (pp. 27–28)?
7 How does the description in verses 5–8 militate against too negative a view of human beings (pp. 29–30)?
8 How does Hebrews 2:8 balance the ideal vision of Psalm 8 and how is that reflected in the world we live in today (pp. 30–31)?
9 In what way does Jesus fulfil the vision of *ultimate* humanity and what is the mystery inherent in that fulfilment (pp. 31–32)?
10 What is meant by creation, de-creation, re-creation and new creation (p. 32)?

Exodus 3 – 4
2. Worship and the story of salvation (pp. 34–47)

1 What factors need to be considered in the quest for freedom (pp. 34–35)?
2 On what grounds can we affirm that the book of Exodus is about freedom to *worship* (p. 35)?
3 How does Moses' experience mirror the plight of the fledgling nation of Israel (pp. 35–37)?

4 What was the sign that God gave Moses and what did the burning bush reveal to him in addition to God's holiness (pp. 37–38)?
5 In what sense was worship a sign of salvation and what were the features of its fulfilment (pp. 36–39)?
6 What were the two key challenges facing Moses and how did he respond (pp. 39–41)?
7 Is 'serve' a more appropriate translation of the Hebrew word *'bd* in this narrative (p. 42)?
8 What is the dual focus of Exodus 20 – 40, giving us 'a key model for what God intends a worshipping community to be' (pp. 43–45)?

'Worship in the Bible is never a bridge that we build out to him but simply a responsive journey we make to cross the bridge he has built out to us. He speaks his word and gives his presence; we his worshipping people simply respond to what he has done' (p. 45).

---

9 How is this dual focus fulfilled in the coming of Jesus (p. 45)?
10 How should worship as the sign and goal of salvation impact on the pastor's task of nurturing a contemporary worshipping community (pp. 46–47)?

Exodus 32 – 34; Isaiah 1
3. Worship catastrophe (pp. 48–62)

1 Which of the two sets of 'worship catastrophes' resonates most with you, and which one should (pp. 48–49)?
2 What is the essence of idolatry and what forms can it take (pp. 49–50)?
3 What features of the golden calf story illustrate the difference between God's perspective and that of the people (pp. 50–51)?
4 What five insights does the golden calf story give us into the nature of idolatry (p. 52)?
5 Can we square the harshness of God's judgment with the turning aside of judgment through the mediation of Moses (pp. 52–55)?
6 Why were Isaiah's words in chapter 1 so shocking (pp. 56–57)?
7 Why was the religious life of Judah such a catastrophe (pp. 57–59)?

'Once the heart to honour God in the obedience of our lives is lost, it is only a matter of time before our worship deteriorates into a dull, mechanical routine, devoid of any true devotion or life' (p. 59).

---

8 How can Isaiah's message to Judah's *national* leaders be interpreted and applied in today's multinational context (pp. 59–60)?
9 'The answer to Judah's hypocrisy lies not with their religious life . . .' Where does it lie and what are the implications for us (pp. 60–61)?
10 What is the 'surprising twist' beyond the worship catastrophes of this chapter (pp. 61–62)?

Matthew 1 – 4
4. The perfect worshipper (pp. 63–73)

1 What positive lessons can we learn about worship from the Old Testament history of Israel (pp. 63–64)?
2 What evidence is there that Israel's calling remained largely unfulfilled (pp. 64–65)?
3 How do the early chapters of Matthew's Gospel present Jesus as the true Israelite (pp. 66–68)?
4 What aspects of Jesus' testing/tempting echo the wilderness experience of Israel (pp. 68–69)?
5 What is the significance of the temptation to turn stones into bread (pp. 69–70)?
6 What is the significance of the testing at the temple (pp. 70–71)?
7 What is the significance of the testing on the mountain (pp. 71–72)?
8 In what three ways is the perfect worship of Jesus of direct interest to us (pp. 72–73)?

John 4:1–42
5. In Spirit and truth (pp. 74–85)

1 'The contrast with Nicodemus could hardly be greater.' In what ways was the Samaritan woman such a contrast (pp. 74–75)?
2 Why would the image of living water have resonated so much in the land of Samaria and how does Jesus develop it (pp. 75–76)?
3 Where else in Scripture do we find the imagery of water and what conclusions can we draw from them (pp. 76–78)?
4 How did Jesus reveal himself to the woman as a prophet and how would she have understood that truth (pp. 78–79)?
5 What was the issue used by the Samaritan woman to redirect the conversation and why did Jesus not try to return to her personal life (pp. 79–80)?

6 What are the features of the new, true worship which Jesus reveals (pp. 80–82)?

'We are not called to worship "God-in-general" but specifically the God who is the Father of our Lord Jesus Christ and who has drawn us into fellowship with himself by the Holy Spirit' (p. 83).

---

7 In what ways should the Christocentric focus of our worship be maintained (p. 83)?
8 What is needed to set the agenda for our worship (p. 84)?
9 'In the original language, one preposition, "in", governs both "Spirit" and "truth".' What conclusions can we draw from this? (pp. 84–85)?

Revelation 4 and 7
6. The ultimate worship (pp. 86–95)

1 What is meant by 'a pilgrim people' and how should it impact on our understanding of worship (pp. 86–87)?
2 Should the concept of whole-life worship make us cautious about describing corporate praise as worship (p. 87)?
3 What is the focus of heaven's worship in (a) chapter 4 and (b) chapter 5 of Revelation (pp. 87–88)?
4 What do the *four living creatures* represent and what is the focus of their worship (p. 88)?
5 What do the *twenty-four elders* represent and in what two ways is their worship expressed (pp. 88–90)?
6 Why is the content of Revelation 7 in the context of chapters 6 to 8 significant (p. 90)?
7 Who are the 144,000 and what is the seal of the living God (pp. 90–91)?
8 What should (and what should not) be the source of our joy in worship (pp. 92–93)?
9 How should we understand the reference to *the great tribulation* (pp. 93–94)?
10 What is signalled by the shift in verb tenses in verse 15 and what aspects of God's presence are highlighted in the remaining verses (pp. 94–95)?

Psalm 100
7. The voice of celebration: A joyful noise (pp. 96–106)

1 What two failures tarnish worship and in what way (p. 96)?
2 Why is the grouping of psalms into 'genres' or types a helpful approach (pp. 96–98)?

'I suggest that the hermeneutical tool of genre analysis in the Psalms can be helpfully recast as a way of identifying a glorious diversity of "voices of worship" which can deeply enrich our experience of worship and move us beyond the deadly turf wars of culture and preference' (p. 98).

---

3 What is the atmosphere in the opening verses of Psalm 100 and what conclusion should we draw from it (pp. 98–99)?
4 In the Bible, what is worship 'never' and what is it 'always'? (pp. 99–100)?
5 In what way do the people of God belong to him twice over and how is this reinforced for us as Christians (p. 100)?
6 Should worship be distinguished from praise and thanksgiving and how does this psalm help us to express the latter (pp. 101–102)?
7 What does it mean to affirm that the Lord is good (p. 102)?
8 What is the overflow of true worship and the 'ache' which accompanies it (pp. 102–103)?
9 Where does true enjoyment of God arise and in what two ways are we guided in verses 2–3 and 4–5 (p. 103)?
10 How is the importance of music and singing affirmed both in culture and Scripture (pp. 104–105)?
11 How far do temperament, life situation, preference and culture limit the breadth of our 'voices of worship' and how far should they (pp. 105–106)?

Psalm 99
8. The voice of adoration: A trembling world (pp. 107–117)

1 In what period do scholars place the compilation of Psalms 90 – 106 and is it possible to square this with the inclusion of earlier authors such as Moses and David (pp. 107–108)?
2 What emphasis in Isaiah 6 reappears in Psalm 99 and how does it affect the tone of the psalm (pp. 108–109)?

3 Why is the positioning of Psalm 99 in this block of psalms remarkable and what does it demonstrate about the faith of the post-exilic community? What parallels can we see with our own worship experience (pp. 109–111)?

'Never did the chasm between their present and their history, between what they experienced and what they had been promised, seem wider' (p. 110).

---

4 What is the referent of God's justice in this context and how can Christian readers make Israel's praise here their own (pp. 111–113)?
5 Is it true to say that 'actions speak louder than words' (pp. 113–114)?
6 In what sense can Moses be described as a 'priest' and what links the incidents alluded to in verse 6 (p. 114)?
7 Is verse 7 primarily about Moses, Aaron and Samuel (pp. 114–115)?
8 In what senses did God 'answer' his people in times of national failure and sin (p. 115)?
9 Why are the 'sobering words' of Ecclesiastes 5:1–7 still relevant against the background of New Testament teaching (pp. 115–116)?
10 What is the starting point for worship and why can 'reverent' and 'traditional' not necessarily be equated (pp. 116–117)?

PART 2. WORSHIP AND THE SUPREMACY OF CHRIST

Hebrews 9:1 – 10:25
9. All fulfilled (pp. 121–134)

1 Where in the New Testament is the relationship of shadows to reality used and to what do these passages refer (pp. 121–122)?
2 What are the features of the sacrificial system as described in the book of Leviticus (pp. 122–124)?
3 How is the subject of *Atonement* dealt with in Ian McEwan's novel of that title and what does it suggest about his pre-suppositions (p. 124)?
4 How does Christ's offering differ from the Levitical offerings in (a) the place where the offering is made, (b) the nature of the offering itself and (c) the approach to God which the offering achieves (pp. 125–126)?
5 What are the 'self-made prisons' from which Christ's offering delivers us (pp. 126–127)?

6 What is the major theme of verses 15–28 and how is it developed in contrast to Leviticus (pp. 127–129)?

7 What was deficient in the sacrifices offered on the Day of Atonement (pp. 129–130)?

8 In what three ways was the sacrifice of Christ superior to those prescribed by Leviticus (pp. 130–131)?

'Old Testament worship could go so far, but it could go no further. It offered no final cleansing of the conscience from sin and therefore no access to this Most Holy Place. However, through offering himself as a sacrifice on the cross, Christ has changed everything, fulfilling all that the structures of Old Testament worship were pointing towards' (p. 132).

9 How do Old Testament and New Testament worship differ regarding God's word, his presence, sacrifices and nearness to him (pp. 132–133)?

10 What three conclusions can we draw from the three imperatives of verses 22–25 (pp. 133–134)?

Colossians 1:15–23
10. All for Jesus (pp. 135–148)

1 What features help us to identify the structure of this passage (pp. 135–136)?

2 What two titles for Christ are used in verse 15 and how should they be understood (pp. 137–138)?

3 What does it mean to say that all things were made 'in him', 'through him' and 'for him' (pp. 138–139)?

4 In what ways do we enjoy creation most fully (p. 139)?

5 What is the function of verses 17–18a and how do they develop Paul's thought (pp. 139–141)?

6 How does the second section from verse 18b mirror the structure of the first and in what ways is Paul's theme developed (pp. 141–143)?

7 How should the reconciliation of 'all things' be understood and what light does Francis Schaeffer throw on Paul's vision here (pp. 143–144)?

8 Who is referred to in the phrase 'reconcile to himself' in verse 20 (p. 144)?

9 Why does Paul follow the note of 'joyful confidence' with 'a more cautious note' (pp. 144–145)?

10 In what three areas do we celebrate Christ's supremacy and what are the implications (pp. 145–148)?

Romans 12
11. All of life (pp. 149–164)

1 What is 'the surprise of Romans 12' (p. 149)?
2 In what way does the word 'therefore' provide a link and what is the connection that is sometimes overlooked (pp. 149–150)?
3 In what way is the Old Testament link between sacrifice and worship transformed in the New Testament (pp. 150–151)?
4 What three distinctive features characterize New Testament sacrifice (pp. 151–153)?
5 What are the negative and positive instructions in verse 2 (pp. 153–154)?

'Transformed living comes out of transformed thinking – Christians need to pay close attention to the life of the mind. Nonetheless, Paul is not talking about a merely intellectual process, but about the work of the Holy Spirit' (p. 153).

---

6 Why can we see the opening two verses of this chapter as a heading for the section 12:1 – 15:3 (p. 154)?
7 In what three ways does worship involve changed attitudes (pp. 154–158)?
8 What three attitudes should govern our use of gifts (pp. 156–158)?
9 How does Paul envisage a transformed life of Christian love in the community of the church (pp. 158–160)?
10 How does Paul envisage a transformed life of Christian love in the wider community (pp. 160–161)?
11 What three characteristics of a whole-life worship perspective are evident in Romans 12 (pp. 161–162)?
12 In what specific areas is there a need to link the worship of the church gathered together and the worship of the church scattered in the world (pp. 162–164)?

Luke 22:7–30
12. Remember me (pp. 165–175)

1 For you personally, is Communion 'a moment of grief to endure or a moment of grace to savour' (pp. 165–166).

2 What was the basic structure of the Passover meal (pp. 166–167)?
3 Why is it important to see Communion as an acted parable (pp. 167–168)?
4 How should we understand the symbolism of the bread (pp. 168–169)?
5 How should we understand the symbolism of the wine and which Old Testament streams of thought influence it (pp. 169–172)?
6 Is it appropriate to use the language of symbolism and recollection when speaking about Communion (pp. 171–172)?
7 Why is self-examination so important (pp. 172–173)?
8 What is the 'terrible irony' of the behaviour of the disciples and what can we learn from Jesus' response (pp. 173–174)?
9 In what way is the Lord's Table linked to the Messianic banqueting table and what aspects of Jesus' earlier teaching illuminate it (pp. 174–175)?

Psalm 51
13. The voice of repentance: A broken man
(pp. 176–188)

1 In what two senses is Jesus the light of the world (pp. 176–177).
2 What are the details of King David's sin, recorded in 2 Samuel 11 – 12 (pp. 177–179)?
3 In what way do the terms used by David describe his failure (pp. 179–180)?
4 Is David right when he says, 'Against you, you only, have I sinned' (pp. 180–181)?
5 What is 'the essence and the ambiguity of human nature in its fallenness' (pp. 181–182)?
6 Why does David ask to be cleansed with hyssop (pp. 182–184)?
7 Why is a decision to turn from sin not enough and what must accompany it (pp. 184–185)?
8 In what three ways are the fruits of repentance evident in the closing verses of this psalm (pp. 185–187)?

'Moral failure never happens in a hermetically sealed space. When we fail, there are always others who are affected in some way or another' (p. 187).

---

9 Why is the voice of repentance so vital for our worship and in what way can we encourage it (pp. 187–188)?

Psalm 96
14. The voice of proclamation: A global call
(pp. 189–202)

1 What is the value of singing 'a new song' (pp. 189–190)?
2 Where other than Psalm 96 does much of this song appear and what insight does Chris Wright bring in his book *The Mission of God* (pp. 190–191)?
3 What insights do Jeremy Perigo and Harold Best contribute to 'the vision of a global community called to the worship of Yahweh' and how did the author's visit to a village in rural East Africa influence his thinking (pp. 191–193)?
4 How should we apply the encouragements in verses 2b–3 in our own cultural context (pp. 194–195)?
5 What two truths about God underlie the call for global worship in verses 4–6 (pp. 195–197)?
6 Why does the cycle of the psalm begin again in verse 7 and in what way does it develop (p. 197)?
7 What do Isaiah 60 and Revelation 21 contribute to the vision of global worship in this psalm (pp. 198–199)?
8 What is the 'one step further' that we are invited to take in Psalm 98 (p. 199)?
9 Why is judgment seen as decidedly good news in the final verses of the psalm (pp. 199–200)?
10 How can the missional task presented in Psalm 96 be implemented in a complex multicultural society (pp. 200–202)?

'Rather than give way to the attitudes of cultural supremacy that we would (rightly) never tolerate in our "missionaries", we need to face the fact that in today's world all of us are called to cross-cultural mission' (p. 202).

PART 3. WORSHIP AND THE LIFE OF THE HOLY SPIRIT

2 Corinthians 3
15. The transformative Spirit (pp. 205–217)

1 What is the connection between Lepe Beach and the life and mission of the Christian church (pp. 205–206)?
2 What is the background to 2 Corinthians (p. 206)?

3 On what grounds was Paul's authority being challenged and how does he respond to the challenge (pp. 206–208)?

4 Which Old Testament passages is Paul alluding to in verse 3 and what light do they throw on the authenticity of his ministry (pp. 208–209)?

5 What three contrasts does Paul present in verses 7–11 as he compares the ministry of the old covenant with that of the new (pp. 210–213)?

6 What setting is introduced by the words *condemnation* and *righteousness* (pp. 211–212)?

7 What contrasts and conclusions does Paul draw from the veiling of Moses' face in verses 12–18a (pp. 213–215)?

8 In what three ways will Christian worship be seen to be authentic (pp. 216–217)?

1 Corinthians 12 – 13
16. The empowering Spirit I: The gifts of the Spirit for the church (pp. 218–229)

1 What three points are clear from 1 Corinthians 12:7 and in what three ways do they shape the church (pp. 218–219)?

2 How can we discern the authenticity of the gifts of the Spirit (pp. 219–220)?

'This breadth of gifting bears witness to the boundless creativity of the Holy Spirit who is able to manifest himself in numerous ways within the church. By contrast, there often seems to be a drive within churches to replace that glorious and creative diversity with a narrow uniformity' (p. 220).

---

3 Why does Paul emphasize the diversity of spiritual gifts and where do we see a tendency to narrow them, both in the Corinthian correspondence and contemporary church life (pp. 220–221)?

4 What three observations can be made about the manifestations of the Spirit in verses 8–11 (pp. 221–222)?

5 What four aspects of the gifts of the Spirit should we value according to verses 12–31 (pp. 222–224)?

6 How should we account for Paul's change of style in chapter 13 (p. 224)?

7 What does Paul emphasize in verses 1–3 and why (p. 225)?

8 In what four ways does Paul expound the nature of love in verses 4–7 (pp. 225–226)?

9 In verses 8–13 Paul's perspective shifts 'from the interpersonal to the eschatological'. What conclusions can we draw from this, both negatively and positively (pp. 226–229)?

1 Corinthians 14
17. The empowering Spirit II: The gifts of the Spirit in the church (pp. 230–239)

1 Why may spiritual gifts be considered a problem? What problems did they present in Corinth and how did Paul respond (pp. 230–231)?
2 How should we understand the gift of tongues in this context (pp. 231–232)?
3 How should we understand the gift of prophecy in this context (pp. 232–234)?
4 What does Paul mean by 'building up' the church (p. 234)?
5 Is there a place for the gift of tongues in public worship (pp. 234–235)?
6 How does the context of Isaiah 28:11–12 help us to understand tongues as a sign for unbelievers (pp. 235–236)?
7 What is the correct balance between order and participation in corporate worship (pp. 236–238)?
8 What difficulties do verses 33b–35 present and how may they be resolved (p. 238)?
9 Why do we need to exercise some caution in approaching this chapter and why may caution be taken too far (pp. 238–239)?

Ephesians 5:18–21; Colossians 3:15–17
18. The dynamic Spirit (pp. 240–251)

1 How is the activity of the Spirit described in the book of Acts and Paul's letters (pp. 240–241)?
2 In what ways does the dynamic Spirit bring the powerful word of God into the life of God's people (pp. 241–242)?

'The New Testament evidence is clear: we should not think of the Holy Spirit only as a one-off endowment whose presence, once received, can be safely ignored and taken for granted. He is rather the dynamic Spirit with whom the people of God are to cultivate a continuing relationship of expectancy, dependence, openness and joy' (p. 241).

---

3 What conclusion can we draw by comparing Ephesians 5:18–21 and Colossians 3:15–17 (p. 242)?
4 What are 'the essential ingredients of authentic worship' and how do they affect our lives (pp. 243–244)?
5 What militates against giving the word of Christ 'a rich welcome' in our worship and what encourages it (pp. 244–245)?
6 What is made clear by the fact that 'Be filled' is a command (p. 246)?
7 How is the command to 'be filled' reflected in Paul's prayers throughout Ephesians (pp. 246–248)?
8 What is the place of music in our ministry to one another (pp. 248–249)?
9 What should characterize the vertical dimension of our worship (pp. 249–250)?
10 What does the author mean by the 'overflow principle' and what are its implications (pp. 250–251)?

Psalms 42 – 43
19. The voice of lament: A troubled soul (pp. 252–263)

1 Why is lament such an important facet of public worship and in what way is that reflected in the Psalms (pp. 252–254).
2 Why has God given us the psalms of lament (pp. 254–255)?
3 What is 'one of the most striking features of the psalm' and what can we surmise about its original setting (pp. 255–256)?
4 What pattern can we discern in Psalms 42 and 43 and what does it teach us (pp. 256–257)?
5 Why does the psalmist feel far from God and how does he respond (pp. 257–258)?
6 How does the psalmist express his feelings of confusion and what factors contribute to his struggle (pp. 258–259)?
7 What is the paradox which the psalmist had to live with (pp. 259–260)?
8 Why is the psalm 'much more than just a grief process (pp. 260–261)?
9 How is confidence seen to be growing (pp. 261–262)?

'We need to learn how to worship in sadness' (p. 262).

---

10 What do the psalms of lament offer (and not offer) and what place do they have in our worship today (pp. 262–263)?

Psalms 63 and 85
14. The voice of desire: A raging thirst (pp. 264–277)

1 What does it mean to settle for 'pitiful pleasures' in worship and what is the greater alternative (pp. 264–265)?

2 What issues do we need to consider when we feel distant from God (p. 265)?

3 Why was thirst for God an apt metaphor for David and how may more mundane desires be directed towards a desire for God (pp. 265–266)?

4 What features of his past encourage David to offer God praise and what is the 'deep conviction' that undergirds such praise (pp. 266–267)?

5 What three stages of worship does John Piper identify and why is satisfaction in God a good thing (pp. 267–268)?

6 'The voice of desiring God has more than one register.' What evidence of that do we find in this psalm (pp. 269–270)?

7 What does the reference to the king in verse 11 draw to the mind of Christian readers (pp. 270–271)?

8 What was the likely occasion of Israel's remembering in Psalm 85 and what dangers are to be avoided in such looking to the past (pp. 272–273)?

9 What element is intriguingly absent in this psalm and how should we account for that (pp. 273–274)?

10 What danger does the Western church face and what response is needed (pp. 274–275)?

11 What is the message of the 'solo voice' in verses 8–9 and how should we understand it (pp. 275–276)?

12 In what three ways can we expect God to respond to prayerful worship and how should we summarize the message of this book (pp. 276–277)?

The Bible Speaks Today: Old Testament series

The Message of Genesis 1 – 11
The dawn of creation
David Atkinson

The Message of Genesis 12 – 50
From Abraham to Joseph
Joyce G. Baldwin

The Message of Exodus
The days of our pilgrimage
Alec Motyer

The Message of Leviticus
Free to be holy
Derek Tidball

The Message of Numbers
Journey to the promised land
Raymond Brown

The Message of Deuteronomy
Not by bread alone
Raymond Brown

The Message of Joshua
Promise and people
David G. Firth

The Message of Judges
Grace abounding
Michael Wilcock

The Message of Ruth
The wings of refuge
David Atkinson

The Message of Samuel
Personalities, potential, politics and power
Mary J. Evans

The Message of Kings
God is present
John W. Olley

The Message of Chronicles
One church, one faith, one Lord
Michael Wilcock

The Message of Ezra and Haggai
Building for God
Robert Fyall

The Message of Nehemiah
God's servant in a time of change
Raymond Brown

The Message of Esther
God present but unseen
David G. Firth

The Message of Job
Suffering and grace
David Atkinson

The Message of Psalms 1 – 72
Songs for the people of God
Michael Wilcock

The Message of Psalms 73 – 150
Songs for the people of God
Michael Wilcock

The Message of Proverbs
Wisdom for life
David Atkinson

The Message of Ecclesiastes
A time to mourn, and a time to dance
Derek Kidner

The Message of the Song of Songs
The lyrics of love
Tom Gledhill

The Bible Speaks Today: New Testament series

The Message of the Sermon on the Mount (Matthew 5 – 7)
Christian counter-culture
John Stott

The Message of Matthew
The kingdom of heaven
Michael Green

The Message of Mark
The mystery of faith
Donald English

The Message of Luke
The Saviour of the world
Michael Wilcock

The Message of John
Here is your King!
Bruce Milne

The Message of Acts
To the ends of the earth
John Stott

The Message of Romans
God's good news for the world
John Stott

The Message of 1 Corinthians
Life in the local church
David Prior

The Message of 2 Corinthians
Power in weakness
Paul Barnett

The Message of Galatians
Only one way
John Stott

The Message of Ephesians
God's new society
John Stott

The Message of Philippians
Jesus our Joy
Alec Motyer

The Message of Colossians and Philemon
Fullness and freedom
Dick Lucas

The Message of Thessalonians
Preparing for the coming King
John Stott

The Message of 1 Timothy and Titus
The life of the local church
John Stott

The Message of 2 Timothy
Guard the gospel
John Stott

The Message of Hebrews
Christ above all
Raymond Brown

The Message of James
The tests of faith
Alec Motyer

The Message of 1 Peter
The way of the cross
Edmund Clowney

The Message of 2 Peter and Jude
The promise of his coming
Dick Lucas and Christopher Green

The Message of John's Letters
Living in the love of God
David Jackman

The Message of Revelation
I saw heaven opened
Michael Wilcock